"For eighteenth-century Particular Baptists, ordination sermons were a key way to publicly communicate pastoral theology and identify spiritual priorities. Published ordination sermons constituted an important genre of applied theology that shaped younger ministers and reinforced the convictions of seasoned pastors. In this helpful book, Nigel Wheeler shows how Andrew Fuller's ordination sermons summarized his own pastoral theology and, by virtue of his role as a leading pastor-theologian in the movement, helped form a generation of Particular-Baptist pastors. Wheeler's work is an important contribution to British Baptist history as well as a gift to contemporary ministers who will benefit from Fuller's pastoral wisdom."

NATHAN A. FINN
Provost and Dean of the University Faculty,
North Greenville University

"When it comes to assessing candidates for the pastoral office, my church focuses on five 'C's': calling (by the Holy Spirit), character (personal piety), competencies (teaching, leading), chemistry (unity), and confirmation (congregational ordination). What a pleasant surprise I encountered in reading this book, which addresses similar ideas from an eighteenth-century perspective. More than prompting surprise, however, this book provides a richness and depth in filling out the biblical standards for these areas and providing examples of pastors who live out their calling to church ministry. In our day in which things from the past are easily dismissed as irrelevant, this book refreshingly offers centuries-old wisdom for pastors and their office today."

GREGG R. ALLISON
Professor of Christian Theology,
The Southern Baptist Theological Seminary

"This lovely little book establishes the ordination sermons of Andrew Fuller in their historical, denominational and theological context. As a jewel nestled in this rich setting, Fuller's sermons show both the continuity and the vitality of his conception of pastoral ministry. Just as he was engaging and interacting with his past, and contributing to his future, so the reader of Nigel Wheeler's book will find his own sense of pastoral ministry, whether viewed from the pulpit or the pew, challenged, stimulated and enhanced. The biblically-framed, carefully-considered, prayerfully-communicated pastoral priorities identified and discussed here remain of enduring value for all who want to understand what it means to care for God's flock and to preach God's Word."

JEREMY WALKER
Pastor, Maidenbower Baptist Church, Crawley, UK
Author, *On the Side of God: The Life and Labors of Andrew Fuller*

"In the past, the ordination of Baptist ministers were times when respected pastors would convene to examine and charge the prospective pastor with a biblical message chock-full with pastoral theology. By mining the ordination sermons of one of the greatest Baptist pastor-theologians of the late-eighteenth and early-nineteenth centuries, Nigel Wheeler has uncovered a goldmine of pastoral theology that is still just as relevant today as when those sermons were preached. Those who desire to know what Baptist pastors once aspired to and still should will find the revelations of this study useful to that end. These sermons shaped a generation of ministers in the past and reveal that which is good and enduring in a Baptist theology of pastoral ministry."

STEVE WEAVER
Senior Pastor, Farmdale Baptist Church, Frankfort, KY
Senior Fellow, Andrew Fuller Center for Baptist Studies

"Andrew Fuller was a rigorously thoughtful and biblical practitioner of pastoral ministry. The frequency with which he was asked to preach ordination sermons bears witness to the confidence his contemporary seasoned ministers had in him. Nigel Wheeler's examination of these ordination sermons in the light of prevailing Particular Baptist theological and pastoral interests is richly rewarding in at least three ways. First, we find Andrew Fuller's deep and biblically founded spirituality expressed in pastoral ministry beneficial to the church in giving voice to the Bible, to confessional theology, and to truth-founded Christian experience. Second, Wheeler lays to rest any false notions that Fuller's corrective emphases on some issues of evangelism and the duty of repentance and faith led into theological shallowness or even infidelity. Wheeler notes that Fuller's deep polemical awareness of the devastating impact of the infidelities of the day sealed his convictions as a clearly orthodox and confessional Particular Baptist. Even so did he admonish pastoral candidates in these deeply serious convictions. Evangelism with a deep sense of oughtness was not a mere pragmatic technique, but a deeply biblical stewardship related to the glory of God as the chief end of man. Third, Wheeler demonstrates Fuller's mature and unwavering loyalty to historic Particular Baptist concerns about the stewardship involved in pastoral ministry. The 'nature and goals of their theological priorities remained essentially the same.' He gives this insightful summary of the lesson from this comparison of ordination sermons: 'For as the priorities of a culture change so does the emphatic expression of certain aspects of a fixed theological dogma which is inherently designed to communicate an unchanging message to an ever-changing world.' This book is a profoundly helpful analysis of a profoundly insightful person giving biblically-grounded expression to an eternally significant calling."

TOM NETTLES
Senior Professor of Historical Theology,
The Southern Baptist Theological Seminary

"Some may look at the title of this book and think it would only be of interest to historians. But those who don't listen to history are in danger of being prisoners to the spirit of their own age. *The Pastoral Priorities of 18th Century Baptists* by Nigel Wheeler gives contemporary Christians a chance to see their blind spots and measure their practice by a glimpse into the practice of eighteenth-century Baptists. Though this work focuses on the themes in ordination sermons, especially in the life and work of their foremost pastor-theologian Andrew Fuller, contemporary Christians will be challenged and instructed by the care, thoughtfulness, and thoroughness in numerous matters of church practice, and commitment to deep piety and biblical orthodoxy. They, of course, had their errors and blind spots, but they were healthier in many areas than are contemporary churches. There is much value here. I highly commend it to pastors and church leaders."

JOHN HAMMETT
John L. Dagg Senior Professor of Systematic Theology,
Southeastern Baptist Theological Seminary

"As a leading nineteenth-century shepherd, theologian, and statesman amongst eighteenth-century Particular Baptists, Andrew Fuller delivered many ordination sermons which offer an important window into their practice and theology. Setting Fuller's sermons amid historic and contemporary ordination sermons, Nigel Wheeler demonstrates continuity within the tradition. What becomes especially clear is Fuller's coupling of the theme "eminent spirituality equals eminent usefulness" with a recovery of real Calvinism (e.g. "a free Gospel offer"). Fuller believed that a revival of personal godliness was the wellspring for wider revival; by making this a priority for pastors, churches under their care would ultimately contribute to Baptist revival. As the shepherd, so the flock. Wheeler's book is rich in interactions with primary sources, and it is an important academic addition to the discontinuity/continuity discussion in nineteenth-century evangelicalism. In addition to offering an historic understanding of Baptist pastoral theology, Wheeler's book is an edifying and practical work for twenty-first century pastors and churches who wish to see revival in our own day."

CHRISTOPHER W. CROCKER
Associate Professor of Church History, Toronto Baptist Seminary
Pastoral-Elder, Markdale Baptist Church, ON

"Many years have passed since the time of Andrew Fuller and his ministerial colleagues, but there are key components of Christian ministry that remain the same and, consequently, they still have much to teach us. Fidelity to the scriptures as the word of God, the centrality of Christ as the only Savior of sinners, the importance of gospel repentance and faith, the nature of the church as the assembly of God's elect, and much more were their pastoral priorities. Dr. Wheeler has done us a great service by letting these spiritual leaders speak in their own words. Here is a work that calls us to remember what it means to be a Christian regardless of when we live in history, and one that I heartily commend to Christian readers everywhere."

KIRK M. WELLUM
Principal & Professor of Systematic Theology,
Toronto Baptist Seminary

The Pastoral Priorities of 18th Century Baptists

An Examination
of Andrew Fuller's Ordination Sermons

Nigel Wheeler

The Pastoral Priorities of 18th Century Baptists

Published by: H&E Academic, Peterborough, Ontario, Canada
www.hesedandemet.com

Front cover group photo: First row, left to right: Carey, Kinghorn, John Ryland Jr, Robert Hall Jr., Andrew Fuller, and John Foster. Second row: Joshua Marshman, William Ward, William Knibb, Thomas Burchell, John Rippon, Dan Taylor, J.G. Pike, William Steadman, and Samuel Pearce.

Paperback ISBN: 978-1-989174-96-8
Hardcover ISBN: 978-1-989174-98-2
Ebook ISBN: 978-1-989174-97-5

Dedication

To my beloved wife Janice
who serves her Lord with such diligence and faithfulness.

Contents

FOREWORD

On an August Wednesday in 1764, John Davis, a descendant of Bible-believing Huguenots on his mother's side, was formally ordained as the pastor of the Baptist cause in Waltham Abbey, Essex, now on the outskirts of north-east London. The famed John Gill spoke at his ordination from Ezekiel 10:20 ("This is the living creature that I saw under the God of Israel by the river of Chebar; and I knew that they were the cherubims," KJV), which, at first glance, hardly seems appropriate as a text for an ordination sermon. Gill well knew the oddity of the choice of text, but he believed that the cherubim were "emblems of ministers of the Gospel" and as such were instructive about the nature of the pastorate.[1] In one pithy remark, Gill summed up the importance that he placed on pastoral ministry: "as ministers be, churches are."[2] This high view of pastoral ministry was a given among his Particular Baptist contemporaries in the so-called Georgian era (1714–1830) as this new study of Andrew Fuller's ordination sermons well reveals.

This study began life, as it were, as a doctoral thesis, and I am personally thrilled that, through this publication, it will reach a wider audience. It deals with a subject that, due to the high premium placed on pastoral ministry by the Particular Baptists, goes to the heart of Baptist ecclesiology and spirituality in the Georgian era, for not only pastors, but also congregations believed Gill's pithy, Puritan-like aphorism cited above: the theology and piety of pastors had a profound impact, conscious and unconscious, upon the communities that they led. And ordination sermons are a fabulous doorway by which we might enter into the thinking of these eighteenth-century men and women about these matters. These sermons revealed the ideal that pastor and people strove to emulate and to experience.

The largest collection of Baptist ordination sermons that we have from the Georgian period comes from the pen of Andrew Fuller and they make an ideal

[1] John Gill, *The Doctrine of the Cherubim Opened and Explained: In a Sermon Preached at the Ordination of the Reverend Mr John Davis, At Waltham-Abbey, August 15, 1764* (London: G. Keith; J. Robinson; W. Lepard, 1764), 4, 15.

[2] Gill, *Doctrine of the Cherubim*, 40.

source to study and to unveil the pastoral piety of that era. And Nigel Wheeler has done a superb job in delineating that piety, which is not simply Fuller's, but as noted, was standard fare in this remarkable Christian community. Hopefully, Dr. Wheeler's study of Fuller's thinking regarding pastoral ministry will not only inform minds about an important bygone facet of church history, but will also help in sharpening our present-day thinking and expectations about what it means to be a pastor today. And given Dr. Wheeler's own pastoral experience, he is an ideal pastor-historian to give us such guidance.

Michael A.G. Haykin
Dundas, Ontario
December 31, 2020.

ABSTRACT

The aim of this study is to investigate one slice of the multifaceted contribution of Andrew Fuller, namely, his ordination sermons, to determine what key theological priorities shaped his understanding of pastoral ministry and what his exact influence on this Baptist community was as it relates to pastoral theology. To put the theology of his ordination sermons in context, this study examines them in relation to other available Particular Baptist ordination sermons of the era.

This study reveals that Fuller's pastoral priorities as expressed in his ordination sermons concerning the character, qualifications, and duties of a pastor, which represented the chief subject matter of the ordination charge, shows a great deal of continuity with his Particular Baptists theological tradition.

There is no doubt that Andrew Fuller is at the heart of a renewal of Particular Baptists in the late eighteenth century which impacted one key element of the pastoral office: offering Christ to all and sundry. But this did not entail a complete revamping of the Particular Baptist perspective on pastoral ministry.

The continuity/discontinuity in pastoral theology between Fuller and his brethren of the earlier part of the century, especially in connection with the defining characteristic of Fuller's pastoral theology of eminent spirituality and eminent usefulness, reveals that there was little change in the sermons prior to when the evangelical revival was thought to have significantly affected the Particular Baptists in 1770. They shared a similar concern as Fuller to communicate that eminent spirituality results in eminent usefulness.

This close connection does not argue in favour of a radical redefinition of pastoral theology transformed by the so-called rise of evangelicalism. The main difference in terms of renewal centred on a return to the biblical precedent of offering the gospel freely to all. The diversion of this emphasis was connected to the rise of High Calvinist dogma precipitated by a defence of the orthodoxy from the attacks of rationalist age. Still, Baptist preaching was consistently plain in style, evangelical in content, and affectionate in application.

Introduction

Andrew Fuller (1754–1815) is considered by many to be the most influential Baptist theologian in the Anglophone world of the latter third of the "long" eighteenth century. His influence is especially known in relation to his polemical work *The Gospel Worthy of All Acceptation*, that demolished the Hyper-Calvinism embedded in certain quarters of his Baptist community and paved the way for the formation of the Baptist Missionary Society. But his impact is broader than this achievement, monumental though it was. His importance is also rooted in other polemical works directed against such products of the Enlightenment as Deism and Socinianism; his pastoral ministry, and the mentoring of an upcoming generation of pastoral leadership, is especially evident in his contribution to ordination services. The aim of this study is to investigate one slice of the multifaceted contribution of this theological giant, namely, his ordination sermons, to determine what key theological priorities shaped his understanding of pastoral ministry and what his exact influence on this Baptist community was as it relates to pastoral theology. To put the theology of his ordination sermons in context, the study will examine them in relation to other available Particular Baptist ordination sermons of the era.

At the beginning of the eighteenth century, far too many of the Particular Baptists were known for a doctrinal rigidity, which so highlighted the doctrines of grace as to deny the propriety of the free offer of the gospel. Many historians regard this as a key contributor to the numerical decline among the Particular Baptists who consequently became characterized by a lack of passionate evangelism and a distinct insularity. In the last quarter of the eighteenth century there was a significant shift among Particular Baptists as the emphasis on doctrinal preciseness gave way to a more outward-looking and evangelistically-centred focus. At the heart of this influence was their pastoral theology.

Although the genre of ordination sermons represents a unique and important reflection on the pastoral priorities of the Particular Baptists of the eighteenth century, they have been largely ignored as a locus of study. There are a few assorted articles in journals like *The Baptist Quarterly*[1] which deal with certain aspects of ordination theology and some brief mention in doctoral theses usually developing other arguments, but, in the past, no major study of Particular Baptist pastoral theology from ordination sermons was attempted,[2] except for the one recent work by Grant.[3]

In my opinion, these studies don't satisfactorily interact with the history of Particular Baptist pastoral theology within the tradition itself. Was there a radical transformation in their thought? There is no doubt that Andrew Fuller is at the heart of a renewal among Particular Baptists in the late eighteenth century. This renewal impacted one key element of the pastoral office: offering Christ to all and sundry. But did this entail a complete revamping of Particular Baptist perspective on pastoral ministry? In other words, when older Particular Baptists heard Andrew Fuller's ordination sermons, did what they hear differ significantly from what they heard as younger men and women? Or did they hear much that was similar? Through a detailed examination of the ordination sermons prior to the evangelical revival among Baptists around 1770, compared with Fuller's sermons, this book seeks to determine to what extent the revival reshaped Particular Baptist pastoral theology by considering what was new and what was different.

---

[1] For example, N. Clark, "The Meaning and Practice of Ordination" *The Baptist Quarterly* 17 (January 1958): 197–205.

[2] A.H. Kirby, "The Theology of Andrew Fuller in its Relation to Calvinism" (PhD diss., Edinburgh University, 1956); E.F. Clipsham, "Andrew Fuller's Doctrine of Salvation" (BD thesis, Oxford University, 1961); Robert Oliver, "The Emergence of a Strict and Particular Baptist Community Among the English Calvinistic Baptist, 1770–1850" (DPhil diss., CNNA, London Bible College, 1986); Thomas South, "The Response of Andrew Fuller to the Sandemanian View of Saving Faith" (ThD diss., Mid-America Baptist Theological Seminary, 1993); Pope Alexander Duncan, "The Influence of Andrew Fuller on Calvinism." (ThD diss., Southern Baptist Theological Seminary, 1917); D.L. Young, "The Place of Andrew Fuller in the Developing Modern Missions Movement" (DPhil diss., Southwestern Baptist Theological Seminary, 1981); John W. Eddins Jr., "Andrew Fuller's Theology of Grace" (PhD diss., Southern Baptist Theological Seminary, 1957); Tom Ascol, "The Doctrine of Grace: A Critical Analysis of Federalism in the Theologies of John Gill and Andrew Fuller" (PhD diss., Southwestern Baptist Theological Seminary, 1989); Harlice E. Keown, "The Preaching of Andrew Fuller" (MTh thesis, Southern Baptist Theological Seminary, 1957); Paul Brewster, "Andrew Fuller (1754–1815): Model Baptist Pastor-Theologian" (PhD diss., Southeastern Baptist Theological Seminary, 2007); Chris Chun, "The Greatest Instruction Received from Human Writings: The Legacy of Jonathan Edwards in the Theology of Andrew Fuller" (DPhi. diss., University of St. Andrews, 2008).

[3] Keith Grant, "Very Affecting and Evangelical: Andrew Fuller (1754–1815) and the Evangelical Renewal of Pastoral Theology" (ThM thesis, Regent College, 2007). This work has recently been published as a book in *Studies of Baptist History and Thought*, Keith S. Grant, *Andrew Fuller and the Evangelical Renewal of Pastoral Theology* (Keynes, UK: Paternoster, 2013).

The question to be answered in light of an increased zeal for evangelism among eighteenth- century Particular Baptists, which led in turn to measurable growth in the latter part of the century is what was Fuller's pastoral theological contribution?

By restricting the sources to ordination sermons, this study represents a manageable and cohesive body of primary source material for the historian. The distinctive significance of ordination sermons as a unique corpus of material lies primarily in their personal practicality. By their very nature they sifted out the extraneous and focused on what was essential with a theologically governed practicality. In the context of public ordination services, which is a covenantal ceremony, a usually more seasoned pastor would instruct the ordinand on the important character, qualities, and duties of the pastor for successful ministry. In other words, he would tell the new minister what was absolutely essential for the successful discharge of the office, based on his own personal experiences in the ministry. This was getting to the heart of the matter of what was personally important for that pastor to impart to the newly appointed minister. This gives the inquirer unique insight into the main concerns of seasoned, influential, and respected pastors, for those chosen to speak at the charge were largely recognized as men with preeminent gifts and graces. Further, they reveal their personal theological emphases as interpreted through their inherited Particular Baptist tradition. These pastors had worked out their own unique theological convictions in day to day ministry within a clearly defined received body of belief beginning in the seventeenth century. By comparing Fuller's sermons with others in his own tradition the researcher can ascertain trends of continuity and discontinuity among Particular Baptists. This inquiry becomes even more valuable in light of Fuller's profound influence among these Particular Baptists.

The importance of pastoral theology within the context of the ordination sermon is also enhanced by the covenantal nature of the proceedings. Because ordination is essentially a covenant between the members of the church and the newly appointed pastor, their mutual pledges to one another reinforced accountability. Enhanced accountability often promotes more careful delineation both in thought and in actual implementation. It is one thing to profess the importance of a particular pastoral theology and quite another to publicly express your determination to live it out in that very community. Further, since every aspect of their pastoral theological tradition could not be expressed due to the time limitations of a ceremony, only the priorities were discussed and openly and mutually agreed upon. This largely neglected corpus of material reveals pastoral priorities uniquely in both an ideological (theological) and pragmatic (practical) way, which makes it an essential source for understanding Particular Baptist theological precedence.

Fuller's significant influence among eighteenth-century Baptists might help to explain their increased zeal for evangelism and the resulting growth that occurred. For at the heart of Fuller's axiom "eminent spirituality produces eminent usefulness" was an activism that was directly tied to the pastor's piety. In other words, he believed that in order for the church to flourish the pastor must be in close communion with God. In addition, he believed that the church member's piety also affected the approbation of God's presence and his accompanying blessing so that the church might become a key means for building the kingdom of God. In this sense the destiny of all human history was directly tied to the holiness in his people. In modern North American Evangelicalism (which is still very activistic in its approach to evangelism but where personal piety rooted in a biblical and doctrinal confessional framework is largely waning), Fuller's balanced approach between an adherence to doctrine combined with an emphasis on personal holiness is instructional.[4] It is possible to be both pious and biblically confessional while effectively seeking to evangelize the world.

The connection between personal holiness and effectiveness in evangelism is a vital aspect of pastoral theology. The connection between piety and growth through evangelism was at the heart of Particular Baptist growth of the late eighteenth century. Prior to this awakening, when the Baptists were more inward focused, piety was understood more in terms of doctrinal precision than through a passion to promote the cause of Christ in the world. As a result, there was measurable numeric decline. Did Fuller's pastoral theological emphasis on eminent spirituality which helped to foster this evangelical growth represent a radical revamping of previous Particular Baptist pastoral theological priorities?

Fuller had such a clear theological stress in his ordination sermons that his thought can be justly compared with other Particular Baptists in light of his unique prominence and influence especially in the latter part of the century.

---

[4] See, for example, David Wells, *No Place for Truth: Or Whatever Happened to Evangelical Theology* (Grand Rapids, MI: Wm. B. Eerdmans, 1993); Kevin J. Vanhoozer, *The Bible, The Reader, and the Morality of Literary Knowledge: Is there meaning in this text?* (Grand Rapids, MI: Zondervan, 1998).

Since this emphasis of eminent spirituality and eminent usefulness is also noticeable in the greater Evangelical Revival, it provides intriguing links between Fuller's own theological transition and the growth of the Particular Baptists with the rise of Evangelicalism. So although a primary goal is to evaluate Fuller's thought within the developing context of his Baptist heritage, this study has implications for the larger church.

Chapters Outline

Chapter 1 will describe an overview of Fuller's life, the forces that shaped him as a man as well as his theology, and the impact of his life and labours in the ministry, particularly in reference to his pastoral theology.

Chapter 2 places Fuller in the larger socio-political, theological tradition of the Particular Baptists beginning in the seventeenth century. Significant events that had a profound impact on Baptist activism in relation to the Established Church (Church of England) such as the Act of Toleration (May 1689) are considered. It places Fuller's origins in the Particular Baptists Puritan-Separatist roots.

Chapter 3 describes the dynamics and the importance of ordination sermons particularly to the Baptists. Their significant influence reflects their importance in authority. The actual procedure of the ceremony is described, which in itself reflects its importance to the Baptists.

Chapter 4 will examine the pastoral theological emphases that emerge from eighteenth-century Particular Baptist sermons. The major themes of their pastoral theology are analysed, reviewed, and collated to describe theological continuity with the tradition.

Chapter 5 will examine Fuller's distinctive emphasis that comes from his ordination sermons to determine what key theological priorities shaped his understanding of pastoral ministry.

The final chapter will conclude with an analysis of the continuity and discontinuity between Fuller and the mainstream thought of his tradition with a view to determine what unique theological contribution he made. The goal is also to determine the extent of renewal among Particular Baptists, especially between the earlier and latter part of the century.

1
The Life & Influence of Andrew Fuller

Birth & Early Childhood

According to one account, when Andrew Fuller (1754-1815) was born in a farming community in the unassuming village of Wicken in Cambridgeshire, England, about seven miles from the cathedral city of Ely, on 6 February 1754, "the fen-ditches were all convulsed, the earth shook to its very centre, and the devils ran frightened to one corner of Hell."[1] Robert Hall Jr. (1764-1831) who recorded this hyperbolical report was referring to the effect that Fuller's theological efforts would have on the influence of High Calvinism in the region. Fuller, who was destined to become one of the foremost Baptist theologians of the eighteenth century in Britain and America, was born in a modest farmhouse in this former marshland that, according to his son Andrew Gunton Fuller, was overshadowed by the ancient Ely Cathedral's majestic octagonal tower.[2] The cathedral tower emblematically reflected the power and dominance of the established church (Church of England), but Fuller was born into a dissenting tradition of Puritanism on both his father's and mother's side.[3]

His father Robert Fuller (1723-1781) and his mother Philippa Gunton (1726-1816) were Baptists and all three of their sons, Robert (b.1747), John (b.1748), and Andrew, would later occupy leadership positions in Baptist churches, with the former two serving as deacons and the latter serving as a prominent pastor. Like their father, the two eldest boys Robert and John were

---

[1] John Greene, "Reminiscences of the Rev. Robert Hall, A. M." in Olinthus Gregory and Joseph Belcher eds., *The Works of the Rev. Robert Hall, A. M. with a Memoir of his Life, by Dr. Gregory; Reminiscences, by John Greene, ESQ.; and his Character as a Preacher, by the Rev. John Foster* (New York: Harper and Brothers Publishers, 1854), IV, 27.

[2] Andrew Gunton Fuller, *Andrew Fuller* (London: Hodder & Stoughton, 1882), 14, "But a vast expanse of country is visible from a rise of a few feet bounded by elevations, on which are to be seen ancient churches, notably those of Swaffham Prior, and that queen of cathedrals, Ely Minster, which is almost everywhere conspicuous. It still serves as a landmark to the whole district."

[3] *The Complete Works of the Rev. Andrew Fuller, With a Memoir of his Life by the Rev Andrew Gunton Fuller* (A.G. Fuller ed., rev. ed. J. Belcher: 3 vols; Harrisonburg, VA: Sprinkle Publications, 1988 [1845]), I, 2.

farmers by profession and Andrew himself would practice what was then called "husbandry" until his "twentieth year."[4] His background in farming formed some of his most dominant characteristics as a man. For example, speaking of taking a challenge to plow a straight line in a field, which was a noteworthy accomplishment among farmers, Fuller says:

> One day I saw such a line, which had just been drawn, and I thought, "Now I have it." Accordingly, I laid hold of the plough, and putting one of the horses into the furrow which had been made, I resolved to keep him walking in it, and thus secure a parallel line. By and by, however, I observed that there were wrinkles in this furrow, and when I came to them, they turned out to be larger in mine than in the original. On perceiving this I threw the plough aside, and determined never to be an imitator.[5]

This commitment to intellectual independence would emerge as a consistent feature of Fuller's later ministry. In fact, Gilbert Laws believes that, "Nothing is more remarkable about Fuller than his independence. He thought for himself, and to great purpose."[6] Especially in regard to his theological works, Fuller did not accept others' ideas uncritically but he consistently evaluated them against the standard of the Bible.[7] Another key characteristic of Fuller's ministry was his great industriousness, which was most probably cultivated on the farms of the Fenland.[8]

In 1761 Robert Fuller moved his family to Soham—about three miles away—where Andrew and his brothers were attending the local grammar school and where his wife Philippa was already a member of the Calvinistic

---

[4] Fuller, *Complete Works*, I, 5.

[5] Gilbert Laws, *Andrew Fuller: Pastor, Theologian, Ropeholder* (London: The Carey Press, 1942), 14.

[6] Laws, *Andrew Fuller*, 14.

[7] William Ward, *A Sketch of the Character of the Late Andrew Fuller, In a Sermon Preached at the Lal Bazar Chapel, Calcutta, on Lord's Day, October 1, 1815* (London: Button and Sons, 1817), 7: "His remarkably strong perceptions, thus assisted by a confident reliance on, and a most extensive knowledge of, divine revelation, enabled him to examine received opinions without that timidity so common to weaker minds, and without those predilections to which so many are the degraded slaves. He did not receive any human creed: he looked into the perfect law of liberty; he walked amongst the sacred penmen as one who had received at least the mantle of Elijah."

[8] A.G. Fuller, *Andrew Fuller*, 18.

Baptist church.[9] Robert Fuller was a regular "hearer,"[10] but Andrew was concerned that his father remained unconverted at his death.[11] The pastor of the Baptist work at Soham was a man named John Eve (d.1782), a High Calvinist,[12] who, reflecting the pervading theology of his day among far too many quarters of Particular Baptists, did not believe in the "free offer" of the gospel.[13] As a result, Fuller would later write in a letter to his Scottish friend Charles Stuart (1745–1826) in 1798, that Mr. Eve "had little or nothing to say to the unconverted."[14]

Conversion

Fuller initially had little concern for his own eternal welfare despite the fact that he regularly attended a Calvinistic dissenting church while he was growing up. Reflecting on his early days Fuller describes his most prevalent sins before his conversion as "lying, cursing, and swearing."[15] Although he periodically experienced a certain amount of success in conquering these deviations, it was only temporary and his repentance was short lived. It seems the preaching he was hearing did not provide Fuller with any satisfactory answers to the questions forming in his mind concerning his eternal state. Always an avid reader, he began to search for answers in Christian literature.[16] The most memorable of these books included *Grace Abounding to the Chief of Sinners* by John Bunyan (1628–1688) and the *Gospel Sonnets* of Ralph Erskine (1685–1752). The former of these works is the spiritual autobiography of John Bunyan, the lowly tinker who became a renowned preacher and author. The book was written during his imprisonment in 1666 and describes Bunyan's spiritual passage from an irreverent life characterized by blasphemy to a new life free of bondage

---

[9] A.G. Fuller, *Andrew Fuller*, 13.

[10] A "hearer" was a person who regularly attended the church but was not a member.

[11] John Ryland, *The Work of Faith, the Labour of Love, and the Patience of Hope, illustrated; in the Life and Death of the Rev. Andrew Fuller*, 2nd ed. (London: Button & Son, 1818), 88.

[12] "High Calvinism," was also known as "hyper-Calvinism," "ultra-Calvinism," or Fuller's terms, "false-Calvinism," or "pseudo-Calvinism." It was characterized mainly by a rejection of the free offer of the gospel, denying it was the *duty* of the unregenerate to believe in Christ and a belief in eternal justification.

[13] "Free offer" refers to an indiscriminate invitation of the gospel to all people.

[14] Letter to Charles Stuart, Edinburgh, 1798 (Transcribed by Joyce A. Booth from a calendar of Fuller's letters prefaced by the Rev. Ernest A. Payne found in manuscript box [4/5/1] (Angus Library, Regent's Park College, Oxford).

[15] "Fuller's Letters," manuscript box *(4/5/1)* (Angus Library, Regent's Park College, Oxford).

[16] A.G. Fuller, *Andrew Fuller*, 24.

to sin and guilt. *Grace Abounding* records a life that begins in despair but ends with a life "full of comfort," and thankfulness for "grace abounding."[17] Bunyan was describing the very condition Fuller was experiencing and as he read he related Bunyan's experience to his own and was overcome with weeping. Yet, he was still not permanently relieved of his inward distress and continued in sin as before.

Again in 1767 he began to feel concern about his spiritual destiny, but because of the influence of a High Calvinistic theology that taught that a sinner needed a "warrant," or special qualification to come to Christ, Fuller was in a state of hopeless despair.[18] But one day as the words of the apostle in Romans 6:14: "Sin shall not have dominion over you; for ye are not under the law, but under grace," came to mind, he felt an overwhelming joy and freedom. According to High Calvinistic dogma this might be the special sign that confirmed salvation.[19] But this latest resolution to fight sin proved to be transitory and Fuller realized there was no real change as his former apathy, especially in the practice of prayer, soon returned. After yet another similar experience in the year 1769, when Fuller was fifteen years old, his former convictions returned but this time resulted in genuine evangelical conversion. The intense conviction of sin that Fuller experienced at this time increased to the point of desperation. Fuller describes feeling like a drowning man:

> looking every way for help, or, rather catching for something by which he might save his life. I tried to find whether there was any hope in the Divine mercy—any in the Saviour of sinners; but felt repulsed by the thought of mercy having been so basely abused already. In this state of mind, as I was moving slowly on, I thought of the resolution of Job, "Though he slay me, yet will I trust in him" (Job 13:15).[20]

---

[17] John Bunyan, *Grace Abounding to the Chief of Sinners and the Pilgrim's Progress*, ed. Roger Sharrock (London: Oxford University Press, 1966), 103.

[18] A "warrant" was a special subjective revelation of God whereby a person's mind was unusually impressed, typically with a particular Scripture text, which served as a sign that he/she were among the elect.

[19] "Fuller's Letters," *(4/5/1)*. "Now the suggestion of a text of scripture to the mind, especially if it came with power, was generally considered by the religious people with whom I occasionally associated, as a promise coming immediately from God. I therefore so understood it, and thought that God had thus revealed to me that I was in a state of salvation and that therefore iniquity should not, as I had feared, be my ruin."

[20] Fuller, *Complete Works*, I, 5.

As he repeated to himself these verses in Job he realized that if he were to be saved he must cast himself on the mercy of Christ alone. When he began to focus on Christ's ability and desire to save rather than his own sin and failure Fuller at last found peace for his troubled soul. He was no longer willing to depend on his own futile efforts to reform himself and according to his friend Dr. Charles Stuart (1745–1826) "perceived now, that if he were saved, he must be saved in spite of himself—that even if God forgave his past sins, he should still destroy his own soul in a day."[21] Andrew Fuller had truly repented this time and determined to consecrate his life to Christ.

Baptism

In March 1770 as Fuller witnessed a public believer's baptism for the first time he was greatly moved by the experience and was convinced that it represented the apostolic mode of baptism:

> The solemn immersion of a person, on a profession of faith in Christ, carried such conviction with it, that I wept like a child, on the occasion. ... I was fully persuaded, that this was the primitive way of baptizing, and that every Christian was bound to attend to this institution of our blessed Lord.[22]

About a month later, Fuller himself was baptized and joined the Soham church as a member. As he matured as a Christian he grew to love the church and the pastor, Mr. Eve. But perhaps the most formative relationship in this early stage of his Christian life was with a man named Joseph Diver (d.1780) with whom he was baptized. Fuller's grandson, Thomas Ekins Fuller, describes Diver at this time as a man about forty years old and somewhat reclusive and thoughtful.[23] He and Fuller soon became close friends and regularly discussed aspects of practical Christianity together.

During these early years at Soham a dispute arose over the power of sinful men to do the will of God and to keep themselves from sin. The issue was precipitated by Fuller's challenge to a church member who drank too much. The member responded that it was not within his power to repent. Eventually he was excommunicated but the basic issues remained contentious. The pastor

---

[21] Charles Stuart, *A Short Memoir of the Late Mr. Andrew Fuller* (Edinburgh, 1815), 3.

[22] Ryland, *Work of Faith*, 22.

[23] Thomas Ekins Fuller, *A Memoir of the Life and Writings of Andrew Fuller* (London: J. Heaton & Sons, 1863), 16.

John Eve argued that there was a difference between internal and external power in relation to a man's response to sin. Fuller recounting Eve's position says, "We certainly could keep ourselves from open sins. We had no power," he observed, "to do things spiritually good; but outward acts, we had power both to obey the will of God and disobey it."[24] He believed that men could not do anything spiritually good but they could keep themselves from blatant acts of sin.[25] But the church rejected his position and because of the dispute the pastor resigned and the church was almost dissolved. This episode provides insight into both Fuller as a Christian in particular and eighteenth-century Calvinistic Baptist life in general. First, there was in Fuller, even at this early stage in his Christian life, a deep desire that the people of God live holy lives. He boldly confronted sin, recognizing that authentic Christianity was more than a mere profession but one that demanded a holy lifestyle to affirm its genuineness and protect its integrity. Similarly, we see in the church at Soham a strong commitment to truth and therefore a willingness and desire to practice church discipline. The Bible was esteemed as the ultimate authority in all church matters, not just as a principle but also as a practical truth. This experience was extremely traumatic for Fuller because he valued peace and harmony in the church, but his personal struggle in answering the questions raised by the dispute would provide the foundation of much of his later apologetic ministry.

Fuller's Ministry

John Eve left Soham in October 1771 and Joseph Diver, who was now a deacon, took over the responsibility of filling the pulpit. However, one morning he was sick and Fuller was given an opportunity to speak extempore to the church. His first sermon lasted about thirty minutes and was well received by the church.[26] Providentially, the day before he had been practicing preaching a sermon to himself on Psalm 30:5 and remembered feeling comfortable that he could expound it publicly. This gave him confidence to agree to the spur-of-the-moment request to preach. Due to his initial success he was asked to speak again, but the next time he preached he felt he did not do as well. Discouraged he did not speak again for over a year.

In January 1774 an elderly lady in the church passed away and requested that Fuller preach her funeral service. In response to her request the church at

[24] Fuller, *Complete Works*, I, 8–9.
[25] Fuller, *Complete Works*, I, 9.
[26] Ryland, *Work of Faith*, 29.

Soham called him as their minister. After a probation period of a year he was officially ordained as the pastor of the Soham church in May 1775. Robert Hall Sr. (1728–1791) of Arnsby, considered one of the wisest and most trusted counselors of the Northamptonshire Association, preached his ordination sermon.[27] Hall would prove to be a life-long mentor for Fuller, who in turn loved him as a father.[28]

From the beginning of his ministry one of Fuller's central tenets as a pastor was the authority of God's Word. He saw the Bible as the infallible rule for Christian living and consistent with this applied himself to learning its doctrines. He believed that complete dependence on God was essential for success in pastoral ministry and made Proverbs 3:5–6, "Trust in the Lord with all thine heart; and lean not unto thine own understanding. In all thy ways acknowledge him, and he shall direct thy paths," a verse he regularly applied to his life.[29] In this period at Soham he also sought to understand and apply the Scriptures to his life by devoting himself to searching for answers to some of the prevailing theological questions of the day. These included debates about the pre-existence of Christ's human soul before his incarnation and the question of whether the title "son" was given to Christ in his pre-incarnate state. The main theological challenge that would engage him for much of his life, though, was the "Modern Question," which he first encountered in a systematic argument in 1775.[30] It dealt with whether or not it was unregenerate man's duty to believe

---

[27] Thornton Elwyn, *Particular Baptists of the Northamptonshire Baptist Association as Reflected in the Circular Letters, 1765–1820,* http://www.rpc.ox.ac.uk/bq/elwyn-2.htm (accessed November 14, 2004), 1–3. The Northamptonshire Association was founded in Kettering in 1765 for the key purposes of unity in fellowship and promotion of the Particular Baptist cause. Michael A.G. Haykin, *One Heart and One Soul: John Sutcliff of Olney, His Friends and His Times* (Durham: Evangelical Press, 1994), 111. The church at Soham had applied for, and had been accepted into membership in, the Northamptonshire Association on 8 June 1775.

[28] Laws, *Andrew Fuller*, 31.

[29] "Amongst others, I was aware of the danger of being drawn into acquaintance with the other sex which might prove injurious to my spiritual welfare. While poring over these things ... I was led to think of that passage: 'In all thy ways acknowledge Him, and He shall direct thy paths.' This made me weep for joy; and for forty-five years I have scarcely entered on any serious engagement without thinking of these words, and entreating the Divine direction" (T. E. Fuller, *Life and Writings*, 15–16).

[30] Matthias Maurice (1684–1738) published a book in 1737 called *The Modern Question Modestly Answer'd*. Sell says, "Here he [Maurice] forsook High Calvinism, and proclaimed the duty of hearers of the Word to believe in Christ" (Alan P. Sell, *The Great Debate: Calvinism, Arminianism and Salvation* [Eugene, OR: Wipf & Stock Publishers, 1998], 78). For more on the "Modern Question" in Northamptonshire, see Geoffrey F. Nuttall, "Northamptonshire and The Modern

the gospel. This inquiry would eventually culminate in a major theological shift in Fuller's theology that in turn would have a lasting and profound effect on the theology and practice of the British Particular Baptists of the eighteenth and nineteenth centuries.[31]

Another important aspect of Fuller's personality and a key to understanding his ministry was his desire and ability to maintain "spiritual" friendships.[32] On 28 May 1776 Fuller met John Sutcliff (1752–1814) at the Northamptonshire Association meeting at Olney. John Sutcliff was the pastor of the Particular Baptist Church at Olney and, as we shall see, his friendship and influence is deeply woven into the fabric of Fuller's story. Shortly afterwards in 1778 Fuller also met John Ryland Jr. (1753–1825), who was at this time co-pastor of the Calvinistic Baptist church at Northampton. Both these men proved to be lifelong friends, working side-by-side in furthering the work of the Baptist denomination especially through the promotion of the Baptist Missionary Society. As E.F. Clipsham notes, Fuller's involvement with the eighteenth-century evangelical revival among the Baptists is essentially a story of teamwork.[33] These men all shared a common theological identity as they were all re-evaluating certain aspects of High Calvinistic theology. In particular, there was a common appreciation for the writings of the New England divine Jonathan Edwards (1703–1758), which they circulated amongst themselves.[34] They all came to believe in, and to actively promote, the theological belief that it was the duty of all who hear the gospel to believe in Jesus Christ. In particular, Jonathan Edwards' theology provided the answers they were seeking, especially in his book, *A Careful and Strict Inquiry into the Modern Prevailing Notions of that Freedom of the Will which is Supposed to be Essential to Moral Agency, Virtue, and Vice, Reward and Punishment, Praise and Blame* (hereafter referred to as *Freedom of the Will*).[35] Edwards' *Freedom of the Will* significantly influenced

Question: A Turning Point in Eighteenth Century Dissent" *Journal of Theological Studies* 16 (1965); Fuller, *Complete Works*, I, 15.

[31] Not all believe that these influences were necessarily positive. For example see George M. Ella, *Law and Gospel in the Theology of Andrew Fuller* (Durham: GO Publications, 1996), 11.

[32] Michael A.G. Haykin ed., *The Armies of the Lamb: The Spirituality of Andrew Fuller* (Dundas, ON: Joshua Press, 2001), 42.

[33] E.F. Clipsham, "Andrew Fuller and Fullerism: A Study in Evangelical Calvinism" *The Baptist Quarterly* 20, no. 6 (April 1964): 270.

[34] Fuller, *Complete Works*, I, 35.

[35] Originally the work was recommended to Fuller by Robert Hall in 1775, but Fuller did not read it until 1777, two years later. Fuller, *Complete Works*, I, 14). Paul Ramsay ed. Jonathan Edwards, *Freedom of the Will* (New Haven, CT: Yale University Press, 1957): 118–119: Edwards'

Fuller's thinking, particularly the distinction between natural and moral inability. For Fuller this distinction clearly articulated a line of thought, towards which he was already moving, which would form the basis of his argument in his influential soteriological magnum opus, *The Gospel Worthy of all Acceptation.*[36]

On 23 December 1776 Fuller married Sarah Gardiner (1756–1792), a member of the Soham church. Together they had eleven children, but only three would survive infancy. As mentioned, one of the remarkable features of Fuller's life was his indefatigable energy and productivity even amidst severe trials. A trial that he often faced was the loss of loved ones and especially of his beloved children. In particular, the death of a daughter named Sarah (1779–1786) sorely grieved him. His good friend and first biographer John Ryland Jr. recalls the deep love Fuller had for the girl. Ryland writes, "With respect to his parental tenderness towards his daughter, I was an eye-witness to the uncommon degree in which it was manifested."[37] Fuller had committed her to God at a very early age and was almost overwhelmed when she died of the measles at six and half years old. While she was dying Fuller describes his anguish in his diary:

> Death! Death is all around me! My friends die ... Death and judgment is all I can think about! ... On the 25th, in particular, my distress seemed beyond all measure. I lay before the Lord, weeping like David, and refusing to be comforted. This brought on, I have reason to think, a bilious cholic: a painful affliction it was; and the more so, as it prevented my ever seeing my child alive again! Yes, she is gone! On Tuesday morning, May 30, as I lay ill in bed, in another room, I heard a whispering. I inquired, and all were silent. ... all were silent. ... but all is well! I feel reconciled to God. I called my family round my bed. I sat up, and prayed as well as I could; I bowed my head, and worshipped, and blessed a taking as well as a giving God.[38]

Freedom of the Will was first published in Boston in the year 1754. A second and third edition was brought out by publishers in London in 1762 and 1768 in the decade following Edwards' death in 1758. To the third edition, the "Remarks" on *Lord Kames' Essays* were added for the first time. The fourth English edition appeared in 1775 and in 1790 two more British editions.

[36] Fuller, "Gospel Worthy" in *Complete Works*, II, 328. In the preface to *Gospel Worthy* Fuller states his interest and dependence on President Edwards' *Freedom of the Will* particularly in reference to the difference between natural and moral inability.

[37] Ryland, *Work of Faith*, 270.

[38] Ryland, *Work of Faith*, 283–284.

Despite these tremendous trials Fuller found strength in God's sovereign and benevolent care and this enabled him to press forward with his duties as a pastor. Later on in his ministry he would remember these trials and use them to minister sensitively and with empathy to others facing similar difficulties.[39]

His wife Sarah died six years later after a bout of mental illness. During certain episodes she thought that Andrew was an imposter who had infiltrated the house. Fuller writes, "'No,' she would say to me, with a countenance full of inexpressible anguish, 'this is not my home ... you are not my husband ... these are not my children.'"[40] She was always trying to "escape" and so Andrew was forced to lock the doors to keep her safe at home. Despite his great love for her, when she eventually died, Fuller characteristically responded with humble resignation: "It is the cup which my Father hath given me to drink, and shall I not drink it?"[41] Fuller married again on 30 December 1794, this time to Miss Ann Coles (d.1825), daughter of the Rev. William Coles (1735–1809), a Baptist pastor from Ampthill in Bedfordshire.[42]

Fuller pastored the church at Soham for seven years. As his theology began to shift further away from its High Calvinist roots, so also his preaching underwent a transformation. Increasingly it was becoming characterized by a passion to share that all sinners were welcomed to trust in Christ without any special sign that they were among the "elect." A small minority of people in the church were alarmed at this change and became disgruntled with this aspect of his ministry.[43] In addition to these conflicts Fuller was also struggling with insufficient finances as the exiguous resources of the poor church could not afford an adequate salary to support his growing family.

At the same time he was struggling with these issues, the congregation of the Baptist church at Kettering who had heard him preach on many occasions approached him to become their full-time pastor. Despite the temptation of the opportunity at the larger Kettering church, which could pay him what he needed and which was more theologically compatible, Fuller agonized long

---

[39] For example, in a letter to his friend Christopher Anderson written in 1809 concerning the death of a niece, Fuller adds his biblical perspective and encouragement remembering the death of his own daughter Sarah. See Joseph Belcher, *The Last Remains of the Rev. Andrew Fuller: Sermons, Essays, Letters, and other Miscellaneous Papers, not included in his Published Works* (Philadelphia: American Baptist Publication Society, 1856), 303.

[40] Fuller, *Complete Works*, I, 59.

[41] Fuller, *Complete Works*, I, 61.

[42] Ryland, *Work of Faith*, 293.

[43] Fuller, *Complete Works*, I, 18.

and hard over the decision to accept their offer. He considered the relationship between a church and its pastor to be a covenant relationship ordained by God, similar to a marriage, and his hesitation was based on a desire to make certain that he was doing the will of God.[44] Ryland says, "Men who fear not God, would risk the welfare of a nation with fewer searchings of heart than it cost him to determine whether he should leave a little dissenting church, scarcely containing forty members besides himself and his wife."[45] Fuller's diary at this time reveals some of his internal struggles. "My heart often aches in thinking of my situation. Lord, what is duty? Oh, that my ways were directed to keep Thy statutes."[46] Fuller loved the people at Soham and was reluctant to leave them without a shepherd, so he sought the Lord in prayer with fasting even as he was considering the counsel of trusted advisors.[47] In May 1781 at the annual association meeting, Fuller asked for the advice of nine assembled ministers.[48] They unanimously advised him to pursue the opportunity at Kettering. Fuller's sense of duty was not satisfied, though, as he was concerned that he may have presented only his side of the story without properly representing the opinions of the Soham church.[49] So both Fuller and the church sought answers through an arbitration committee consisting of three ministers. The results were that one justified his removal, another condemned it, and the third was neutral.[50] As the issue of whether he should leave or stay was still not decided, the case was referred to Robert Robinson (1735–1790) from Cambridge, a businessman, farmer, and pastor, who advised that Fuller should continue at Soham for a full year and the congregation should raise his income to twenty-six pounds a year clear of all deductions.[51] Fuller was making about

---

[44] Laws, *Andrew Fuller*, 41.

[45] Fuller, *Complete Works*, I, 19.

[46] A.G. Fuller, *Andrew Fuller*, 46.

[47] Fuller, *Complete Works*, I, 31.

[48] Fuller, *Complete Works*, I, 29: The ministers were Abraham Booth, Caleb Evans, John Gill, Jr., Thomas Guy, Robert Hall, Sr., Richard Hopper, John Ryland Sr., John Ryland Jr., and John Sutcliff.

[49] A.G. Fuller, *The Principal Works and Remains of the Rev. Andrew Fuller: with a New Memoir of his Life, by his Son* (London, Henry G. Bohn, 1828), 29.

[50] A.G. Fuller, *Andrew Fuller*, 49.

[51] Laws, *Andrew Fuller*, 42. Laws feels that Robinson may have thought that Fuller could engage in multiple occupations like himself to supplement his income. Fuller tried bi-vocational ministry by setting up a school, which had failed by April 1780. J.W. Morris, *Memoirs of the Life and Writings of the Rev. Andrew Fuller, Late Pastor of the Baptist Church at Kettering, and Secretary to the Baptist Missionary Society* (London: Paternoster Row, 1816), 29.

thirteen pounds a year salary at the time.[52] It is indicative of Fuller's character that even though the counsel of men was sought, the Word of God was the final arbitrator. In a diary entry of 10 January 1780 Fuller prayed:

> Nor do thou suffer my own fancy to misguide me. Lord, thou hast given me a determination to take up no principle at second-hand; but to search for everything at the pure fountain of thy word. Yet, Lord, I am afraid, seeing I am as liable to err as other men, lest I should be led aside from truth by mine own imagination. Hast thou not promised, "The meek thou wilt guide in judgment, and the meek thou wilt teach thy way"?[53]

Appropriating the promise of Psalm 25:9, he trusted that ultimately the Lord would guide him.

In October 1782 Fuller moved to Kettering to the church known as the "Little Meeting House," a term that distinguished it from an independent church known as the "Great Meeting House."[54] Following another probation period of a year he was formally installed as their pastor. He ministered at the "Little Meeting House" in Kettering for the next thirty-two years, but there was a certain irony underlying this transfer. It is noteworthy that John Gill (1697–1771), whose parents were founding members of the Baptist church at Kettering, and John Brine (1703–1765), both considered the fathers of High Calvinism among the Baptists, were both born in Kettering.[55] Now the man credited with bringing down the strongholds of High Calvinist dogma was pastoring the church that had nurtured young Gill and Brine in the faith.

The Baptist church at Kettering had eighty-eight members when Fuller was called, but the number of "hearers" was much higher than the membership numbers indicated. At the time of Fuller's death the membership numbered one hundred and seventy-four, with about one thousand hearers,[56] and at this time the population of Kettering was only about three thousand and

---

[52] Fuller, *Complete Works*, I, 19.

[53] Fuller, *Complete Works*, I, 20.

[54] Laws, *Andrew Fuller*, 43.

[55] Robert W. Oliver, "John Gill (1697–1771)" in Michael A.G. Haykin, ed., *The British Particular Baptists 1638-1910* (Springfield, MO: Particular Baptist Press, 2000), 1:145.

[56] Peter J. Morden, *Offering Christ to the World: Andrew Fuller (1754–1815) and the Revival of Eighteenth Century Particular Baptist Life* (Carlisle, UK: Paternoster Press, 2003), 110.

three hundred people.[57] According to Laws many were afraid to commit to membership because they doubted if they were truly among the elect.[58] He quips, "The door-step of the church was very high indeed," which he feels may account for the high number of hearers.[59] This interpretation is open to challenge however, as it is hard to imagine that this many people would sit under Fuller's ministry so long and still maintain a High Calvinist position. Perhaps Fuller's views on strict communion might also have contributed to this state of affairs. Regardless, the situation at Kettering was typical of the period. The elder Robert Hall gave the charge to Fuller from 1Timothy 4:12 with John Ryland Jr. preaching to the people from Acts 20:31.

The move put Fuller into closer and more frequent contact with John Sutcliff, John Ryland, and Robert Hall, men who would emerge as the key leaders of the British Calvinistic Baptists and who greatly influenced the direction and growth of the denomination.[60] Perhaps their main influence on Fuller's theology would be introducing him to the New England theology of Jonathan Edwards. On 23 April 1784[61] Ryland received from John Erskine (1721–1803)[62] a copy of Edwards' *An Humble Attempt to Promote Explicit Agreement and Visible Union of God's People in Extraordinary Prayer for the Revival of Religion and the Advancement of Christ's Kingdom on Earth, Pursuant to Scripture Promises and Prophecies concerning the Last Time.*[63] He immediately shared it with Sutcliff and Fuller and as a result they committed to spend every second Tuesday of every other month to "seek the revival of real religion, and the extension of

---

[57] R.L. Greenall, "After Fuller: Baptists in Nineteenth Century Kettering," *The Kettering Connection—Northamptonshire Baptists and Overseas Missions*, R.L. Greenall, ed. (Leicester, UK: Department of Adult Education, 1993), 33.

[58] Laws, *Andrew Fuller*, 44.

[59] Laws, *Andrew Fuller*, 44.

[60] George M. Ella disagrees that their influence, especially Fuller's, was positive. Ella, *Law and Gospel*, 193.

[61] Haykin, *One Heart and One Soul*, 158.

[62] John Erskine was a Scottish Presbyterian divine involved in transatlantic letter writing. See the discussion of transatlantic evangelical correspondence in relation to Erskine in Susan O'Brien, "A Transatlantic Community of Saints: The Great Awakening and the First Evangelical Network, 1735-1755," *The American Historical Review* 91 (1986), 811–832.

[63] The influence on Fuller is reflected in his diary where he comments, "Some serious tenderness of spirit, and concern for the carnality of my heart, for some days past. Read to our friends, this evening, a part of Mr. Edwards's *Attempt to Promote Prayer for the Revival of Religion*, to excite them to the like practice. Felt my heart profited, and much solemnized by what I read." This extract is found in Fuller's Diary, now at Bristol Baptist College, written 9 July 1784. Andrew Fuller, *Diary and Spiritual Thoughts [1784–1801].*

Christ's kingdom in the world."[64] At the annual association meeting of that year Fuller preached a sermon on 2 Corinthians 5:7 entitled "The Nature and Importance of Walking by Faith." Following Fuller's sermon Sutcliff proposed the churches of the association meet to pray that God would send revival. They met every first Monday of the month for one hour.[65] Soon other Particular Baptist churches in other associations throughout England began similar corporate prayer regiments.[66] These prayer meetings continued for another forty years and were directly linked to renewal among British Particular Baptists[67] while at the same time nurturing thoughts of expansion beyond Britain.[68] This renewed interest in corporate prayer may provide evidence of a shift among the Particular Baptists from "a garden enclosed"[69] that primarily looked within towards an interest in influencing the wider church and the world in general. They now seemed more concerned to pray that all evangelicals experience success in the spread of the gospel.[70]

Fuller continued to remain very active in the Northamptonshire Association and his leadership became so significant that J.W. Morris describes him as functioning as a kind of unofficial "bishop" of the Baptists.[71] One of the ways he contributed was regularly writing some of the circular letters distributed annually to the churches of the association. For example, shortly after the "1784 Call to Prayer," Fuller wrote a circular letter entitled *Causes of Declension in Religion, and Means of Revival*. In it he called for self-examination among the churches to remove any potential cause for a decline in spiritual vitality. He challenged them to consider whether or not there existed in their churches a contentedness with only a superficial acquaintance with the gospel and also

---

[64] Ryland, *Work of Faith*, 96.

[65] Haykin, *One Heart and One Soul*, 164.

[66] In 1786 these prayer meetings began among the Warwickshire churches and in the Western Association by 1790. See Peter Morden, "Andrew Fuller as an Apologist for Missions" in Michael A.G. Haykin, ed., '*At the Pure Fountain of Thy Word': Andrew Fuller as an Apologist* (Carlisle, UK: Paternoster Press, 2004), 240.

[67] Haykin, *Armies of the Lamb*, 109.

[68] S. Pearce Carey, *William Carey: The Father of Modern Missions* (London: The Wakeman Trust, 1993), 9–11.

[69] Haykin, *One Heart and One Soul*, 20. Haykin describes how early eighteenth-century Particular Baptists had "limited their horizons to the maintenance of congregational life" as a means of self-preservation and "delighted in describing themselves as 'a garden enclosed' (Song of Solomon 4:12)."

[70] Haykin, *One Heart and One Soul*, 165.

[71] Morris, *Memoirs*, 83.

if they were satisfied with only a surface level concern of holiness and prayer.[72] He was anxious to encourage churches to repent as a necessary precursor to revival.[73]

Another important role Fuller played in the Northamptonshire Association was his involvement in the ordination sermons of new pastors. Through this means he could challenge a new generation of leadership, and in turn the community they influenced, to, among other things, participate in effective evangelism based on the evangelical Calvinism carefully articulated in his *The Gospel Worthy of all Acceptation.*

The Gospel Worthy of all Acceptation

The Gospel Worthy of all Acceptation was published in two editions. It was originally written in 1781 to confirm in Fuller's own mind whether men needed a warrant to come to Christ. At this time he had no thoughts of publishing it.[74] The first edition, published in 1785, was entitled *The Gospel of Christ Worthy of all Acceptation: or the Obligations of Men Fully to Credit, and Cordially to Approve, Whatever God Makes Known. Wherein is Considered the Nature of Faith in Christ, and the Duty of Those Where the Gospel Comes in that Matter.*[75] The second edition, which represents the more mature soteriology of Fuller, was published in 1801 under the title *The Gospel Worthy of all Acceptation, or the Duty of Sinners to Believe in Jesus Christ, with Corrections and Additions to which is added an Appendix, On the Necessity of a Holy Disposition in Order to Believing in Christ.* As mentioned, the initial key motivation for exploring these theological issues stemmed from his original situation at Soham when John Eve resigned over the question of whether a person could keep himself from sin. As Fuller delved deeper into the issue he noticed that Scripture often exhorts and commands all people to repent.[76] In Fuller's mind Edwards' distinction between moral and natural inability in his *Freedom of the Will* was one of the keys to understanding the errors both of Arminianism and of High Calvinism. Both of

---

[72] Fuller, "Declension in Religion" in *Complete Works*, III, 318.

[73] Fuller, "Declension in Religion" in *Complete Works*, III, 323.

[74] Fuller, "Gospel Worthy of all Acceptation" in *Complete Works*, II, 328–329.

[75] Andrew Fuller, *The Gospel of Christ Worthy of all Acceptation: or the Obligations of Men Fully to Credit, and Cordially to Approve, Whatever God Makes Known. Wherein is Considered the Nature of Faith in Christ, and the Duty of Those Where the Gospel Comes in that Matter* (Northampton: T. Dicey & Co., 1785). This first edition is not found in his *Complete Works*.

[76] Fuller, "Gospel Worthy of all Acceptation" in *Complete Works*, II, 328.

these assumed that if God commands something, men and women must possess certain capabilities to obey, or it would be unjust. Whereas Arminians reasoned that in order for God to be just, man must have the innate ability to respond to his commands; High Calvinists argued that in order to be just, God simply does not require unregenerate man to obey God's spiritual commands. "Where no grace is given, they are united in supposing that no duty can be required; which, if true, 'grace is no more grace.'"[77] Here Edwards' distinction between moral and natural inability was helpful to Fuller. Edwards argues that all men have the natural ability to respond to the gospel, but morally they will not because of the imputation of sin from the "fall" of Adam.[78] As Peter Morden summarizes, "a person could not come" to Christ "because they would not come" to Christ.[79] Fuller also found support from older Puritan divines like John Bunyan and John Owen (1616–1683) in that he found evidence that they regularly made indiscriminate calls to repent and turn to Christ.[80] Arminians and High Calvinists alike sought to refute *The Gospel Worthy* in print. Against both of these camps, Fuller found in Edwards' theology a defense of the biblical balance between the antinomic realities of the divine sovereignty of God and human responsibility.

The subtitle *The Duty of Sinners to Believe in Jesus Christ* effectively summarized the main thesis of *The Gospel Worthy*, for, at the time of publication, a central purpose of the book was to provide the theological rationale to motivate churches to share the gospel through evangelical appeals to all and sundry to repent and believe in Christ.[81] The work itself is divided into three parts. In part one, Fuller stressed the importance of a correct understanding of the true nature of biblical faith. High Calvinists like Lewis Wayman (fl. 1730–1740) had argued that faith must contain "a persuasion of our interest in spiritual blessings."[82] Fuller agreed that true faith may indeed contain assurance of salvation, but that it was not the central aspect of saving faith. An unbeliever may be convinced that he is in a state of salvation, but this in itself does not validate his faith as authentic. Under the High Calvinist scheme a person tended to

---

[77] Fuller, "Gospel Worthy" in *Complete Works*, II, 330.

[78] Romans 5:12.

[79] Morden, *Offering Christ*, 44.

[80] Arthur H. Kirkby, *Andrew Fuller (1754–1815)* (London: Independent Press, 1961), 11. See Andrew Fuller, "Gospel Worthy" in *Complete Works*, II, 367.

[81] Fuller, "Gospel Worthy" in *Complete Works*, II, 386.

[82] Fuller, "Gospel Worthy" in *Complete Works*, II, 333.

place his trust in faith itself rather than the gospel. Fuller, on the other hand, believed that true faith trusts what God has revealed in Scripture about Christ and his salvation.[83] As a result biblical faith must be directed outwards with Christ as its focus. High Calvinism encouraged people to gaze inward for assurance seeking to see if they were among the "elect." They looked for a "warrant" as evidence to apply for Christ's mercy, while for Fuller the "warrant" was the gospel offer itself.[84]

Part two of *The Gospel Worthy* is concerned with Fuller's main thesis that faith in Christ is the duty of all who hear, or who have the opportunity to hear, the gospel. He provided six arguments to support his position. First, Fuller argued that "unconverted sinners are commanded, exhorted, and invited to believe in Christ for salvation."[85] It followed that those who hear the gospel are expected to respond in faith. "All who hear" includes not only the elect, but unbelievers also, as evidenced in passages like Psalm 2:12 and John 12:36. The second main argument is that every person is required to accept and obey whatever God reveals.[86] If God reveals something as true, his creatures should not doubt it. To neglect God's revelation is a violation of duty and those who do not choose Christ are condemned in Scripture as being disobedient.[87] Third, "though the gospel, strictly speaking, is not a law, but a message of pure grace, yet it virtually requires obedience, and such an obedience as includes saving faith."[88] The gospel by virtue of its content requires obedience to it. So Fuller says for example that just as the goodness of God is not a law yet deserves a reaction of gratitude, so the gospel requires an appropriate response of obedience.[89] Fourth, "the want of faith in Christ is ascribed in the scriptures to men's depravity, and is itself represented as a heinous sin."[90] The lack of faith itself is considered as sin in the Bible so it must be a duty to believe. Fifth, "God has threatened and inflicted the most awful punishments on sinners for

---

[83] E.F. Clipsham, "Andrew Fuller and Fullerism: A Study in Evangelical Calvinism" *The Baptist Quarterly* 20 (January 1964): 215; Fuller, "Gospel Worthy" in *Complete Works*, II, 332–342.

[84] Gerald L. Priest, "Andrew Fuller, Hyper-Calvinism, and the Modern Question" in Michael A.G. Haykin, ed., *'At the Pure Fountain of Thy Word': Andrew Fuller as an Apologist* (Carlisle, UK: Paternoster Press, 2004), 54.

[85] Fuller, "Gospel Worthy" in *Complete Works*, II, 343.

[86] Fuller, "Gospel Worthy" in *Complete Works*, II, 349.

[87] Fuller, "Gospel Worthy" in *Complete Works*, II, 352.

[88] Fuller, "Gospel Worthy" in *Complete Works*, II, 352.

[89] Fuller, "Gospel Worthy" in *Complete Works*, II, 352.

[90] Fuller, "Gospel Worthy" in *Complete Works*, II, 354.

their not believing on the Lord Jesus Christ."[91] Only sin can be the cause of God's punishment and sin is a breach of duty.[92] Finally, "other spiritual exercises which sustain an inseparable connection with faith in Christ are represented as the duty of man in general."[93] Repentance, which is a general duty of all men, is thus a spiritual exercise resulting in spiritual blessing but is inseparable from faith. The third section of *The Gospel Worthy* responds to seven major arguments against Fuller's theology.[94]

The importance of *The Gospel Worthy* can be seen through its continuing influence in the nineteenth century. Among the Calvinistic Baptists two opposing theological ideologies emerged, the one known as "Fullerism" and the other known as "Gillism." The former system, based on the arguments in *The Gospel Worthy*, made it theologically consistent to call all men to repentance, while the latter system viewed such universal calls as a perversion of the true gospel.[95] The second edition of *The Gospel Worthy* received fierce opposition not only from some High Calvinists, but also from some more sympathetic and moderate Calvinistic Baptists like Abraham Booth (1734–1806).[96] It should be noted that despite the controversy between Booth and Fuller, both men as leading Particular Baptists of the latter eighteenth century[97] remained cordial

---

[91] Fuller, "Gospel Worthy" in *Complete Works*, II, 358.

[92] Fuller, "Gospel Worthy" in *Complete Works*, II, 358.

[93] Fuller, "Gospel Worthy" in *Complete Works*, II, 360.

[94] Fuller, "Gospel Worthy" in *Complete Works*, II, 366–382. These arguments relate to such things as the principle of holiness possessed by man in innocence, the decrees of God, particular redemption, sinners under the covenant of works, the inability of sinners to believe in Christ and do what is spiritually good, the work of the Holy Spirit, and the necessity of a divine principle to believe.

[95] Thomas J. Nettles, *By His Grace and for His Glory: A Historical, Theological, and Practical Study of the Doctrines of Grace in Baptist Life* (Lake Charles, LA: Cor Meum Tibi, 2002), 110. George M. Ella would not consider *Gillism* to represent the charges often laid against Hyper-Calvinism in that he would deny the charge that they did not evangelize. Ella, *Law and Gospel*, 193.

[96] For Fuller's response see, "Six Letters to Dr. Ryland Respecting the Controversy with the Rev. A. Booth" in *Complete Works*, II, 699–715.

[97] Abraham Booth was a leading Particular Baptist minister who pastored Prescot Street Baptist Church in London for almost thirty-seven years. See Robert W. Oliver, "Abraham Booth (1734-1806)" in Michael A.G. Haykin, ed., *The British Particular Baptists 1638-1910* (Springfield, MO: Particular Baptist Press, 2000), 2:31.

to one another.[98] Fuller could still refer to Booth as a "good man and upright."[99] In turn Booth gave his support to the Baptist Missionary Society.

The Gospel Worthy in its second edition represented the crystallization of Fuller's thought and provided clear and concise theological rationale for what many Particular Baptists already believed. As a result it had significant influence on British Particular Baptists in reminding them of, and consequently restoring them back to, their seventeenth-century Particular Baptist evangelistic heritage.[100] Many consider *The Gospel Worthy* to be the key factor in rejuvenating evangelistic activity among British Particular Baptists. Doyle Young writes, "This book, more than any other single influence, drew the attention of Baptists back to the importance of evangelism. Its significance was monumental."[101] In regard to emancipation from High Calvinism, Morris noted at this time:

> A considerable revolution has in consequence taken place in the sentiments of the Baptist denomination, and a greater relish excited for spiritual and practical religion. A wider separation has been made between real and nominal Christians of the same community; between Antinomian Calvinists and Calvinistic believers; while a closer union has been effected amongst the genuine friends of evangelical truth.[102]

Thus, by positively influencing the milieu of the Particular Baptists, *The Gospel Worthy* paved the way for evangelical preaching, personal evangelism, and overseas missions by providing these Christians with the biblical justification to make appeals for souls.[103] The new evangelistic environment contributed to an era of expansionistic optimism where confidence was mounting that God was about to enlarge his kingdom on earth.[104]

---

[98] Robert W. Oliver, "Andrew Fuller and Abraham Booth" in Michael A.G. Haykin, ed., *At the Pure Fountain of Thy Word: Andrew Fuller as an Apologist* (Carlisle, UK: Paternoster Press, 2004), 203.

[99] Letter to William Carey, November 26, 1802 (Transcribed by Joyce A. Booth from a calendar of Fuller's letters prefaced by the Rev. Ernest A. Payne found in manuscript box [4/5/1]) (Angus Library, Regent's Park College, Oxford).

[100] Kenneth Dix, *Strict and Particular: English Strict and Particular Baptists in the Nineteenth Century* (Didcot: Baptist Historical Society, 2001), 269.

[101] Doyle L. Young, "The Place of Andrew Fuller in the Developing Modern Mission Movement" (PhD diss., Southwestern Baptist Theological Seminary, 1981), 130.

[102] Morris, *Memoirs*, 272.

[103] Morden, *Offering Christ,* 139.

[104] Morden, "Andrew Fuller as an Apologist for Missions," 240.

Other Theological Controversies

Throughout his career Fuller was involved in a variety of debates combating theological errors of his day. An important work refuting the Socinianism[105] of Joseph Priestly (1733–1804) entitled *The Calvinistic and Socinian Systems Examined and Compared, as to their Moral Tendency* was written in 1793.[106] Fuller effectively argued that Socinianism, which denied the trinity of the Godhead and the deity of Christ, produced a vastly inferior form of morality to that of orthodox Christianity.

Another influential work and one of his most popular apologetic works was a defense against the Deism of men like Thomas Paine (1737–1809).[107] In 1800, the work *The Gospel its Own Witness* was published (and subsequently reprinted numerous times) and represented the most significant eighteenth-century Baptist defense against Deism.[108]

Finally, his *Strictures on Sandemanianism* in Twelve Letters to a Friend (1810) countered the arguments of the doctrine of Robert Sandeman (1718–1771) who taught that faith was an intellectual consent to the doctrines of Scripture.[109] Fuller argued that true knowledge of Christ necessarily involves the affections of the heart where a proper understanding of doctrine leads to a love and delight in the living resurrected person of Jesus Christ. In other words, true Christianity for Fuller was a relationship with a person rather than a mere assent to certain truths about a person.

---

[105] *Evangelical Dictionary of Theology 3rd ed.*, Walter A. Elwell, ed. (Grand Rapids, MI: Baker Book House, 1984), s.v. "Socinus, Fautus (1539-1604)," by P. Kubricht: Faustus Socinus (1539-1604) believed Scripture should be interpreted rationally. "This philosophical framework led him to deny the deity of Christ." He did not believe the cross bought forgiveness of sins, he denied the Trinity, original sin, predestination, and the resurrection of the body. His ideas were the root of later Unitarian movements.

[106] Fuller, "Socinian Systems Examined" in *Complete Works*, II, 108.

[107] *Evangelical Dictionary of Theology, 3rd ed.*, Walter A. Elwell, ed. (Grand Rapids, MI: Baker Book House, 1984), s.v. "Deism," by M.H. Macdonald: Deism was a movement of rationalistic thought in the eighteenth century. Deists differ from orthodox Christianity in that they "deny the Trinity, the incarnation, the divine authority of the Bible, the atonement, miracles, any particular elect people such as Israel, and any supernatural redemptive act in history."

[108] Fuller, "The Gospel Its Own Witness" in *Complete Works*, II, 1; *Biographical Dictionary of Evangelicals*, ed., Timothy Larsen (Downers Grove, IL: Inter-Varsity Press, 2003), s.v. "Fuller, Andrew (1754-1815)" by Michael A.G. Haykin.

[109] Fuller, "Strictures on Sandemanianism" in Complete *Works*, II, 561. See also the online article by Michael Haykin, "Defenders of the Faith: Andrew Fuller and the Sandemanians," http://www.evangelical-times.org (accessed November 9, 2004); and Michael A.G. Haykin, "Andrew Fuller and the Sandemanian Controversy" in Michael A.G. Haykin, ed., *At the Pure Fountain of Thy Word: Andrew Fuller as an Apologist* (Carlisle, UK: Paternoster Press, 2004), 226.

Other Writings

Mention should also be made of Fuller's memoir for his good friend Samuel Pearce (1766–1799) entitled *Memoirs of the Rev. Samuel Pearce, M.A.* (1800).[110] Pearce was the pastor of Cannon Street Baptist Church in Birmingham. He was well loved in the group of friends that consisted of John Ryland Jr., John Sutcliff, Robert Hall Jr. (1764–1831), William Carey (1761–1834), and Fuller. They all recognized his exceptional piety and he became known as "the seraphic Pearce" for his chief characteristic of "holy love."[111] The descriptive of "holy love" referred not only to his great love to God, but also to his concomitant evangelistic passion for the salvation of souls. When funding for the Baptist Missionary Society seemed only like a quixotic ideal, Pearce managed to raise the munificent amount of seventy pounds for the society. He himself earnestly desired to go out as a missionary but his ministerial peers felt he was needed more at home.[112] When their verdict was pronounced, Pearce humbly submitted to their counsel despite his enormous personal disappointment.[113] This self-sacrificing Christian submission was one of the traits that endeared him so much to his colleagues. Fuller was on a fundraising trip to Scotland when he heard of the death of Pearce. He was so overcome he cried, "O Jonathan, very pleasant hast thou been unto me. I am distressed for thee, my brother Jonathan ... God of Samuel Pearce be my God."[114] Pearce died young, at the age of thirty-three, and Fuller's memoirs portray him as a kind of Baptist David Brainerd (1718–1747) who was known by all for his deep love of God, personal holiness, and effectiveness as an evangelistic preacher.[115] Fuller's memoir of Pearce proved to be a very popular work gaining a high place "in the public estimation."[116]

In addition to his controversial works and Pearce's memoirs, Fuller also authored much personal correspondence, circular letters to the

---

[110] Fuller, "Memoirs of the Rev. Samuel Pearce" in *Complete Works*, III, 367. For a recent publication see Andrew Fuller, *The Life of Samuel Pearce* (Peterborough, ON: H&E Publishing, 2020).

[111] Tom Wells, "Samuel Pearce (1766–1799)" *The British Particular Baptists 1638-1910*, Michael A.G. Haykin, ed. (Springfield, MO: Particular Baptist Press, 2000), 2:183. See also *Complete Works*, III, 429.

[112] Fuller, "Memoirs of the Rev. Samuel Pearce" in *Complete Works*, III, 380.

[113] Fuller, "Memoirs of the Rev. Samuel Pearce" in *Complete Works*, III, 384, 389.

[114] Laws, *Andrew Fuller*, 81.

[115] Jonathan Edwards, *The Life of David Brainerd*, Norman Pettit, ed. (New Haven, CT: Yale University Press, 1985). David Brainerd, whose biography was written by Jonathan Edwards, was a missionary to the North American Indians of Pennsylvania, New Jersey, and New York.

[116] Morris, *Memoirs*, 181. See also T.E. Fuller, *Life of Fuller*, 214.

Northamptonshire Association, numerous sermons, evangelistic tracts, various essays, book reviews, answers to queries in journal articles, a personal diary, articles on various theological topics, and he even began a systematic theology. He also produced two major expository works, one on Genesis and one on Revelation. What is particularly remarkable about this prodigious literary output is that it was written while pastoring a growing church in addition to all his duties as the secretary of the Baptist Missionary Society.

Baptist Missionary Society

By 1792, the Particular Baptists in Britain were growing stronger. This set the stage for the formation of The Particular Baptist Society for Propagating the Gospel Among the Heathen (afterwards called the Baptist Missionary Society and abbreviated BMS).[117] William Carey, one of the first missionaries of the BMS and often credited as the "founder of the modern missionary movement,"[118] was born in the small village of Paulerspury in the Midlands of England. He was converted at the age of seventeen and in October 1783 John Ryland Jr. baptized Carey in the River Nene at Northampton.[119] Six years later in 1789 Carey accepted a call to become pastor of the church at Harvey Lane in Leicester. This would put him in the company of like-minded men who would nurture and facilitate his desire for a missionary society to reach the world with the gospel.[120]

The formation and success of the BMS was a result of the perseverance and vision of Carey, the industriousness of Fuller and his friends, as well as an evangelical climate where churches and individuals were willing to provide prayer and financial resources for the cause.[121] However, the focus here is on Fuller's important contribution. John Ryland Jr., who himself was a key figure in the development of the BMS wrote:

---

[117] Morden, *Offering Christ*, 129–130.

[118] Morden, *Offering Christ*, 129. Morden points out that this nomenclature is in some ways misleading as Carey was not the first protestant missionary sent from Europe. Also Carey was greatly influenced by the American missionary David Brainerd.

[119] S. Pearce Carey, *William Carey*, 26.

[120] John C. Marshman, *The Life and Times of Carey, Marshman, and Ward* (London, 1859), I, 7.

[121] F.A. Cox, *History of the Baptist Missionary Society, from 1792 to 1842* (London: T. Ward & Co. and G. & J. Dyer, 1842), I, 5; Ryland, *Work of Faith*, 147–148.

> With regard to Mr. Fuller's active concern for the welfare of the Baptist Mission, from his appointment as Secretary, at its first formation, till his death, it is impossible to do full justice to his indefatigable zeal, his assiduous attention to whatever could promote its welfare, and the uncommon prudence with which he conducted all measures that related to it at home, and gave counsel to those that needed it most abroad.[122]

Formation of the BMS

At the Clipstone ministers meeting on 27 April 1791 two important sermons were delivered. The first was John Sutcliff's sermon "Jealousy for the Lord of Hosts Illustrated," based on 1 Kings 19:10.[123] The second sermon was given by Fuller and was entitled "The Instances, Evil, and Tendency of Delay, in the Concerns of Religion." It was based on Haggai 1:2.[124] In this address Fuller challenged Christians to consider whether they were guilty of procrastination, which had resulted in halfhearted efforts in world evangelization:

> There is something of this procrastinating spirit that runs through a great part of our life, and it is of great detriment to us in the work of God. We know of many things that should be done, and cannot in conscience directly oppose them; but still we find excuses for our inactivity.[125]

Fuller was appealing for action in addition to prayer. He recognized that God ordained "ordinary means" like evangelistic preaching as the outworking of his sovereign plan. This reminder countered a High Calvinist dogma that emphasized God's sovereignty almost to the exclusion of any human responsibility. Fuller writes:

> We pray for the conversion and salvation of the world, and yet neglect the ordinary means by which those ends have been used to be accomplished. It pleased God, heretofore, by the foolishness of preaching, to save them that believed; and there is reason to think it will still please God to work by that distinguish means. Ought we not then at least to try

122 Ryland, *Work of Faith*, 147.

123 Ryland, *Work of Faith*, 149. For the entire text of the sermon, see Haykin, *One Heart and One Soul*, 355–365.

124 Fuller, "Delay in Religious Concerns" in *Complete Works*, I, 145–151.

125 Fuller, "Delay in Religious Concerns" in *Complete Works*, I, 145.

> by some means to convey more of the good news of salvation to the world around us than has hitherto been conveyed?[126]

Morris viewed this sermon as highly influential in the formation of the BMS. He commented:

> The latter of these sermons [Fuller's] made such an impression on the minds of the ministers present, and the audience in general, as will not easily be forgotten. Every heart was penetrated with the subject; and the ministers retired, scarcely able to speak to one another. A scene of such deep solemnity has seldom been witnessed. Mr. Carey, perceiving the impression on all around him, could not suffer the company to separate until they had come to some resolution on the forming of a missionary society; and a society would then have been formed, but for the well-known deliberative prudence of Mr. Sutcliffe.[127]

The founding of a missionary society was to be delayed despite Carey's impassioned pleas. Instead, a resolution was made suggesting that Carey publish something on the subject of world missions. The pamphlet he published the following year on 12 May 1792 was entitled *An Enquiry into the Obligations of Christians to use Means for the Conversion of the Heathens*, which seemed to draw on some ideas presented in Fuller's *The Instances, Evil, and Tendency Of Delay, In The Concerns OfReligion.*[128] Here Carey argued that the "Great Commission," a common descriptive for a text found in Matthew 28:18–20 where Christ commands his disciples "to make disciples of all nations," was as binding on all believers as it was on the apostolic church.[129]

The next key event in the formation of the BMS was on 30 May 1792,[130] when Carey delivered the annual sermon at the Northamptonshire associational meeting at Friar Lane in Nottingham. His text was taken from Isaiah

---

[126] Fuller, "Delay in Religious Concerns" in *Complete Works*, I, 148.

[127] Morris, *Memoirs*, 98–99.

[128] Morden, *Offering Christ*, 134.

[129] Matthew 28:18–20: "And Jesus came and spake unto them, saying, All power is given unto me in heaven and in earth. Go ye therefore, and teach all nations, baptizing them in the name of the Father, and of the Son, and of the Holy Ghost, teaching them to observe all things whatsoever I have commanded you: and, lo, I am with you always, *even* unto the end of the world. Amen."

[130] Brian Stanley, *The History of the Baptist Missionary Society 1792–1992* (Edinburgh: T&T Clark, 1992), 13. Stanley points out the fact that often the date is often given incorrectly as 31 May 1792.

54:2–3: "Enlarge the place of thy tent, and let them stretch forth the curtain." Carey's two main points were "expect great things," "attempt great things."[131] John Ryland commented on the effects the sermon had on the congregation:

> If all the people had lifted up their voice and wept, as the children of Israel did at Bochim, (Judges ii.) I should not have wondered at the effect: it would have only seemed proportionate to the cause; so clearly did he prove the criminality of our supineness in the cause of God. A resolution was printed, in this year's Letter, "That a plan be prepared, against the next Ministers' Meeting at Kettering, for forming a Baptist Society for propagating the Gospel among the Heathen."[132]

Yet after the sermon it initially appeared that again nothing concrete would be done. John C. Marshman (1794–1877) depicted the scene thus: "Carey seized Fuller by the hand in desperation, inquiring whether 'they were again going away without doing anything?' Carey's appeal evidently moved Fuller who then took the initiative from which others had held back."[133] So with Carey's prompting, Fuller submitted the above-mentioned resolution, "that a plan be prepared against the next ministers meeting at Kettering, for forming a Baptist Society for Propagating the Gospel among the Heathen."

The BMS was officially formed in Kettering on 2 October 1792 by fourteen men crowded into Martha Wallis' parlor. She was the widow of a deacon from the Kettering church, Beeby Wallis (1735–1792), who had been so influential in Fuller's coming to Kettering, and who had died earlier in April.[134] Fuller was the best qualified to be the society's first secretary. Duly appointed as such, he served from its inception until his death in 1815.[135] Indeed, his level of commitment to the role of secretary was such that some saw it as a chief

---

[131] Ryland, *Work of Faith*, 150. Ryland remembers it as "expect great things from God, and to attempt great things for God." See Haykin's discussion of the theories of what exactly was said. Haykin, *One Heart and One Soul*, 217.

[132] Ryland, *Work of Faith*, 150.

[133] Brian Stanley, "The Origins and Early Work of the Baptist Missionary Society" in *The Kettering Connection—Northamptonshire Baptists and Overseas Missions*, ed., R.L. Greenall (Leicester: Department of Adult Education, 1993), 20.

[134] John Rippon, *A Brief Memoir of the Life and Writings of the Late John Gill*, D. D. (Harrisonburg, VA: Sprinkle Publications, 1991 [1838]), 2. William Wallis (d. 1712), Beeby's great-grandfather, was the first pastor of the congregation. Haykin, *One Heart and One Soul*, 219.

[135] E.F. Clipsham, "Andrew Fuller and the Baptist Mission" *Foundations*, 10, no.1 (January–March, 1967): 5.

cause of his death. Morris says of Fuller that he "lived and died a martyr to the mission."[136] Fuller's vision for the mission was of a group of men penetrating into a previously undiscovered mine. With no guide but God, though dangerous and frightening, they were determined to "attempt great things." Carey would go down, as it were, to the mission field and Fuller and their colleagues would "hold the rope."[137] They all viewed their responsibilities as a sacred oath. It is vital to note that for these men an oath was not simply a casual verbal agreement, but a binding covenant that they would attempt to fulfill no matter the personal cost. As mentioned, in Fuller's case this commitment most probably cost him his life. Fuller's main responsibilities as secretary included theological and letter writing, wide ranging administrative duties, fundraising for the mission, various pastoral obligations, and frequent polemical justifications for the mission both home and abroad.

The Theologian

Fuller's theological writings, and especially *The Gospel Worthy*, had contributed to the creation of a sympathetic evangelical environment among the British Baptists, which helped to justify and sustain a society like the BMS. In this sense Fuller was the chief "thinker" behind the mission.[138] He possessed a common-sense practicality that helped guide the mission through uncharted waters. His no-nonsense wisdom was based on certain key theological underpinnings. First, Christ is the unique revelation of God in the gospel and God has freely offered Christ to the world through his obedient servants.[139] Fuller's great confidence in the mission's ability to overcome all obstacles—spiritual, political, and financial—was reinforced by an Edwardsean post-millennial optimism which supposed that God's eschatological plan for mankind's salvation could not be thwarted.[140]

These theological convictions were communicated and reinforced through regular correspondence to the missionaries, encouraging, exhorting, and sometimes rebuking them. When Fuller gave a sermonic charge to new missionaries going to the field he encouraged them to develop and maintain a deep

---

136 Morris, *Memoirs*, 49.

137 Ryland, *Work of Faith*, 157.

138 Clipsham, "Fuller and the Baptist Mission," 6.

139 Clipsham, "Fuller and the Baptist Mission," 6–7.

140 Fuller, "The Promise of the Spirit" in *Complete Works*, III, 363. See Morden, "Andrew Fuller as an Apologist for Missions," 240.

spirituality as they went as representatives of God. In a charge delivered to the first missionaries of the BMS in 1793, for example, Fuller admonished them, saying, "The heathen will judge of the character of your God, and of your religion, by what they see of your own character."[141] As Timothy George, a foremost Baptist historian, rightly argues, Fuller was the leading theologian of the fledgling missionary movement.[142]

The Administrator

Fuller was also the chief administrator of the mission, managing its affairs mostly from his manse at Kettering for twenty-two years.[143] Bureaucracy was always kept to a minimum and consisted mainly of an annual conference and occasional committee meetings.[144] The reluctance to expand the formal organization of the mission was based on its philosophy to care for the missionaries as "ropeholders." Consequently Fuller would spend upwards of eleven hours a day at his desk personally managing the affairs of the mission.[145] His main duties as secretary included letter writing and issuing regular periodical accounts of the society,[146] supplying missionary news to Rippon's Baptist Annual Register, as well as contributing pieces to the *Evangelical* and *Baptist Magazine*. He was even involved in the minutiae of details concerning the delivery and tracking of missionary supplies.[147]

The Fundraiser

Obviously, the mission needed significant amounts of money and so one of Fuller's key tasks as secretary was to raise funds. The whole initiative of a foreign mission was founded on a solid base of at least nine years of prayer and, in like manner, prayer was at the foundation of their fundraising activities.[148] Fuller's chief method for fundraising was through individual and corporate

---

[141] Fuller, "The Nature and Encouragements of the Missionary Work" in *Complete Works*, I, 511.

[142] See Morden, *Offering Christ*, 139.

[143] Clipsham, "Fuller and the Baptist Mission," 8.

[144] Clipsham, "Fuller and the Baptist Mission," 8.

[145] Clipsham, "Fuller and the Baptist Mission," 9.

[146] Ryland, *Work of Faith*, 147.

[147] T.E. Fuller, *Life of Fuller*, 102. Thomas Fuller, Andrew Fuller's grandson, describes the discovery of an undelivered cask sitting in a warehouse filled with supplies intended for the missionaries. Fuller was sent to London to investigate.

[148] John Fawcett, *An Account of The Life, Ministry And Writings Of The Late Rev John Fawcett* (London: Baldwin, Craddock and Joy, 1818), 294.

appeals, which included preaching, personal visits, and letter writing. A strong confidence that God would complete what he had begun gave Fuller great boldness when soliciting funds. In a letter to John Fawcett (1740-1817), who at that time was a stranger, Fuller writes:

> Any sums of money conveyed to me, brother Carey of Leicester, Sutcliff of Olney, Ryland of Northampton, or Hogg of Thrapstone, will be thankfully received. The sooner the better, as time is short—Mr. Carey will be in your part in the course of a week or two on a visit to a relation. Hear him preach, and you will give him a collection.[149]

In addition to these individual appeals, Fuller also traveled extensively raising funds for the mission through preaching tours. These tours included five trips to Scotland during the years 1799-1813,[150] one to each of Ireland (1804), and Wales (1812), as well as many to London, Lancashire, Yorkshire, Norfolk, Essex, and to the West of England. These tours often covered great distances and kept him away from his church at Kettering for up to three months a year.[151] These herculean efforts took their toll on his health. Morris later noted, "In serving the mission, he had no idea of sparing himself; but while his health was constantly impaired by the greatness of his exertions, he persevered in them with unabating ardour to the very last."[152] Not only did Fuller preach extensively during these tours, but he also conducted numerous individual meetings with pastors and congregational members. He could travel up to forty miles a day[153] visiting and collecting while preaching up to three times a day on a Sunday.[154] In addition he would often stay up late into the evening talking to ministers or writing letters and all this despite failing health in the

---

149 Fawcett, *Account*, 294-295. This is found in a letter from Fuller to Fawcett dated 28 January 1792 (Cited in Morden, *Offering Christ*, 146). John Fawcett (1740-1817) was John Sutcliff's pastor in Yorkshire at Wainsgate Baptist Church and author of the popular hymn *Blessed be the Tie that Binds*.

150 The dates of the Scotland trips were 1799, 1802, 1805, 1808, and 1813. Ryland, *Work of Faith*, 156.

151 Morden, *Offering Christ*, 147.

152 Morris, *Memoirs*, 157.

153 Between the years 1750-1759 the average journey time in England was just under three miles per hour. It had risen to approximately seven miles per hour at the time of Fuller's death in 1815. See Dan Bogart, "Turnpike Trusts and the Transportation Revolution in 18th Century England" (http://orion.oac.uci.edu/~dbogart/transportrev_oct13.pdf (accessed January 21, 2005), 38.

154 Ryland, *Work of Faith*, 197; Morden, *Offering Christ*, 153.

last dozen years of his life.[155] Fuller himself believed that a paralytic stroke he suffered in January 1793 and that caused a loss of muscle control in his face was related to his exhausting labors.[156] Truly no one in England did more than Fuller to support the mission.[157]

The Pastoral Advisor

From its inception, there was a concern that the BMS might develop into an impersonal institution, possibly threatening the personal covenant between the missionaries and the representatives of the Particular Baptists at home in England. They wanted the BMS to be a mission owned by the churches. For Fuller the issue was not primarily a fear of losing control as it was a concern to honour his commitment to God and the missionaries in fulfillment of his oath as a "ropeholder." In this sense the mission was to be an extension of the church and so Fuller viewed his primary role as pastoral. Undeniably his theological, administrative, polemical, and fund-raising tasks were an outworking of his pastoral concern. He was involved in selecting and preparing the missionaries, delivering charges to them through ordination sermons, and encouraging, exhorting, and rebuking them through frequent correspondence while they were in the field. For example, he did not hesitate to send a strong letter of encouragement when missionaries were feeling discouraged over their apparent lack of success.[158] Sometimes these letters came with the promise of a classic theological treatise like John Owen's *On the Mortification of Sin* being sent to them.[159] Nor did he shrink back from admonition. On one occasion he rebuked the missionary John Fountain (1767–1800) who was thought to be jeopardizing the success of the mission because of radical political views.[160]

In fine, as the chief pastoral advisor for the missionaries, Fuller was concerned for the spiritual welfare of the missionaries as individuals. In other

---

155 Morden, *Offering Christ*, 153.

156 Ryland, *Work of Faith*, 155.

157 James M. Renihan, "Out from Hyper-Calvinism: Andrew Fuller and the Promotion of Missions" *Reformed Baptist Theological Review* 1 (January 2004): 46.

158 Clipsham, "Fuller and the Baptist Mission," 11.

159 Ryland, *Work of Faith*, 159.

160 *Letter to John Fountain* 25 March 1796 (Transcribed by Joyce A. Booth from a calendar of Fuller's letters prefaced by the Rev. Ernest A. Payne found in manuscript box [4/5/1]) (Angus Library, Regent's Park College, Oxford).

words, he directed them not only in terms of vocational oversight, but with a pastoral concern for their souls.[161]

The Polemical Defender of Rights

The political position of the BMS was always precarious. The British East India Company was a monopolistic trading business that had become heavily involved in British politics in the eighteenth century.[162] As a result it had a good deal of political clout in India. At times both the company and the British government itself threatened the ongoing work of the mission.[163] The British East India Company feared that the missionaries were interfering with the Indian culture[164] which in turn might harm their business interests.[165] As the chief advocate of the mission at home, Fuller was ever ready to defend its interests and to ensure its ongoing success. In fact, Clipsham feels that this was the "most outstanding aspect of Fuller's achievement as secretary of the Baptist Missionary Society."[166] Fuller's specific involvement in the defense of the mission included advocacy with cabinet ministers, Members of Parliament, and East India directors to protect the rights and privileges of the BMS abroad. With characteristic common sense, a fund of patience, and biblical wisdom, he not only provided sound judgment and advice on practical matters such as transporting money and goods to the missionaries, but he also produced a major theological treatise in defense of the mission.

In particular, two main threats against the mission became so ominous that Fuller felt a public written defense was required. The first threat concerned a mutiny of East India troops in Vellore (1807). The missionaries were accused of interfering with the Hindu religion, thus precipitating an attack on the soldiers.[167] The second involved a vitriolic tract published by a Muslim convert to Christianity accusing Islam of perverting the commands of God.[168] Back in England the missionaries were assailed in print as intolerant radicals who threatened Britain's economic interests in Asia. These changes resulted in a

---

[161] Clipsham, "Fuller and the Baptist Mission," 11.
[162] J.H. Plumb, *England in the Eighteenth Century* (Middlesex: Penguin, Books, 1983), 25.
[163] S. Pearce Carey, *William Carey*, 247.
[164] S. Pearce Carey, *William Carey*, 245.
[165] S. Pearce Carey, *William Carey*, 253.
[166] Clipsham, "Fuller and the Baptist Mission," 11.
[167] Morden, "Andrew Fuller as an Apologist for Missions," 247.
[168] Morden, "Andrew Fuller as an Apologist for Missions," 248.

motion in Parliament to expel them.[169] Fuller visited privately with friends and directors of the East India Company and prepared a statement defending India's mission and the motion was defeated. The tract written against Islam became known as *The Persian Pamphlet* and it provided polemical ammunition for the enemies of the mission in Britain. In response to these events, Fuller wrote the *Apology for the Late Christian Missions to India* (1808). Its main purpose was to vindicate the character of the missionaries and set forth a plea for toleration where people were free to propagate their convictions.[170] Fuller's sagacity, skill, energy, and self-sacrifice in defense of the mission on the home front were essential not only for its continued effectiveness, but also for its very existence.

Pastoral Duties

In the above description of Andrew Fuller, we have seen a man of unfaltering energy capable of extraordinary activity. His exceptional exertions influenced the course of the Particular Baptist cause in the late eighteenth and nineteenth centuries and paved the way for a renewed concern for world missions by providing solid answers to many of the key theological disputes of his generation. His writings had such an impact that he was awarded two honorary doctorate degrees, though he declined both of them.[171] This achievement in itself is noteworthy, yet he accomplished all this while successfully pastoring a growing congregation at Kettering.

---

[169] Young, "Developing Missions," 222.

[170] Fuller, "Apology for the Late Christian Mission to India" in *Complete Works*, II, 763–836.

[171] Fuller, *Complete Works*, I, 81–85. He was offered one from the College of New Jersey (which became Princeton University in 1896) in 1798. The second was offered by Yale in 1805. "Andrew Fuller" in Timothy George and Davis Dockery, eds., *Theologians of the Baptist Tradition* (Nashville, TN: Broadman & Holman Publishers, 2001), 37: Phil Roberts believes that Fuller accepted Yale's degree out of politeness but never used the title. He bases this on Gilbert Laws' comments in, *Pastor, Theologian, Ropeholder*, 95–96: "In May of 1805 the great esteem in which Fuller's writings were held in the United States was shown in the conferring upon him the honorary degree of Doctor of Divinity by Yale College. This had been done before, as early as 1798, by Princeton. But Fuller had respectfully declined to use the degree. ... Having taken this position he adhered to it when Yale also granted him their honorary D.D. in 1805, notwithstanding that they sent over Professor Silliman to present the honour in person and urge its acceptance. For Ryland, as head of the College, and for other reasons, Fuller thought it might be well. For himself he preferred to be Brother, not Doctor, Fuller. To Dr. Timothy Dwight, President of Yale, and grandson of the beloved President Edwards of Princeton, Fuller sent a gracious letter of appreciation of the honour and a renewed assertion of his reasons for not using the degree."

His pastoral influence on the BMS has been briefly surveyed, but there needs to be a closer look at the discharge of his pastoral responsibilities in his home church in Kettering. He was without official help until 1811 when John Keen Hall (1786–1829) joined as the assistant pastor.[172] Until that time, as has already been noticed, Fuller was away from his congregation for up to three months a year, mostly raising funds for the BMS. At times Fuller himself feared he might be neglecting his pastoral responsibilities at Kettering. He lamented on 27 October 1794, "I long to visit my congregation, that I may know more of their spiritual concerns, and be able to preach their cases."[173] Despite his long absences, the church at Kettering continued to grow, which led to the rebuilding of their Meeting House in 1805. In fact, an epitaph written by the Kettering congregation at Fuller's death praises his life and ministry:

> His ardent piety, the strength and soundness of his judgment, his intimate knowledge of the human heart, and his profound acquaintance with the scriptures, eminently qualified him for the ministerial office, which he sustained amongst them thirty-two years. The force and originality of his genius, aided by undaunted firmness, raised him from obscurity to high distinction in the religious world.[174]

These words give the impression that his people genuinely loved him and were well satisfied with the discharge of his pastoral responsibilities. It seems they understood that Fuller's calling, reinforced by his unique giftedness, inevitably extended his ministry beyond their local church. This love was mutual. Fuller believed that the great secret for ruling a church was to love them and make sure they knew they were loved.[175] In a letter to a young ordinand written in 1810 Fuller could say, "I have been pastor of the church which I now serve for nearly thirty years, without a single difference."[176] He attributes this mutual harmony to his practice of periodically yielding to the advice his deacons,

---

[172] Fuller mentions to Carey that he had an assistant for the summer in 1802: "We shall have an unusual load of business and expense this summer. I must get an assistant, as I had last summer in Stennet. He is now in Ireland." *Letter to William Carey* 28 February 1803 (Transcribed by Joyce A. Booth from a calendar of Fuller's letters prefaced by the Rev. Ernest A. Payne found in manuscript box [4/5/1]) (Angus Library, Regent's Park College, Oxford).

[173] Ryland, *Work of Faith*, 155.

[174] Ryland, *Work of Faith*, 385.

[175] Fuller, "Counsels to a Young Minister" in *Complete Works*, III, 497.

[176] Fuller, "Counsels to a Young Minister" in *Complete Works*, III, 497.

even when his opinion differed. He humbly recognized that as a pastor he was not infallible and that others' opinions were truly valuable.

The epitaph refers both to his knowledge of the human and heart and to his knowledge of Scripture. As a preacher Fuller was preeminently expositional, practical, evangelical, and experiential. Throughout his career Fuller would preach through most of the books of the Bible.[177] His main theme was the glory of God revealed in the cross of Christ and lived out in experiential religion.[178]

In addition to enduring the deaths of many friends and loved ones, Fuller also had to cope with a chronic illness caused by a diseased liver.[179] As a result, throughout his life he was susceptible to illness, especially "bilious affections."[180] Also, the more he wrote in the latter years of his ministry, the more severe were the headaches he experienced.[181] In the closing years of his life he often had difficulty breathing accompanied with a violent cough, indigestion, bilious sickness, and fever.[182] As remarkable as his productivity was, one must carefully consider the context in which it was accomplished, amidst not only extraordinary grief and suffering including many deaths of family and friends, living with a wayward son, and opposition from friends and foes, but also amidst intense physical suffering bordering on near incapacitation.[183] He truly lived one of his favourite maxims, "Whatsoever thy hand findeth to do, do it with thy might."[184] Despite all this illness he still worked up to twelve hours a day at his desk. His wife complained about his excessive labours and Fuller answers:

> Ah, my dear, the way for us to have any joy is to rejoice in all our labour, and then we shall have plenty. "But you allow yourself no time for recreation," continues the pleading wife. "Oh, no," he replies; "all my recreation is a change of work." She tries once more: "Yes, but you will wear yourself out." He replies, slowly and solemnly: "I cannot be worn out in a better cause; we must 'work while it is day.'"[185]

---

[177] Ryland, *Work of Faith*, 382.
[178] Ryland, *Work of Faith*, 382; Morris, *Memoirs*, 69.
[179] Morris, *Memoirs*, 441.
[180] Morris, *Memoirs*, 441.
[181] Morris, *Memoirs*, 441.
[182] Morris, *Memoirs*, 442.
[183] Fuller, *Complete Works*, I, 70–73.
[184] T.E. Fuller, *Life of Fuller*, 293. This maxim is found in Ecclesiastes 9:10.
[185] T.E. Fuller, *Life of Fuller*, 302–303.

He could press on in the midst of these severe trials because he truly believed what he taught: that God was both good and sovereign and would provide grace to support him. On his death bed Fuller wrote to his friend John Ryland Jr.:

> I have preached and written much against the abuse of the doctrine of grace; but that doctrine is all my salvation and all my desire. I have no other hope, than from salvation by mere sovereign, efficacious grace, through the atonement of my Lord and Saviour. With this hope, I can go into eternity with composure. Come, Lord Jesus! Come when thou wilt! Here I am; let him do with me as seemeth him good![186]

The doctrine of the cross was central to Fuller's theology, and with Christ as his example of suffering he expected no less for himself. At his conversion he had submitted his will and his life to God and his cause.

DEATH

Andrew Fuller died in his manse in Kettering on 7 May 1815, a Sunday, at the age of sixty-one. As he lay dying he could hear hymns being sung in his adjoining chapel and he whispered to his child by his bedside, "I wish I had strength enough," "To do what father?" she replied, "To worship child!"[187] He died about half an hour later. Robert Hall was preaching at the time when someone interrupted his sermon with a whisper about Fuller's death. "An audible wail went up" as the congregation "quickly interpreted the movement. The service was closed with a few tender and touching words, and a short pouring out of the heart to Him who gave and had taken away."[188]

His funeral service was attended by about two thousand people with John Ryland Jr. preaching on Romans 8:10. An earlier biographer and once friend of Fuller, J.W. Morris, summarized Fuller's life as follows:

> He possessed a most sincere desire to glorify God, and his whole life was devoted to that all-important object. It may be doubted whether, since Luther's time any man could be found on this side of the globe, who had laboured more to cultivate and extend the knowledge of the truth than Mr. Fuller.[189]

---

[186] Ryland, *Work of Faith*, 355.
[187] T.E. Fuller, *Life of Fuller*, 310.
[188] Fuller, *Andrew Fuller*, 190–191.
[189] Morris, *Memoirs*, 496.

It is almost universally accepted that Fuller was among the greatest Baptist theologians of the eighteenth century in America and Britain. He accomplished great things for the cause of Christ. Yet, in the words of his fellow Kettering minister Thomas Toller, he died, not great in his own eyes, but merely as "a penitent sinner at the foot of the cross."[190]

Conclusion

All these factors contributed to the formation of his pastoral theology which was at the centre of late eighteenth century Baptist renewal. But Fuller did not stand alone and was a part of a clearly defined tradition beginning in the seventeenth century. The next chapter will consider that tradition and its roots to help further understand Fuller's theological and socio-political underpinnings.

---

190 Ryland, *Work of Faith*, 363: Mr. Toller was a close friend of Fuller. He pastored the Independent church at Kettering.

2
Origins of Particular Baptists

Andrew Fuller was a part of a larger Particular Baptist theological tradition which was influential in determining his understanding of pastoral ministry. This chapter provides a brief overview of the origins of the Particular Baptists from their Puritan-Separatist roots and includes a description of the socio-political and theological forces that shaped Fuller's understanding of the ministerial office. Some factors that affected the decline and subsequent numerical rise of the Particular Baptists in the latter part of the eighteenth century will also be briefly discussed.

Particular Baptist Beginnings

Two traditions of Anglophone Baptists emerged in the seventeenth century. They were designated either "General" or "Particular" Baptists according to their views of the atonement of Christ.[1] Both sect's belief that the true church is comprised of those who profess Christ as their Saviour and their steadfastness in favour of water baptism, usually by full immersion, distinguished them as Baptists. Even though this departure from their immediate forebears over the issue of infant baptism resulted in the pejorative labels of "Antipaedo Baptists" or "Anabaptists" by some in the broader reformation tradition,[2] their conviction in this regard was positively motivated by a desire for biblical fidelity. As Roger Hayden observes, "It was the Bible that brought these Christians to radical faith."[3] Yet despite their general agreement on Believer's Baptism,

---

[1] John Ryland, *Work of Faith*, 3.

[2] David Bogue and James Bennett, *History of Dissenters from the Revolution to the Year 1838. Vol.1* (Stoke-on-Trent: Tentmaker Publications, 2000), 1:134. Daniel Defoe uses both these terms to describe Baptists. See Daniel Defoe, *A Tour Through the Whole Island of Great Britain* (Harmondsworth, UK: Penguin Books Ltd., 1971), 71.

[3] Roger Hayden, *English Baptist History and Heritage: A Christian Training Programme Course* (Oxfordshire: The Baptist Union of Great Britain, 1990), 10.

the two communities had different origins as well as different theological emphases.[4]

The General Baptists, named for their belief that Christ died for all men and that anyone who put his/her faith in Christ would be saved, have their roots in the Amsterdam ministries of John Smyth (*c.*1570–1612) and Thomas Helwys (died *c.*1615).[5] John Smyth was a Separatist, originally an Anglican who left England for Amsterdam, Holland due to the persecution of James I (r.1603–1625) around 1607. He came to accept Believer's Baptism as biblical truth in 1609. Initially, he baptized himself and his congregation, but after criticism that his self-baptism was unbiblical, he was baptized again by the Waterlander Mennonite Church.[6] By this time he had also rejected Calvinism and adopted the views of Jacob Arminius (1560–1609) who taught that Christ had died for all people not just the elect. Whereas Smyth most likely died before being fully absorbed into the Mennonite Waterlander Church,[7] Thomas Helwys and a small group from Smyth's original congregation moved back to England where they eventually set up the first Baptist Church on English soil and would become the first congregation in the General Baptist denomination.[8]

The second representative group of Baptists, and the focus of the following study, is the Particular Baptists. The Particular Baptists differed from their General Baptist counterparts primarily through their Calvinism, and were so named because of their belief in a "particular" or "limited" atonement. The doctrine of Particular Redemption states that "the saving purpose of Christ's

---

[4] Some historians like Thomas Crosby (1685–1752), the son-in-law of Benjamin Keach (1640–1704), at times seem to wish to minimize the differences for the sake of unity prior to the union in 1813. Thomas Crosby, *The History of the English Baptists, From the Reformation to the Beginning of the Reign of King George 1, Vol. 3* (London, 1740), III, 271–272. On the formation of the Baptist Union in 1813 see Ernest A. Payne, *The Baptist Union: A Short History* (London: The Carey Kingsgate Press Limited, 1959), 147.

[5] B.R. White, *A History of the English Baptists, Volume 1, The English Baptists of the Seventeenth Century* (London: The Baptist Historical Society, 1983), 7.

[6] John Smyth and about thirty-one others sought membership in February 1610 but they were not accepted immediately.

[7] Tom Nettles, *The Baptists: Key People Involved in Forming a Baptist Identity: Volume One Beginnings in Britain* (Ross-shire: Christian Focus Publications, 2005), 68–69.

[8] M. Dorothea Jordan, "John Smyth and Thomas Helwys: The Two First English Preachers of Religious Liberty. Resemblances and Contrasts," *The Baptist Quarterly* 12 (April-July, 1947): 189, 195.

sacrifice on the cross was for the salvation of the elect alone."[9] They became the more dominant of the two groups in the eighteenth century as many General Baptists adopted Unitarianism.[10] In fact, Thomas Nettles argues that the theology of these Calvinistic Baptists continued to be highly influential among Baptists up to the second decade of the twentieth century.[11]

The Particular Baptists of England arose during the reign of Charles I (r.1625–1644/49), descending from the Puritan-Separatist tradition.[12] In their case, the mainly Paedobaptist ecclesiology of the Independents evolved into the foundational Baptist tenet of Believer's Baptism.[13] That they retained the Calvinistic theology of the Reformed tradition is clearly seen in their early confessions. In 1616, a congregation in London was established that became known as the Jacob-Lathrop-Jessey church, so named for their first three Pastors who were Puritans turned Separatist.[14] From this group a man named John Spilsbury (1593–*c.*1668)[15] emerged to lead the first Particular Baptist church that was founded in 1638. He was a cobbler in London by trade and a member of the church of Henry Jessey (1601–1663) prior to his secession to begin this

---

[9] Robert W. Oliver, *History of the English Calvinistic Baptist (1771-1892) from John Gill to C.H. Spurgeon* (Edinburgh: Banner of Truth, 2006), 166. See also, Fuller, "Gospel Worthy" in *Complete* Works, II, 373–375; cf. John Gill, *A Body of Doctrinal Divinity* (Paris, AK: The Baptist Standard Bearer, 1984), 461–467; William L. Lumpkin, *Baptist Confessions of Faith* (Valley Forge, PA: Judson Press, 1969), 255.

[10] Ryland, *Work of Faith*, 3; R. Philip Roberts, *Continuity and Change: London Calvinistic Baptists and the Evangelical Revival 1760-1820* (Wheaton, IL: Richard Owen Roberts Publishers, 1989), 15; Peter Naylor, *Picking Up a Pin for the Lord: English Particular Baptists from 1688 to the Early Nineteenth Century* (London: Grace Publications, 1994), 49; A.C. Underwood, *A History of the English Baptists* (London: The Baptist Union Publications Department, 1947), 127.

[11] Thomas J. Nettles, *By His Grace and For His Glory: A Historical, Theological, and Practical Study of the Doctrines of Grace in Baptist Life* (Lake Charles, LA: Cor Meum Tibi, 2002), 13.

[12] Underwood, *English Baptists*, 56; R.W. Oliver, "Emergence of a Strict and Particular Baptist Community Among the English Calvinistic Baptists 1770-1850" (DPhil diss., CNAA [London Bible College], 1986), 9. Haykin notes that this generally accepted thesis has been challenged most notably by E.A. Payne (Michael A.G. Haykin, *Kiffen, Knollys, and Keach: Rediscovering Our English Baptist Heritage* [Peterborough, ON: H&E Publishing, 2019], 6–7. See, for example, Ernest A. Payne, "Who were the Baptists?" *The Baptist Quarterly* 16 (October 1956): 339–342.

[13] H. Wheeler Robinson, *The Life and Faith of Baptists* (London: The Kingsgate Press, 1946), 12–14.

[14] Henry Jacob (1563-1624), John Lathrop (1584-1653), Henry Jessey (1601-1663).

[15] Also spelled "Spilsbery," see B.R. White, "Samuel Eaton (d. 1639) Particular Baptist Pioneer" *The Baptist Quarterly* 24 (January 1971): 12. "Spilsberie," see B.R. White ed., *Association Records of the Particular Baptists of England, Wales and Ireland to 1660 Part III* (London: The Baptist Historical Society), 131.

early Baptist work.[16] As the Particular Baptists continued to grow, he became an influential leader among them, sometimes functioning as a polemicist in defense of Baptist distinctives.[17] In 1643 he published a book on baptism entitled *A Treatise Concerning the Lawful Subject of Baptism* to combat criticism that Believer's Baptism was scripturally illegitimate.[18] At the very least he was a signatory of the important *First London Confession of Faith*, but he may have contributed more than just his name.[19] The extent of his contribution to the *First London Confession*[20] is unclear; however Underwood feels he played a significant role in its actual formulation.[21]

By 1644 there were seven congregations in London and forty-seven in the rest of England.[22] By 1660 there were one hundred and thirty-one Particular Baptist churches with the majority located in the Midlands, London, and the southern counties.[23] The impressive growth of the Baptists in this period parallels the development of associations of individual churches in a district or region that cooperated to further their mutual objectives.[24] These associations provided accountability for orthodoxy and a means for providing necessities for ministers of poorer churches.[25] This resulting "strength in numbers" cooperation facilitated evangelism and the spread of Baptist principles.

---

[16] James M. Renihan, "John Spilsbury (1593–*c.*1662/1668)" in Michael A.G. Haykin, ed., *The British Particular Baptists 1638–1910* (Springfield MO: Particular Baptist Press, 1998), 1:22–23.

[17] B.R. White, ed., *Association Records of the Particular Baptists of England, Wales and Ireland to 1660. Part 1. South Wales and the Midlands* (Didcot, Oxfordshire: The Baptist Historical Society), 42. Here we see an example where he commended a tract published by Daniel King called, *A Way to Sion* (1650) which was also commended by other known Particular Baptists leaders Thomas Patient and William Kiffin (See B.R. White, *The English Baptists of the Seventeenth Century, A History of the English Baptists, Volume 1* [London: The Baptist Historical Society, 1983], 71). The Abingdon Association sent a letter to Kiffin and others, including Spilsbury (White, *Association Records*, 131). Also they regularly held the meetings at his house: "It is also agreed that the particular churches be desired to returne their answeres respectively to the messengers at London meeting weekely at brother Spilsberie's house in Cole-Harbour in Thames Street upon the 3rd day of the weeke at two of the clocke; and that it be done with as much speed as may be" (White, *Associational Records*, 175).

[18] White, *English Baptists of the Seventeenth Century*, 71.

[19] Lumpkin, *Confessions*, 154–156.

[20] The *First London Confession* is discussed in more detail below.

[21] Underwood, *English Baptists*, 60.

[22] Underwood, *English Baptists*, 85.

[23] Underwood, *English Baptists*, 85.

[24] White, *Baptists Seventeenth Century*, 65.

[25] Haykin, *Kiffen, Knollys, and Keach*, 44.

Particular Baptist Decline

The establishment of a parliamentary government not only contributed to the climate of social and political unrest, but it also provided a new sense of optimism for religious freedom. During this period of rapid Baptist growth, the Particular Baptists were often incorrectly associated with the radical Anabaptism of continental Europe, which resulted in charges of heresy and political dissention.[26] As a result, they felt compelled to produce a statement of faith vindicating themselves from this false connection with the continental Anabaptists and the Arminianism of the General Baptists. The *First London Confession* is clearly Calvinistic in theology. This is especially clear in the articles outlining its Christology, and these twelve sections have been interpreted by some as an indirect denial of Arminianism.[27] Also many of its articles come directly from the *Independent Separatist Confession* of 1596.[28] But despite these similarities with their Calvinistic brethren, the Baptist Confession stresses that full immersion in water is the proper mode of baptism.[29]

In 1661, influenced by the Established Church's perception that all sects were inherently dangerous to the state, Charles II (r. 1660–1685) released a declaration proscribing all illegal and subversive meetings under the facade of worship.[30] The Clarendon Code (1661–1665) was subsequently enacted to re-establish Episcopal power and to achieve a uniformity of creed. It was comprised of several acts aimed mostly at Presbyterians, but of course it affected all Dissenters, including the Baptists. The first Act of Parliament was called The Corporation Act (1661), which stated that members of civic groups must take oaths of loyalty to the crown or they would be removed from office. Those wishing to hold an office were required to take the sacrament of the Church of England at least one year prior to their election.[31] The Act of Uniformity in 1662 required all clergy to agree to the precepts of *The Book of Common Prayer*,

[26] They were often charged with Pelagianism, named after Pelagius, a late fourth-century British monk who taught that "their native powers are such that men are capable of doing everything God requires of them for their salvation" (Reymond, *Systematic Theology*, 468). It also denied the concept of original sin. They were also labeled as "Arminians." Ernest A. Payne, "Who were the Baptists?" *The Baptist Quarterly* 16 (October 1956): 339–342. Lumpkin, *Confessions*, 144.

[27] Lumpkin, *Confessions*, 146.

[28] White, *English Baptists of the Seventeenth Century*, 61. They borrowed twenty-six of fifty-three of the articles from the Independent confession.

[29] Lumpkin, *Confessions*, 167. See, for example, article XL.

[30] Basil Williams, *The Whig Supremacy (1714–1760)* (Oxford: Oxford University Press, 1949), 66.

[31] Underwood, *English Baptists*, 95.

and if they refused, their benefice was revoked.[32] The Conventicle Act (1664) punished people for attending a Nonconformist church service.[33] Finally, The Five Mile Act (1665) prohibited dissenting clergy from coming within five miles of a place where they had previously ministered.[34] Because of these various Acts, all Dissenters, including the Baptists, were denied full legal rights in the state and experienced persecution. It was not uncommon for Baptists to have their meeting houses demolished by angry mobs.[35]

A measure of relief came in 1672 with a Declaration of Indulgence suspending ecclesiastical legal penalties and allowing the licensing of Dissenting meeting places.[36] These privileges would be withdrawn a year later with the Test Act (1673), which prevented Dissenters from entering civil and military office.

In 1677, the Particular Baptists, who shared Calvinism in common with the Independents and Presbyterians, sought to demonstrate their essential theological union with these other Nonconformists, to help present a unified and powerful dissenting voice in response to state persecution.[37] The Particular Baptists in London made one of the most significant of all Anglophone confessions, *The Westminster Confession*,[38] the basis of their own in *The Second London Confession*, albeit with their own distinctions included.[39] Lumpkin notes that there were also some significant differences from the *First London Confession* (1644, 1689) especially in articles describing the Scriptures, the Sabbath, and marriage, while its teaching on Calvinism became even more pronounced.[40] Other changes included statements that the Lord's Supper is not restricted to baptized people, the discarding of the term "sacrament," and an added provision justifying lay preaching.[41] Two months after an Act of Toleration (May 1689), a general meeting was held by Particular Baptists in London. Baptists

---

[32] Underwood, *English Baptists*, 95. *The Book of Common Prayer* is the prayer book of the Church of England. It has been through several revisions over the last few centuries, but it includes the order to be followed in church services.

[33] Underwood, *English Baptists*, 95.

[34] Underwood, *English Baptists*, 96.

[35] W.T. Whitley, *A History of British Baptists* (London: Charles Griffen & Co. Ltd., 1923), 107.

[36] Lumpkin, *Confessions*, 235.

[37] Lumpkin, *Confessions*, 236.

[38] *The Westminster Confession* was created by the Westminster Assembly and published in 1646. It became the official Confession of Scotland and of the English Parliament. It was adopted by both Congregationalists and Presbyterians.

[39] Austin Walker, *The Excellent Benjamin Keach* (Dundas, ON: Joshua Press, 2004), 215.

[40] Lumpkin, *Confessions*, 237.

[41] Lumpkin, *Confessions*, 238.

from one hundred and seven churches in England and Wales sent messengers. At this meeting they approved the Confession of 1677 for use in their churches. A second revised edition was published in 1689.[42]

With the abolishment of compulsory service at the Church of England after the so-called Glorious Revolution of William III and Mary II (1688)[43] and with the passing of the Toleration Act (1689),[44] Dissenters were permitted to worship with relative freedom in their meeting places, although with unlocked doors. They were still required to take oaths of allegiance to the state and to sign the *Thirty-Nine Articles*[45] excepting the article affirming infant Baptism.[46] However, the optimism of this new-found freedom generated by the hopeful confidence of expected growth soon gave way to a melancholy reality of regression.[47] Paradoxically, this period became a season of decline for the Baptists for a variety of social, economic, and theological reasons. Socially many Dissenters were still second-class citizens, which initially may have hindered the development of a more educated ministry. In addition, there were still communication and transportation challenges that made close-knit cooperation and interdependency between different Baptist congregations unfeasible, as many Particular Baptists remained isolated from one another in remote villages. At this time in England the transportation system was still cumbrous and inefficient.[48]

Ideologically, the eighteenth century represented the "Age of Enlightenment" where, for some, human reason eclipsed divine revelation as the preferred basis for epistemology. After enduring years of religious wars and

---

[42] Roger Hayden, "The Particular Baptist Confession 1689 and Baptists Today," *The Baptist Quarterly* 32 (October 1988): 403.

[43] James issued his Declaration of Indulgence in 1687 in which he sought more freedoms for Catholics. Motivated by an increased repression of Anglicanism, and the birth of the King's son, a potential catholic heir, seven leaders invited William of Orange to England "to maintain liberties." James fled the country and Parliament offered the throne to William and Mary. Whitley, *British Baptists*, 164–165.

[44] The Toleration Act abolished compulsory attendance at Church of England services.

[45] The *Thirty-Nine Articles* are the essential statements of Anglican doctrine. They were issued by an assembly of clergy of the Church of England in 1571. They are contained in the Book of Common Prayer.

[46] Walker, *Excellent Benjamin Keach*, 204.

[47] Michael A.G. Haykin, "'A Habitation of God, Through the Spirit': John Sutcliff (1752–1814) and the Revitalization of the Calvinistic Baptists in the Late Eighteenth Century," *The Baptist Quarterly* 34 (July 1992): 304.

[48] Daniel Defoe refers to the poor road conditions especially in the Midlands. Defoe, *Tour*, 407, 430.

persecutions, many people had grown tired of theological wrangling.[49] As the influence of Deism and Socinianism arose to challenge theological orthodoxy, many churches, especially those among General Baptists, adopted their heterodox creed. Whereas the pressure of rationalism caused many General Baptists to question an orthodox Christology, it may have influenced Particular Baptists to intensify their convictions concerning the Doctrines of Grace,[50] leading to High Calvinism.[51] In an effort to protect doctrinal fidelity, some Particular Baptists adopted a form of Calvinism that adhered too rigidly to the logic of a system, resulting in a denial of any offers of free grace.[52] This seemed to quench evangelistic fervour and is believed by many earlier Baptist historians to be the chief cause of decline among the Particular Baptists.[53]

Between 1689 and 1715 the number of churches fell from 300 to 220, with a further decline to 150 by 1750.[54] Even though the Evangelical Revival began around 1730,[55] it was not until the 1770s that the effects of the Evangelical Revival took hold among the Particular Baptists.[56] Initially they were suspicious

---

[49] Underwood, *English Baptists*, 117.

[50] "Doctrines of Grace" refers to the "Five Points of Calvinism." Total Depravity, Unconditional Election, Particular Redemption, Effectual Calling, and Final Perseverance of the Saints.

[51] Raymond Brown, *The English Baptists of the 18th Century* (London: The Baptist Historical Society, 1986), 5.

[52] See chapter one footnotes numbers 12 and 13.

[53] Ryland, *Work of Faith*, 5-8. It should be noted that this assumption has been recently challenged by Clive Jarvis in his doctoral thesis where he maintains that between 1715 and 1773 there "was tangible growth amongst English Baptist Churches, a fact which required a reassessment of the true impact of hyper-Calvinism, and in particular to question the extent to which it truly gripped English Particular Baptists." Clive Robert Jarvis, "Growth in English Baptist Churches: With Special Reference to the Northamptonshire Particular Baptist Association (1770-1830)" (PhD Thesis, University of Glasgow, 2002), 248. Of course, in Particular Baptist theology numerical growth, which is quantifiable, is not as significant an indicator of decline as the more qualitative issues of holiness, love, a burden for the lost, etc. In this way decline can be measured in terms of evangelistic vitality, or desire, which of course would eventually lead to numerical decline. Contemporaries like John Ryland (Ryland, *Work of Faith*, 5-8), Andrew Fuller (Fuller, *Complete Works*, I, 37). "Surely the system of religion [false Calvinism] which he, with too many others, has imbibed, enervates every part of vital godliness;" and John Rippon (Ken R. Manley, *Redeeming Love Proclaim: John Rippon and the Baptists* [Carlisle: Paternoster Press, 2004], 2-3.) were convinced that the form of evangelism that Gill embodied lacked in evangelistic rigor and vitality. So High Calvinism, even if there was no numerical decline, could still negatively affect evangelistic enthusiasm eventually resulting in decline.

[54] Haykin, *One Heart and One Soul*, 25.

[55] David Bebbington, *Evangelicalism in Modern Britain: A History from the 1730's to the 1980's* (Grand Rapids, MI: Baker Book House, 1989), 21.

[56] Underwood, *English Baptists*, 160.

of the "enthusiasm" of the Methodists, their Paedo-baptism, their connection to the state church, as well as their Arminianism.[57]

PARTICULAR BAPTIST GROWTH

During the years 1770–1815 the Baptists were expanding steadily.[58] As a newer generation of Particular Baptists emerged, they adopted a more evangelical form of Calvinism with a strong desire to spread the gospel, not only throughout England, but to the whole world. Significantly, Dr. Kenneth Manley believes that the evangelical revival also affected worship styles among Dissenters, especially in preaching and hymn singing, as doctrinal rigidity was relaxed in favour or more evangelistic concerns.[59] We have already noted how the life and writings of Andrew Fuller are usually given much of the credit for the adoption of this more moderate Calvinism, especially among the Baptists.[60]

In the west of England Edward Terrill (1635–1686), an Elder of the Broadmead Church in Bristol, bequeathed a portion of his estate to the church to fund a school to train gifted leaders. He was particularly concerned that they learn Hebrew and Greek as he believed this training would better equip them to minister the gospel.[61] Although Baptists were divided on the need for an educated ministry, as they are today, many believed that it was necessary to ensure their prosperity. It is significant that the money was bequeathed to the care of the church, for this ensured a continued and close relationship between academia and ecclesia. Bristol Academy became a significant influence among Particular Baptists as it produced a continuous stream of gifted, evangelical men intent on propagating the gospel. Since its inception in 1679, Bristol Baptist College has also produced many exceptional Baptist leaders. Roger Hayden believes that outside London, evangelical or moderate Calvinism was

---

[57] Enthusiasm was a negative term describing, supposedly, those who experienced special revelation and/or empowerments of the Holy Spirit. It also contained the idea of extreme subjective religious excitement which was not appreciated by all in the so-called Age of Reason. Joseph Ivimey, *A History of the English Baptists: Comprising the Principal Events of the History of Protestant Dissenters, from the Revolution in 1688 till 1760; and of the London Baptist Churches, During that Period* (London: B. J. Holdsworth, 1823), III, 290.

[58] W.T. Whitley, *A History of British Baptists* (London: Charles Griffen & Company Limited, 1923), 245.

[59] Manley, *Redeeming Love*, 3.

[60] See introduction.

[61] Norman S. Moon, *Education for Ministry: Bristol Baptist College 1679-1979* (Bristol: Bristol Baptist College, 1979), 1.

centred in Bristol, where over 177 students were trained for the Baptist ministry between 1720 and 1790.[62]

Bernard Foskett (1685–1758), a minister at Broadmead Baptist Church from 1728 to 1758, trained over eighty ministers in Wales and England.[63] Among them were outstanding leaders such as Benjamin Beddome at Bourton-on-the-Water (1717–1795),[64] John Ash at Pershore (1724–1779),[65] and Benjamin Francis at Nailsworth (1734–1799).[66] Welshman Hugh Evans (1713–1781) was invited by the Broadmead Church to continue as senior pastor and principal of the College after the death of Foskett in 1758.[67] The church also appointed his son to assist him in the work. Caleb Evans (1737–1791) co-pastored with his father and ministered together with him at the church and school for the next twenty-three years.[68] When Hugh died in 1781 Caleb assumed responsibility for both aspects of the ministry.

In response to the need for more Baptist ministers, the Bristol Education Society was formed in 1770, which allowed other churches to contribute funds to help pay the expenses for potential Baptist ministers.[69] The work of the college remained closely connected to the church, for the aims of the society were to supply able evangelical ministers to help gifted men develop their gifts, to involve the churches in the selection of potential ministers, and to encourage

---

[62] Roger Hayden, "Evangelical Calvinism among Eighteenth-Century British Baptists with Particular Reference to Bernard Foskett, Hugh and Caleb Evans and the Bristol Baptist Academy, 1690–1791" (PhD diss., University of Keele, 1991), Abstract. Evangelical Calvinism is a term often used to describe a form of Calvinism that is vitally interested in evangelism.

[63] *Dictionary of Evangelical Biography 1730–1860 Volume I*, Donald M. Lewis, ed. (Peabody, MA: Hendrickson Publishers, 2004), s.v. "Foskett, Bernard" by Roger Hayden, 399–400. Hayden, *Baptist History and Heritage*, 88.

[64] *Dictionary of Evangelical Biography 1730–1860 Volume I*, Donald M. Lewis, ed. (Peabody, MA: Hendrickson Publishers, 2004), s.v. "Beddome, Benjamin," by Karen E. Smith, 74.

[65] For Biographical information see *Dictionary of Evangelical Biography 1730–1860 Volume I*, Donald M. Lewis, ed. (Peabody, MA: Hendrickson Publishers, 2004), s.v. "Ash, John," by Roger Hayden, 34. At his funeral address Caleb Evans described his preaching as, "plain, practical, powerful, and thoroughly evangelical." G.H. Taylor, "The Reverend John Ash, LL.D. 1724–1779," *The Baptist Quarterly* 20 (January, 1963): 13. For further information on Ash's background, the church at Pershore, Ash's friendship with Caleb Evans and his descendants (including Joseph Ash) see G.F. Nuttall, "John Ash and the Pershore Church" *The Baptist Quarterly* 22 (January 1968): 271–276.

[66] *Dictionary of Evangelical Biography 1730–1860 Volume I*, Donald M. Lewis, ed. (Peabody, MA: Hendrickson Publishers, 2004), s.v. "Francis, Benjamin," by D. Densil Morgan, 404. Moon, *Education for Ministry*, 8.

[67] *Dictionary of Evangelical Biography*, s.v. "Evans, Hugh" by Roger Hayden, 368–369.

[68] *Dictionary of Evangelical Biography*, s.v. "Evans, Caleb" by Roger Hayden, 366–367.

[69] Moon, *Education for Ministry*, 11–12.

evangelistic work in the churches.[70] These teachers taught a liberal education at a very high standard, but their goal was not just to create excellent scholars, but to produce effective ministers. They wanted to produce "able, evangelical, lively, zealous ministers of the Gospel."[71]

From its beginning, the school was a proponent of moderate Calvinism that encouraged the free offer of grace and the preaching of the gospel.[72] Caleb Evans was urging students to preach a gospel of Christ where he would save all that came to God by him.[73] As one might expect, many of its students imbibed this evangelistic concern and propagated it. Through his publication, *The Baptist Annual Register*, men like John Rippon (1751–1836) disseminated vital information on the state of the various churches, which had a unifying effect among the Baptists.[74] His stories about the BMS fueled growing interest and support for missions among the Baptists. Also, through his collection of *Hymns in Selections* he provided a standard for hymnology among the Particular Baptists which helped propagate certain Baptist theological emphases.[75] Bristol Baptist Academy also produced noteworthy ministers like Thomas Dunscombe (1748–1811), who significantly contributed to Baptist growth in Oxfordshire,[76] and John Sutcliff, who, following Jonathan Edwards' example, initiated the "Prayer Call of 1784."[77] Samuel Pearce was a strong proponent of missions and was extremely disappointed when he was unable to go to the mission field himself. William Staughton (1770–1829)[78] was present at Kettering at the founding of the BMS. He entered Bristol Academy in 1791 from Cannon Street Church in Birmingham, where he was baptized by Samuel Pearce. He was chosen to succeed Ryland at College Lane, Northampton, but declined. Instead he moved to America and became known for his passionate interest in

---

[70] Moon, *Education for Ministry*, 11–12.

[71] Moon, *Education for Ministry*, 11.

[72] Moon, *Education for Ministry*, 18.

[73] Brown, *The English Baptists*, 115.

[74] *Dictionary of Evangelical Biography*, s.v. "Rippon, John" by K.R. Manley, 941. "From 1790 to 1802 Rippon edited the *Baptist Annual Register*, the first periodical among Particular Baptists. Through this influential medium Rippon both reflected and stimulated the new evangelical vitality in the churches of both England and America."

[75] In regard to the influence of Rippon's *Selection*, Manley writes, "Any good hymn-book helps to interpret and define the Christian faith for its own generation." K.R. Manley, "The Making of an Evangelical Baptist Leader," *The Baptist Quarterly* 26 (April, 1976): 256.

[76] Moon, *Education for Ministry*, 15

[77] See introduction.

[78] Roger Hayden, "What are the Qualifications of a Gospel Minister?" *Baptist Quarterly* 19 (October 1962): 352.

Christian missions and Christian education. He was a regular correspondent of Carey and an ardent supporter of missions. He also founded the Philadelphia Baptist Education Society.[79] William Steadman (1764–1837) was actively involved as an itinerant preacher. He was also a great proponent of missions, the president of an academy, an evangelist, and a leader among Baptist associations.[80] He entered the Bristol Academy in 1788 and would go on to become the president of Horton Academy in 1806.[81] Joseph Kinghorn (1766–1832) spent his entire ministry at St. Mary's Baptist Church, Norwich after graduating from Bristol.[82] He was a key leader among the Baptists and a keen supporter of the BMS. This evangelical Calvinistic concern was continued in the leadership of John Ryland who succeeded Caleb Evans. During his thirty-two years as principal of the college, twenty-six of his students became missionaries in the BMS.[83]

CONCLUSION

Between the years 1780–1830 a discernible shift occurred in the mindset of Particular Baptists.[84] A renewed interest in evangelism by key leaders, supported by important institutions like the BMS and Bristol College, played a significant role in the growth of the Particular Baptists in the latter part of the eighteenth century. Factors influencing the nature of this change include not only a theological shift in the area of the free offer, but also an increase in itinerant preaching,[85] the formation of Sunday Schools, and an increased

---

[79] Moon, *Education for Ministry*, 26.

[80] Sharon James, "William Steadman (1764–1837)" in *The British Particular Baptists 1638–1910*, Michael A.G. Haykin, ed., (Springfield, MO: Particular Baptist Press, 2000), 2:163. When he first read of the BMS he wrote in his journal, "It revived me, and did my heart good to think that God had put it into the heart of any to attempt that good work; and I cannot but look upon this as one of the many favorable indications of the approach of the universal spread of the Gospel and of the latter day glory" (Walter Fancutt, "William Steadman's Hampshire Years" *The Baptist Quarterly* 16 [October 1956]: 366–367).

[81] James, *Steadman*, 169.

[82] Dean Olive, "Joseph Kinghorn (1766–1832)" in *The British Particular Baptists 1638–1910*, Michael A.G. Haykin, ed., (Springfield MO: Particular Baptist Press, 2003), 3:85.

[83] Moon, *Education for Ministry*, 35.

[84] W.R. Ward, "The Baptists and the Transformation of the Church, 1780–1830," *The Baptist Quarterly* 25 (October 1973): 167.

[85] "From the first appearance of this new emphasis upon itinerant preaching the leadership and impetus came from those who were ordained ministers. Among those raised in the older Dissenting tradition of the settled pastorate and its associated responsibilities the concern for itinerancy was slow to develop, but in this as in many other aspects of evangelism the 1790s proved to be the crucial decade and by 1800 many Baptist ministers were endeavouring to combine

participation in associational life and foreign missions.[86] But the question to be answered is how was their pastoral theology itself affected? Accompanying this theological shift in the area of the free offer, was there a significant renewal in their understanding of the ministry? To begin to answer these questions, the pastoral theology of the Particular Baptists, and in particular their theology prior to the revival, must be carefully analysed in light of Fuller's pastoral theological emphasis. But before these questions are tackled, the ordination service itself must be examined. Why was it so important to these Baptists? The next chapter will describe the importance as well as the dynamics of Particular Baptist ordination sermons in the long eighteenth century.

---

effectively both pastoral and evangelistic roles" (Deryck W. Lovegrove, "Particular Baptist Itinerant Preachers During the Late 18th and Early 19th Centuries," *The Baptist Quarterly* 28 [July 1979]: 128).

86 Ward, "The Baptists," 167.

3
Baptist Ordination Sermons

The goal of this chapter is to review the dynamics of the ordination sermon to consider their value and to describe the nature and importance of the main sermonic addresses. These ordination services, and particularly the charge, were a very significant expression of Baptist pastoral ministry and so the actual procedure and content must first be understood.

Their Value

At the ordination of the Rev. W. Belsher in 1797 to the pastorate of the Baptist Church in Worcester, the Rev. G. Osborn explained that, "according to scriptural example, and apostolic practice, we are met [*sic*] together this day, to help each other by our mutual prayers and advice, to recognize the solemn designation of our brother to the work of the ministry."[1] He believed, first of all, that the ordination ceremony was rooted in obedience to Scripture. Second, he recognized that it was a public interaction where the congregation, pastor elect, and the visiting elders were gathered to confirm God's call of a man to the ministry. But it was more than just a confirmation of call as it represented the time when a minister is truly made a minister, that is, set apart, in the Church of God. Neville Clark says, "As to be a Christian is to be baptized, so to be a minister is to be ordained,"[2] therefore "the assurance of the call of God must never stand alone, and individual conviction must be tested and confirmed by the community."[3]

---

[1] G. Osborn, *Introductory Address*, in John Ryland and Samuel Pearce, *Declaration of Religious Sentiments in John Ryland and Samuel Pearce, The Duty of Ministers to be Nursing Fathers to the Church; and the Duty of Churches to Regard Ministers as the Gift of Christ* (London: Button/Worcester: Baskerfield/Birmingham: Belcher/Bristol: James, 1796), 6. The comments of N. Clark are helpful, "But the assurance of the call of God must never stand alone, and individual conviction must be tested and confirmed by the community."

[2] N. Clark, "The Meaning and Practice of Ordination," *The Baptist Quarterly* 17 (January 1958): 202.

[3] Clark, "The Meaning and Practice of Ordination," 198.

In the year 1705, at the ordination of Rev. David Rees, Joseph Stennett explained that to "ordain" means "constitute," "to create," or "establish" a man in office.[4] There were two offices in the Baptist church: elders and deacons. The elder (Acts 14:23) was also known as "bishop" (1 Timothy 3:1), "overseer" (Acts 20:28), "pastor" (Ephesians 4:11), "guide," "teacher," "ruler," and "governor" (Hebrews 13:17).[5] As elders they are given authority by the head of the church, Jesus Christ.[6] They are called "pastors" because they function as shepherds, metaphorically feeding the flock of Christ with the Word of God.[7] They are called "bishops" or "overseers" because they have responsibility to see that the church is administered orderly according to the divine will of God.[8] An overseer signifies a steward who is put in charge of the church of whom Christ is the head.[9] They are called "guides" or "leaders" because they lead the people into spiritual warfare, encouraging them in their duties, and exercise discipline to maintain purity.[10] They are called "teachers" because this represents a chief aspect of their work. They believed that essentially the terms "bishop" and "elder" signified the same thing, as did the terms "pastor" and "teacher."[11] In all of these descriptions it becomes apparent that the preaching ministry of a pastor was central to the successful discharge of the office.

Historian Raymond Brown, speaking of the importance of preaching in the early part of the eighteenth century, says, "In any account of religious life and thought in post-reformation England it is almost impossible to exaggerate the influence of the sermon."[12] Published sermons were in great demand as they represented a chief means of disseminating religious "intelligence."[13] Sermons covered a broad spectrum of thought including religion, politics, ethics,

---

[4] Joseph Stennett, *Sermon III. Preach'd at the Ordination of the Revd. Mr. David Rees, and two deacons; in a Church of Christ at Limehouse, Feb. 19, 1705-6* in *The Works Of the late Reverend and Learned Mr. Joseph Stennett* (London, 1731), II, 81. See Acts 6.

[5] Stennett, *Sermon III*, 81.

[6] Stennett, *Sermon III*, 83.

[7] Stennett, *Sermon III*, 83.

[8] Stennett, *Sermon III*, 84.

[9] Stennett, *Sermon III*, 84.

[10] Stennett, *Sermon III*, 84.

[11] Stennett, *Sermon III*, 85–86. More specific details about the purpose, function, and duties of elders and deacons are discussed below.

[12] Raymond Brown, "Baptist Preaching in Early 18th Century England," *The Baptist Quarterly* 31 (January 1985): 4.

[13] This term was often used in the eighteenth century to describe previously unknown, or not yet disseminated information.

and science. But among Particular Baptists, ordination sermons were regarded as uniquely important and were frequently published. Many Particular Baptists believed that their churches' fortunes were tied directly to the appointment of God-called men to their pulpits.[14] Not surprisingly, these ordination services were generally well attended and generated interest even beyond Baptist circles. At the ordination of Abraham Booth on 16 Feb 1769 even the "Countess of Huntingdon was among the large number who attended the service."[15] These ordination services were noteworthy for a variety of reasons.

Particular Baptist esteem for the ordination of their pastors was rooted in their high regard for the Bible and the concomitant obligation to faithfully adhere to its precepts. They felt that Scripture taught the necessity of the perpetuity of the ordination rite in accordance with apostolic precedent.[16] Also, for Baptists, preaching the Word of God, the Scriptures, was central to their concept of worship. William L. Lumpkin, describing the contents of the *London Confession of 1644*, says, "There is a strong emphasis throughout the Confession on preaching ..."[17] The goal of all ministry was the magnification of the glory of God as demonstrated primarily through his redemptive purposes in Christ. They were following in the doctrinal footsteps of their Reformed forefathers, echoing the cry of *sola fide*.[18] Salvation is by faith and faith comes primarily through hearing the Word of God.[19] Article XXIV of the confession states that, "faith is ordinarily begot by the preaching of the Gospel, or word of Christ"[20] Preaching was the responsibility of the pastor and so the church's success in fulfilling her mandate to glorify God was integrally related to the ministry of the pastor.[21] In all that they did they sought to obey God through the Scriptures, or in their parlance, to maintain "orderliness."

---

[14] John Rippon, *The Baptist Annual Register: For 1794, 1795, 1796-1797. Including Sketches of the State of Religion Among Different Denominations of Good Men at Home and Abroad* (London: Dilly, Button, Thomas, 1796), 521.

[15] Ernest A. Payne, "Abraham Booth, 1734-1806," *The Baptist Quarterly* 26 (January 1975): 32. Selina Countess of Huntington (24 Aug. 1707-1717 June 1791) was a well-known, wealthy Calvinist Methodist leader and generous financial supporter of the Methodist cause. *Dictionary of Evangelical Biography 1730-1860, Volume I*, Donald M. Lewis, ed. (Peabody, MA: Hendrickson Publishers, 2004), s.v. "Huntington, Selina" by Peter J. Lineham, 585-586.

[16] See Introductory Discourse below for an expansion of this assertion.

[17] Lumpkin, *Confessions*, 146. See article XXVI.

[18] Latin for "faith alone." This doctrine teaches that salvation is by faith alone.

[19] They based this on Romans 10:17: "So then faith cometh by hearing, and hearing by the word of God."

[20] Lumpkin, *Confessions*, 163. See article XXIV.

[21] Lumpkin, *Confessions*, 168. See article XLV.

A unique feature of the charge[22] in the ordination service was that it represented an admonition from one pastor to another pastor on how the office of elder should function effectively. These sermons embody a uniquely practical exposition of the goals, purposes, encouragements, challenges, and execution of the pastoral office. Beyond a systematic exposition of a Particular Baptist pastoral theology, they contain an elucidation of pastoral theology purified in the crucible of practiced ministry. Pastors who had learned to implement their inherited Particular Baptist theological convictions in their own unique context strove to transmit what they had learned to a new generation of pastoral leadership. Therefore ordination sermons served inimitably to further shorten the gap between orthodoxy and orthopraxy—that's between a written practical theology and practiced theology. For example, although John Gill's *Practical Divinity* clearly articulated a pragmatic theology written by an active pastor, ordination sermons were delivered by active practitioners admonishing other ministerial practitioners with the fervor of a shared interest in a divine cause. This intensified the complementary realities of the pragmatism of ministry and the relatively more abstruse concerns of practical theology.

Further, the solemn designation of a pastor to the ministry occurred in the public milieu of a local church as the charge was delivered in a covenantal context. This exchange between practitioners was expressed openly. The church and their newly ordained pastor were voluntarily binding themselves together in a covenantal relationship that produced an increased accountability and commitment towards one another. For the pastor especially this necessitated the manifestation of a blameless character. It was the pastor's duty to admonish people to obey certain theological precepts to which he, as both a Christian and member of the church, was also accountable. In this role, where his life was regularly exposed to sustained public scrutiny, any discrepancies between his words and actions were amplified. As a leader he had an even greater responsibility than the average church member to maintain a consistent example of practicing what he preached.

As the ordination service typically included a separate address to the church, they outlined their responsibilities to support the pastor in his ministry. This mutual accountability made the ordination ceremony even more significant in terms of its effect of functionalizing theology. Both pastor and

[22] The charge represents the address of a visiting pastor to the newly ordained pastor outlining his duties and responsibilities as a Minister of the church.

congregation were mutually accountable to scriptural precepts ratified in a public ceremony. In this sense it was not unlike a marriage bond with all the accompanying privileges, duties, commitments, and responsibilities.[23]

Ordination Procedure

John Rippon's *The Baptist Annual Register* (1790–1802), the first English Baptist periodical, is an important source for the historian studying eighteenth-century Particular Baptist ordinations.[24] Geoffrey Nuttall states that, "No other denomination has such a fine contemporary record of its churches and their ministers as exists for the 1790s in Rippon's Baptist Annual Register."[25] Ken Manley believes that the thirteen years that it was published cover the most important period in the history of the Particular Baptists.[26] So we have a unique record of Particular Baptists' ministerial activity during a crucial phase of their saga in the eighteenth century.

The Register functioned as a unifying document for Baptists by sharing valuable information of common interest including records on lists of churches, associational letters, personal correspondences, reports from Europe, missionary news, list of books and other miscellaneous facts that would be of interest particularly to Calvinistic Baptists. One of these sections entitled, "Intelligence," included descriptions of over one hundred ordinations services, demonstrating further the great interest and significance of these proceedings to the Baptists. Of these one hundred sermons, five were of American Baptists, one of a General Baptist, three of Independent pastors, and the rest were of Particular Baptists.[27] But they not only indicate the worth of these ordination services for Particular Baptists, they also provide valuable

[23] Benjamin Wallin, *A Charge Delivered at the Ordination of the Rev. Mr. Abraham Booth Feb.16, 1769, in Goodman's Fields* in *A Charge and Sermon together with an Introductory Discourse and Confession of Faith Delivered at the Ordination of the Rev. Mr. Abraham Booth Feb.16, 1769, in Goodman's Fields* (London, 1769), 35. "The office of pastor is relative to a particular church, gathered according to divine appointment; and results from a solemn contract and covenant with one another." William Nash Clarke, who delivered the Introductory Discourse, was at the time the minister at Unicorn Yard Church. Seymour Price, "Abraham Booth's Ordination, 1769," *The Baptist Quarterly* 9 (October 1938): 242.

[24] Ken R. Manley, *Redeeming Love Proclaim: John Rippon and the Baptists* (Carlisle, UK: Paternoster Press, 2004), 139. Rosemary Taylor, "English Baptist Periodicals, 1790–1865," *The Baptist Quarterly* 27 (April 1977): 54.

[25] Geoffrey F. Nuttall, "The Baptist Churches and their Ministers in the 1790s Rippon's Baptist Annual Register," *The Baptist Quarterly* 30 (October 1984): 383.

[26] Manley, *Redeeming Love*, 139.

[27] Manley, *Redeeming Love*, 186.

information on the participants, the order of service, the length of service, and other important details.

Outline of Service

There was flexibility in the modus operandi of an ordination service due to a variety of mainly pragmatic factors. The accessibility of an appropriate meeting place might affect the number of ministers able to participate, which in turn would influence its length. If time were really short, for example, the address to the Church might be eliminated. Or the number of pastors from other Particular Baptist churches available to conduct the service might be influenced by prior commitments or geographical isolation. Nevertheless, a survey of Rippon's *Register* indicates a homogeny of observance in Particular Baptist ordination ceremonies.[28]

Timeline Before Ordination

Part of the tacit responsibilities of a congregation in a Particular Baptist church in the eighteenth century was to constantly look within their own ranks for men with ministerial potential.[29] If a man was suspected of having the necessary moral character and ministerial gifts he was called to exercise his talents before the church.[30] He would preach over a certain period of time, usually on a Lord's Day evening, for evaluation by the members.[31] Rippon records the testing cycle of a man called Rushton in September 1795. He first was asked to demonstrate his preaching abilities before the church on a Sunday. Judging his exhortation acceptable, they asked him to continue preaching for six to seven weeks more to allow all the church members opportunity to hear and evaluate his abilities properly. After this trial period they set apart a day for prayer and fasting to seek the Lord's will in the matter. By 8 November 1795 the entire

[28] "Ordinations are recorded in both volumes ... The order followed in the service, which was virtually invariable, continued to be a traditional into the present century" (Nuttall, *Baptist Churches and Ministers*, 385).

[29] John Gill, *The Duty of Churches Respecting the Encouragement of Spiritual Gifts. The Circular Letter from the Baptist Ministers and Messengers, Assembled at St. Albans, May 31, and June 1, 2, 1796* (n.p., 1796), 3.

[30] G. Reid Doster tells the interesting story of a General Baptist named Widmer who went through a seven-year period between his proposal to the office and the ordination. The delay was largely a result of some members questioning his character based on 1 Timothy 3:7, 8. G. Reid Doster, "Discipline and Ordination at Berkhamsted General Baptist Church, 1712-1718," *The Baptist Quarterly* 27 (July 1977): 128-138.

[31] Rippon, *Register*, 483.

church agreed to call him to the work of the ministry and after prayerful consideration he accepted the call.[32] The actual ordination procedure usually came even later.

In the case of the Rev. William Pain who was ordained in April 1794, it occurred a year and ten months after his probation period.[33] The Rev. Thomas Sowerby was called to ministry in 1788 and was ordained the following October,[34] whereas, the Rev. Robert Hyde was sent into ministry in 1785, and was ordained on May 1787.[35] Another example was the ordination of the Rev. Joseph Swain of Walworth near London, who was for eight years a member of John Rippon's church and was called to the work of the ministry on 2 June 1791 and ordained 8 February 1792.[36] The Rev. James Barnett had an eighteenth-month probation period before being ordained.[37] There seems to be no formally established length of time before a man was ordained to the ministry. Rather the main criterion was that the church was satisfied that he was God's chosen minister for them. In many cases, the ordinand was already functioning successfully as a *de facto* pastor. There was also the possibility that he may have been ordained previously and was being re-ordained. An example of this was Robert Hyde, who was first ordained in May 1787, and was re-ordained in August 1795.[38] Re-ordination took place when a minister changed pastorates.

Following what they believed was the scriptural precedent set in Acts 6:1–7 and Acts 13:1–3, pastors from other churches were invited to preside over ordination services. Particular Baptists believed that only elders were qualified to ordain for the ministry.[39] Usually, these were Particular Baptists ministers, but sometimes Independent ministers also participated[40] although typically

---

[32] Rippon, *Register*, 483.
[33] Rippon, *Register*, 345.
[34] Rippon, *Register*, 346.
[35] Rippon, *Register*, 349.
[36] Rippon, *Register*, 521.
[37] Rippon, *Register*, 119.
[38] Rippon, *Register*, 349.
[39] John Sutcliff, *Introductory Address* in John Ryland and Andrew Fuller, *The Difficulties of the Christian Ministry, and the Means of Surmounting them; with the Obedience of Churches to their Pastors Explained and Enforced* (Birmingham: J. Belcher/London: Button and Son, 1802), 6.
[40] Rippon, *Register*, 482. Usually ministers were from the same county unless they were very well known nationally. An exception to the dominance of participation by Particular Baptist ministers was the case of William Hoddy in 1795 at Bildeston in Suffolk, who had only one Baptist minister take part. The other five ministers were all Independents. Nuttall, *Baptist Churches and Ministers*, 385.

their involvement was restricted to reading Scripture, singing, and prayer.[41] There could be thirteen to fourteen ministers attending as witnesses with upwards of seven participating in the service.[42] Typically, at least three or four visiting ministers were actively involved in the speaking and praying aspects of the service,[43] but other ordained men would join in when it came time to lay on hands at the ordination prayer.[44] Ordination services were considered important events that would often attract other clergy in the area. Rippon even records the unanticipated attendance of a "Popish priest" at one.[45]

Normally the service would be held in the Baptist Meeting House, but poorer congregations who had inadequate facilities were sometimes forced to request the use of another Dissenter's Meeting Place. Usually these were owned by either Independents or General Baptists, but sometimes they asked to borrow the facilities of Quakers or Methodists.[46] If no church building was available, they were forced to be more creative. An interesting anecdotal account in Rippon's *Register* illustrates such a need at the ordination of Rev. William Terry, at Snare Yorkshire 13 November 1793:

> This service was conducted in a dwelling house, the poor people not having a meeting house; a barn being too dark and cold; and their friendly neighbours the Quakers and the Methodists at Massam, being so unfriendly as each to deny the use of their respective houses upon this occasion: But it was pleasing to recollect, that the throne of grace is everywhere accessible, and that the people were within the promise, Matthew xviii.20.[47]

It seems that the lack of availability of an adequate building sometimes necessitated the use of someone's home. In another instance, due to a lack of space, they were forced to use the "meeting-house-yard."[48]

---

[41] Rippon, *Register*, 117, 121. John Rippon, *The Baptist Annual Register: For 1790, 1791, 1792, and Part of 1793. Including Sketches of the State of Religion Among Different Denominations of Good Men at Home and Abroad* (London: Dilly, 1791), 518, 521. Jarvis makes mention of Abraham Tozer who was ordained by Philip Doddridge, a Congregationalist minister on 20 June 1745. Jarvis, "Growth in Baptist Churches," 14–15.

[42] Rippon, *Register*, 345.

[43] Rippon, *Register*, 345, 346.

[44] Rippon, *Register*, 122.

[45] Rippon. *Register*, 481.

[46] Rippon, *Register*, 117, 192.

[47] Rippon, *Register*, 122.

[48] Rippon, *Register*, 480.

Day/Length of Service-Morning

Often the formal service began at 10:00 am or 10:30 am, usually on a Tuesday, Wednesday, or Thursday.[49] The congregation would frequently assemble at 8:00 am to pray for God's presence and blessing at the impending service.[50] The ceremony would last anywhere from three to four hours, sometimes even longer. There is reason to suspect that longer was the norm.[51] Thomas Hunt describes his ordination service on 12 September 1793 which began at 10:30 am with John Sutcliff opening with prayer. He says, "The whole service proved very pleasant; it was compressed within three hours and a half; and the conducting of it gave general satisfaction."[52] It appears that "general satisfaction" was derived, at least partially, from the relative brevity of the service, for in a footnote to these comments, John Rippon the editor adds,

> The brevity of this service is to be attributed, in some measure, to the following circumstance. The church at Watford had laid their plan after the old method, to have two sermons at the ordination; and hence Mr. Hunt came to town, and requested his pastor to preach one, and me the other: I said to him, "My good brother, I am sure I would gladly shew

[49] For example; Tuesday—William Payne 8 April 1794 (Rippon, *Register*, 345); Rev. Holmes 7 July 1795 (Rippon, *Register*, 347); Wednesday—Benjamin Evans 16 July 1794 (Rippon, *Register*, 345); Hugh Williams 24 June 1795 (Rippon, *Register*, 346); Samuel Pearce 18 August 1790 (Rippon, *Register 1790*, 517); Thursday—Joseph Hobbs 30 April 1795 (Rippon, *Register*, 346); Benjamin Dickinson 25 February 1790 (Rippon, *Register 1790*, 517); George Braithwaite 28 March 1734 (note this is calculated under the Julian calendar prior to Britain's conversion to the Gregorian calendar in 1752). John Gill, *The Work of a Gospel-Minister recommended to Consideration* in his *A Collection of Sermons and Tracts: In Two Volumes*. (London: George Keith, 1773), II, 1. At the ordination of Richard Machin at the Particular Baptist Church at Bridlington in 1737, the service was held on a Saturday. Stephen Copson, "Two Ordinations at Bridlington in 1737," *The Baptist Quarterly* 33 (July 1989): 146.

[50] Rippon, *Register*, 345, 482. Nathan Smith 1790 met at 9:30 am (Rippon, *Register 1790*, 518).

[51] At the ordination service of William Steadman, Broughton, Hampshire, 2 November 1791 the service began at half past ten and concluded a little after 2:00 pm (Rippon, *Register 1790*, 520, 521). At the Rev. John Bain's ordination at Downton, 1794, The service began at 10:00 am and was concluded at 3:00 pm (Rippon, *Register*, 189). At the Rev. William Newman's ordination at Old Ford near London, on 15 May 1794 the service began at 10:30 am and the service lasted three and a half hours (Rippon, *Register*, 190, 191). Higgs describes a General Baptist Ordination service in 1811 that lasted from 11:00 am to 3:15 pm (Lionel F. Higgs, "The Calling and Ordination of Ministers in the Eighteenth Century," *The Baptist Quarterly* 16 [April 1956]: 279). At the ordination of David Kinghorn in 1771 at Bishop Burton, "The whole service lasted from a quarter-past ten till half-past two: four hours and a quarter! But still the good friends were not satisfied: for at four they assembled again, when Mr. Gawkrodger preached from Eph. v, 2, after which three deacons were ordained by prayer and laying on of hands" (Terry Wolever, ed., *The Life and Works of Joseph Kinghorn* [Springfireld, MO: Particular Baptist Press, 1995], 1:19).

[52] Rippon, *Register*, 121.

> you any respect in my power, but it is not probable that I can be with you at the time you have fixed; besides, why should we always have two sermons at an ordination, and tire the people to death? Must we forever groan and go on in the road of impropriety? Do give my love to friend Booth, and beseech him to break the neck of a custom of which everybody complains. He has done so much good that if he takes upon him, I mean, if he innovates a little, nobody will blame him: a distinction will be made by all, but idiots, between reformation and revolution." Mr. Hunt, I suppose, carried the message, and only one sermon was preached; and so pleased were the people with the manner in which the business was conducted, that Brother Hunt hopes, when it is generally known, it will become, in some respect at least, a model for future ordinations, and form a new era in the history of these services.[53]

Procedure

The ordination service typically opened with the reading of Scripture, prayer, and singing. As a high regard for the Word of God characterized eighteenth-century Particular Baptists, it is not surprising that such an important ceremony should include the reading of Scripture. Some commonly read texts included 1 Timothy 3, Titus 1, Psalm 132, and Ephesians 4.

It is perhaps expected that 1 Timothy 3 would be a popular choice of a text as it deals with the qualifications of the officers of the church, namely deacons and elders. In this passage, the apostle Paul begins by commending the office of elder as an admirable work (1 Timothy 3:1). He then describes the qualifications and character of an elder in verses 2 through 7. Next, in verses 8 through 13, he outlines the qualification of deacons. Paul concludes the chapter in verses 14 to 16 by explaining to Timothy that he has given him these qualifications for guidance to appoint officers in the church. Likewise, Titus 1, another so-called Pastoral Epistle, is concerned mainly with the qualifications of an elder (verses 5–9).

The common use of Psalm 132 might seem a bit inappropriate for modern-day readers. A casual appraisal may suggest that the Psalm had more to do with

---

[53] Rippon, *Register*, 121. "In 1793, John Rippon, of Carter Lane, was asked to share with Abraham Booth in the ordination of Thomas Hunt at Watford. The day fixed was inconvenient, so Rippon suggested that Booth's sermon be a joint charge to minister and church. Booth's pre-eminence and authority might, Rippon thought, make this a valuable precedent which would be followed. Hunt was a member of the Goodmans Fields church. It was more than a century and a half before the practice of one sermon replaced the traditional two at ordinations and inductions" (Payne, *Abraham Booth*, 33).

ancient Jewish liturgy than an eighteenth-century English Baptist ordination service. But this Psalm was used—both read and sung—regularly.[54] Why was this Psalm so popular at ordination services?

John Gill was the first Baptist to write a verse-by-verse commentary on the whole Bible, and according to Timothy George, "Gill influenced an entire generation of younger ministers through his remarkable preaching and pastoral labours."[55] Speaking of Gill's commentary on the entire Bible, his successor at Carter Lane, John Rippon, writes, "In, short, this Exposition is of unquestionable celebrity in the Republic of Letters, as well for its unparalleled learning, as for its profound research; and has obtained the affluence of fame, among all the evangelical denominations, at home and abroad."[56] Gill's work was highly esteemed and frequently used among the Baptists.[57] Therefore, as one of the most respected Baptist biblical expositors, particularly of the middle of the eighteenth century, his interpretation of Psalm 132 may provide clues to help us understand the Psalm's popularity at Particular Baptist ordination services.

Gill understands the Psalm to be inherently Messianic.[58] Therefore references to the tabernacle (Psalm 132:3) are understood typographically as

---

[54] Rippon, *Register*, 118, 191, 482. For example: (read). Rippon, *Register*, 480 (sung); Rippon, *Register 1790*, 519 (sung).

[55] Timothy George, "The Ecclesiology of John Gill" in *The Life and Thought of John Gill (1697-1771): A Tercentennial Appreciation*, Michael A.G. Haykin, ed. (Leiden: Brill, 1997), 225.

[56] John Rippon, *Life and Writings of the Late Rev. John Gill, D.D.* (Harrisonburg, VA: Sprinkle Publications, 1992), 77.

[57] Tom K. Ascol, "John Gill's Approach to New Testament Exposition" in *The Life and Thought of John Gill (1697-1771): A Tercentennial Appreciation*, Michael A.G. Haykin, ed. (Leiden: Brill, 1997), 114.

[58] "Moreover, respect in all this may be had by the authors of this psalm, or those herein represented, to the Messiah, who is the antitype of David; in his name, which signifies 'beloved;' in his birth, parentage, and circumstances of it; in the comeliness of his person, and in his characters and offices, and who is often called David, Psalm 89:3; see Jer. 30:9, Hos. 3:5; and so is a petition that God would remember the covenant of grace made with him; the promise of his coming into the world; his offering and sacrifice, as typified by the legal ones; and also remember them and their offerings for his sake; see Psalm 20:3. Likewise 'all his afflictions' and sufferings he was to endure from men and devils, and from the Lord himself, both in soul and body; and so as to accept of them in the room and stead of his people, as a satisfaction to his justice. Or, 'his humility' in the assumption of human nature, in his carriage and behaviour to all sorts of men, in his ministrations to his disciples, in seeking not his own glory, but his Father's, and in his sufferings and death, which was foretold of him, Zec. 9:9. ... And indeed the Messiah is meant, the antitype of the ark and temple; of whom the saints or believers in him, a chorus of which is here introduced, had heard that he should be born at Ephratah, which is Bethlehem; see Gen 35:19" (John Gill, *An Exposition of the Old Testament*, The Baptist Commentary Series [London: Mathews and Leigh, 1810], 4:264).

allusions to the church.[59] Psalm 132:7 which says, "We will go into his tabernacles: we will worship at his footstool," is speaking of the church, where Christ

> has his residence, takes his walks, and dwells; and which are very lovely, amiable, and pleasant, and so desirable by believers to go into; because of the presence of God in them, the provisions there made for them, the company there enjoyed; the work there done, prayer, praise, preaching, and hearing the word, and administration of all ordinances.[60]

With David as the Messiah and the Tabernacle as the Church, it may be expected that the priesthood anticipates the pastorate. Psalm 132:9, "Let thy priests be clothed with righteousness; and let thy saints shout for joy," may refer to

> the ministers of the word; who may be said to be clothed with righteousness when they perform their work righteously, and faithfully dispense the word, keep back nothing that is profitable, and administer the ordinances according to the rules of Christ; and when their lives and conversations are agreeable to the Gospel they preach.[61]

For Gill and the Particular Baptists, this Psalm was a grand expression of God's love for his church with a concomitant pledge of his ongoing care revealed in a declaration of his desire for her prosperity.[62]

---

59 "...the temple, which is meant, consisting of three parts, the court, the holy place, and the holy of holies; this was typical of the human nature of Christ, the temple of his body, the tabernacle of God's pitching, John 2:19; in which the fulness of the Godhead dwells, the glory of God is seen, and through whom he grants his presence to his people; and also of the church of God, the temple of the living God, where he dwells and is worshipped: and that this might be a fit habitation for God was the great desire of the Messiah, and not only the end and issue of his sufferings and death, but also the design of his preparations and intercession in heaven, John 14:2" (Gill, *Exposition of the Old Testament*, 4:265).

60 Gill, *Exposition of the Old Testament*, 4:266.

61 Gill, *Exposition of the Old Testament*, 4:266.

62 Verse 13. "For the Lord hath chosen Zion, ... Not only to build upon it the temple in a literal sense, and for the place of his worship; but also for the seat of his majesty, and over which he has set his Son as King; and all this from the love he bears to Zion, which, in a figurative and spiritual sense, is his church; whom he has chosen to privileges, to grace and glory, and for his service and honour; see Ps.78:67; he hath desired [it] for his habitation; heaven is the habitation of his holiness and glory; Christ is his dwelling place, in whom all the fulness of the Godhead dwells bodily: yet his desire is to his church and people; his heart is set upon them, and upon their salvation; his delight is in them, and he takes pleasure in walking with them, and dwelling among

Another commonly read passage at the opening of an ordination service was Ephesians 4:1–16. The passage begins by discussing the unity of the church, but verses 11–13 specifically speak of a leadership, given by God, for the edification and growth of the church. This important connection between the Church and a God-given leadership gets to the heart of the reason for an ordination service. Instruction in the knowledge of the Word of God was the primary means for the growth of the church and this instruction was the most important responsibility of the pastor. As the shepherd, it was his duty to feed the sheep with instruction and knowledge leading to godliness and Christian maturity. The installation of a new pastor was such an exciting event because it heralded the hope of prosperity as a result of God's blessing. At the ordination of Joshua Burton on 8 December 1791 the extract reflects this excitement: "The opportunity was acknowledged to be pleasant and profitable: and the hopes of serious friends were revived, that the Lord would raise up again the ancient church at Foxton, which was nearly lost, having had no pastor for 9 or 10 years."[63]

Also the rationale and necessity for the continuance of the office of elder is found in these verses from Ephesians. While some of the gifts described in verses 11–13 given to edify the church ceased with the apostolic era (apostles, prophets, and evangelists), the work is to be continued through pastors and teachers.[64] Apostolic miracles, whose purpose was to confirm the gospel, have ceased, and have been replaced by the guidance of pastors through the Word.[65] It should be noted that even though there was a general agreement with this interpretation of Ephesians 4 among later eighteenth-century Baptists, there were variations in their understanding of the level of continuity or discontinuity between the present day offices of elder's relationship to the scriptural apostolic office. Some saw the contemporary pastor as a direct continuation of the office of apostle reinterpreted without the need or use of miraculous gifts, while others saw the office of pastor as completely separate.

After the reading of Scripture, they would usually sing a hymn or a Psalm. A common example of a hymn, from later on in the century, was chosen from

---

them; they being built up an habitation for God through the Spirit; see Ps.68:16" (Gill, *Exposition of the Old Testament*, 4:267).

[63] Rippon, *Register*, 521.

[64] Nehemiah Coxe, *A Sermon Preached at the ordination of an Elder and Deacons in a Baptized Congregation in London by Nehemiah Coxe* (London, 1681), 16.

[65] Coxe, *Sermon Preached*, 17.

Rippon's *Selection* numbers 410 or 411.[66] For example in 1795 at the Rev. Joseph Belcher's ordination they sang Rippon's *Selection* 410.[67] Singing would occur at various intervals throughout the service, and in the example given above Rippon's 410 was sung after the pastoral call to office and the subsequent acceptance.[68] Singing also often followed the ordination prayer (laying on of hands).[69] Again it was common to sing after the charge to the pastor[70] and if a prayer followed the charge, it was sung after the prayer.[71] There was also sometimes singing after the address to the church.[72] If there was a separate address to the deacons, as the third sermon of the ceremony, they would follow by singing,[73]and they also usually sung a Psalm or hymn before the closing prayer.[74]

Likewise prayer was conducted at different intervals throughout the service.[75] At the ordination of Joseph Burroughs, Crosby describes the prayer of a Mr. Foxwell who, after reading 1 Timothy 3 and 4, "prayed for that church, for the persons called to offices in it, for the presence of God, and the assistances of his grace, in the duties to be that day performed."[76] The usual times for prayer were at the opening of the service, during the laying on of hands, and to close the service. The most important prayer was the ordination prayer where a visiting pastor "implored the divine blessing" on the new relation which church and pastor had formed accompanied by "laying on of hands" in which the other ministers joined.[77] On 20 February 1717 at the ordination of Mr. Joseph Burroughs of the Church at Barbican, Benjamin Stinton prayed,

---

66 Rippon, *Register*, 482.

67 Rippon, *Register*, 482. Sometimes the hymns were read.

68 Rippon, *Register*, 480. They sang the 132nd Psalm (Rippon, *Register*, 190).

69 Rippon, *Register*, 121 (Psalm 132), 190 (Psalm 132), 482, 522 (410 Rippon's *Selection*).

70 Rippon, *Register*, 122 (sung 410 Hymn of Rippon's *Selection*), 190 (Sung 103rd hymn), 191 (Sung Rippon's *Selection* 410), 519 (sung Rippon's *Selection* 407), 522 (sung Rippon's *Selection* 411).

71 Rippon, *Register*, 519.

72 Rippon, *Register*, 191 (sung Psalm 132 4, 5, 6, 7, 8), 480 (Sung a hymn, Rippon's 411th *Selection*), 522 (Dr. Watt's 132nd Psalm and the whole 410th hymn of Mr. Rippon's *Selection*).

73 Rippon, *Register*, 408, 519.

74 Rippon, *Register*, 190 ("The 132nd Psalm was sung and the opportunity concluded in prayer."), 346 ("in the course of the service hymns sung from bro. Rippon's Selection"), 349.

75 Rippon, *Register*, 346.

76 Thomas Crosby, *The History of the English Baptists* (London, 1740), 184.

77 Rippon, *Register*, 122. ("The Minister laid on hands and was joined by seven or eight of his ordained brethren"), 347, 348, (Hands were laid on the ministers and deacons by four other ministers), 349, 479, 482 ("implored the divine blessing on the relationship then formed between me and the church. With laying on of hands-Brother Steadman offered Ordination prayer with

"Brother Joseph Burroughs, we do, in the name of our Lord Jesus Christ, and with the consent of this church, ordain thee, to be an elder, bishop, or overseer of this church of Jesus Christ." Mr. Stinton then, while their hands rested upon the head of Mr. Burroughs, offered a short and appropriate prayer to God for him, and for the church over which he was now the recognized pastor.[78]

Four Main Addresses of Ordination Service

There were typically four main addresses in the ordination service of Particular Baptists, including the introductory discourse, the ordinand's statement of faith, the charge to the new pastor, and a pastoral address to the Church on their rights and duties as the body of Christ.

The Introductory Discourse

The visiting elder delivering the discourse would begin this aspect of the proceedings with a few words indicating both the solemnity and the joy of the day.[79] They were solemn events because these Baptists were convinced that they stood before an almighty and holy God who had condescended to save mankind from their sin, formed the Church through redemption in Christ, and gave them the task of proclaiming the gospel to the world. His chief means to accomplish this—through the Church—was by means of chosen pastors in every generation to minister the Word in ordinance and preaching.[80] The pastor, as a steward of God, was particularly accountable to the Judge. But they were also joyous events because the gift of a pastor was an indicator of the Lord's blessing and favour on the congregation. There was often a feeling of optimism, excitement, and hope that prosperity and growth would soon follow.

The aim of the introductory discourse was to "open the work of the day" by explaining the nature and purpose of ordination ceremonies, answering the

imposition of hands and he also delivered the charge"), 517 (At Samuel Pearce's ordination with Fuller praying—"Mr Fuller implored the divine blessing on the new relationship which the church and I then formed. Prayer was made with the laying on of hands, in which all the ministers joined him." Also five members were set apart for deacons, whom John Ryland prayed laying on hands), 521 (Mr. Sutcliff prayed with laying on of hands with the rest of the ministers present).

[78] Ivimey, *History of the English Baptists*, I, 148–149.

[79] Hugh Evans, *Introductory Discourse* in *A Charge and Sermon, Together with an Introductory Discourse, and Confession of Faith, Delivered at the Ordination of the Rev. Mr. Caleb Evans, August 18, 1767, in Broad-Mead, Bristol* (Bristol: Broadmead Baptist Church, 1767), 3.

[80] Evans, *Introductory Discourse*, 3–5.

question, "why do we observe this rite?"[81] Although these discourses covered a wide range of topics, there were commonly reoccurring themes.

Throughout the ceremony, there was an emphasis on simplicity as they wished to stress the internal aspects of religion above the sacerdotal, reflecting what they believed was the biblical precedent.[82] This desire to obey the Scripture in all they did is evident in every aspect of the ordination service. Oftentimes the introductory discourse began with a proclamation that Scripture alone was the rule for all church practice and formed the foundation of the ordination service. Yet at least one pastor conceded that "we do not find in the Word of God, any positive command for us formally to ordain."[83] Although the lack of a direct admonition to ordain did mean that there was no biblical precedent to continue the practice of ordination, these Particular Baptists were convinced that the pattern for the continuation of the ordinance was amply demonstrated in Scripture by the example of the apostles and the early church. And so they saw no biblical reason to discontinue the process.[84]

Another common element of the introductory discourse was a sincere profession of fidelity to the civil government. They lived in an age of fear, on the part of the civil government of incitement to rebellion from some Dissenting groups. It was important for the Particular Baptists to demonstrate their sincere desire to observe the scriptural injunction to obey those in authority over them. They desired peace in the world. Yet they also believed that the State had no right to legislate in the church and so they always emphasized the fundamental right of the church to choose her own officers.[85] The Act of Toleration had permitted churches to administer themselves with a newfound freedom.[86] For the Baptists, freedom of conscience was a fundamental axiom of

---

[81] Rippon, *Register*, 345.

[82] Osborn, *Introductory Address*, 6.

[83] Osborn, *Introductory Address*, 5.

[84] Stennett, *Sermon III*, 121.

[85] This assertion reveals "a deep distrust" for a coalition of Church and State. Ernest A. Payne, "The Ministry in Historical Perspective," *The Baptist Quarterly* 17 (April 1958): 263.

[86] "Blessed be God, for our happy Constitution, whereby we enjoy the free exercise of our Religion, as our Judgment and Conscience direct: This must appear to every Protestant, especially to every Protestant *Dissenter*, to be an inestimable Privilege, and of the last Importance. A Privilege this, which our Progenitors groaned under the Want of—but which our Gracious God, had in Reserve, to introduce with the glorious Revolution, and to *entail* it upon us and our Children, by the *Happy* Accession of the *Illustrious* House of *Hanover* to the *Throne* ... and Act of Toleration as Dissenters. Our rightful Sovereign *King George* has given us Liberty so to do; and so has our Gracious God and Saviour, King Jesus ... Then, let us call no Man on earth, the *Master* of our *Consciences*; but strenuously assert our Right to judge of, and chuse our Spiritual Guides: for it belongs

Christianity and some felt that other forms of church government, like Presbyterianism and Episcopalianism, represented a form of tyranny of conscience. Choosing a pastor was the inherent right of the local church.[87]

They would also frequently emphasize God's sovereign authority over his church and his marvelous grace in the salvation of sinners.[88] He had redeemed a people for himself based on his eternal decree to form a mutual and voluntary society as means of executing his will in the earth.[89] Elders were appointed by God alone as a gracious gift for the edification of the church through the Word and the ordinances. The Particular Baptists believed that people must be taught the Scriptures to be effective in evangelism, to grow in holiness, and to glorify God.[90] All believers had the right and duty to search the Scriptures for themselves, but God had especially ordained teachers in the church (Ephesians 4:11–13). Therefore, it is incumbent on the church to take great care when they determine the will of the Lord in choosing their pastor. A potential candidate had first to be tested and proved both as to his moral character as well as his ministerial gifts. Prayer was an essential part of this process.

The visiting elder would often discuss a few theological points concerning the ordination service. A commonly used text was Acts 6, which they viewed as the first New Testament example of an ordination service. They frequently stressed that in the early church it was the apostles who appointed officers, but it was the brethren who choose them.[91] This was the basis for their understanding that only elders could perform the rite of ordination.[92] They were concerned to follow the scriptural precedent because they wanted to maintain

---

only to the People to appoint their Ecclesiastical Officers; since 'tis for their Sake that any such are instituted, and 'tis the Peoples Interest which is concern'd., and their Good or Ill greatly depends upon their choice of Ministers" (James Fall Sr., *The Charge of God to Feed the Flock of Slaughter. A Sermon Preach'd at the Ordination of the Reverend Mr. James Fall, [Jr.] of Goodman's-Fields, London* [London, 1754], ix–x).

[87] Fall, Sr., *Charge of God*, iii, viii, xi.

[88] Evans, *Introductory Discourse*, 3.

[89] William Clarke, "Introductory Discourse" in *A Charge and Sermon together with an Introductory Discourse and Confession of Faith Delivered at the Ordination of the Rev. Mr. Abraham Booth Feb.16, 1769, in Goodman's Fields* (London, 1769), 3.

[90] Clarke, *Introductory Discourse*, 4.

[91] Clarke, *Introductory Discourse*, 6. Acts 6:3 KJV: "Wherefore, brethren, look ye out among you seven men of honest report, full of the Holy Ghost and wisdom, whom we may appoint over this business."

[92] Osborn, *Introductory Address*, 6, 7.

order in the church by prohibiting, as much as possible, the ordination of unqualified ministers.[93]

They also argued for the practice of laying on of hands as a central part of the ordination service.[94] In the New Testament, the chosen men stood before the apostles who prayed, fasted, and laid hands on them.[95] The laying on of hands was defended as a continuing practice for Baptists, but they stressed that it conveyed no extraordinary gifts.[96]

Finally, the qualifications necessary for the pastor elect were discussed. Specific details of the qualification of the elder were usually expounded in the

---

93 Evans, *Introductory Discourse*, 9. (Acts 6:1, 2; Acts 13:1, 2; Titus 1:5).

94 Ivimey, *History of the English Baptists*, I, 434. "The early Baptists, who desired to keep close to scripture, saw no reason to depart from Christian tradition in this matter" (Underwood, *English Baptists*, 131). See also Ernest A. Payne, "Baptists and the Laying on of Hands," *The Baptist Quarterly* 15 (January 1954): 203. This practice was also endorsed in the *Second London Confession*: "The way appointed by *Christ* for the Calling of any person, fitted, and gifted by the Holy *Spirit*, unto the Office of Bishop, or Elder, in a Church, is, that he be chosen thereunto by the common suffrage of the Church itself; and Solemnly set apart by Fasting and Prayer, with imposition of hands of the Eldership of the Church, if there be any before Constituted therein; And of a Deacon that he be chosen by the like suffrage, and set apart by Prayer, and the like Imposition of hands" (Lumpkin, *Confessions*, 287). Hercules Collins wrote, "Ever retain and never part with that Rite and Ceremony in Ordination of Imposition of Hands, with prayer, on the Person ordained. Some think that the Ceremony of laying on of Hands may be omitted," but, "This hath been the ordinary way of the Ordination of Ministers in the Church of God" (Hercules Collins, *The Temple Repair'd: Or, An Essay to revive the long-neglected Ordinances, of exercising the Spiritual Gift of Prophecy for the Edification of the Churches; and of ordaining Ministers duly qualified. With proper Directions as to Study and Preaching, for such as are inclined to the Ministry* [London: William and Joseph Marshal, 1702], 59).

95 Stennett, *Sermon III*, 107. Acts 6:6 KJV: "Whom they set before the apostles: and when they had prayed, they laid *their* hands on them."

96 Evans, *Introductory Discourse*, 9–10. Acts 13:3: "And when they had fasted and prayed, and laid *their* hands on them, they sent *them* away." "In this business there was no mystery, no superstitious right [sic], no ceremonious pomp, no usurpation of prelatical authority: but there evidently appears great simplicity; pure devotion; love of order; submission to divine teaching; and true benevolence to men" (Osborn, *Introductory Address*, 6). The practice of laying on of hands was often defended in an "Introductory Discourse," which suggests that there was some opposition to the practice (Clarke, *Introductory Discourse*, 8–9). Regarding the controversy on imposition of hands Crosby comments, "That there are some among the Baptists, who object against this form of ordination, tho' it is thus usually performed in their churches, believing it favours too much of men's assuming great power to themselves, in their setting others apart to the ministry; and also believing, the apostles themselves in ordinations, used not this form, *we ordain thee.* And therefore decline pronouncing any words of ordination, and only pray to God for a blessing on the pastor elect, laying their hands upon his head, which they hold is ordination sufficient, and all that they know with certainty respecting the practice of the Apostles, who laid their hands over the persons whom they set apart, and prayed to God in their behalf" (Crosby, *English Baptists*, 187). Far and away laying on of hands was practiced during eighteenth-century Particular Baptists Ordination services.

charge to the newly ordained pastor, yet general credentials were sometimes outlined in the preamble. Things such as moral goodness, Biblical competence, spiritual gifts, passion for the gospel, and separation from the world were essential necessities for aspiring ministers.

Near the end of the introductory discourse they would transition into the other proceedings of the service. A visiting pastor would ask what are called "the usual questions"[97] to the church.[98] These questions were addressed to both the members of the church and the ordinand. First, the ordinand would be asked if he was in full communion with the church.[99] This was to ensure that church order was preserved and everything done according to Scripture. The visiting elders would then require a step-by-step account of the process the church had undergone to procure the pastor. The response was usually delivered by a deacon and included a brief history of the church since their previous pastor's departure[100] with an account of God's providential leading which brought the new pastor elect and church together.[101]

Then the non-members were separated from the members of the church. The non-members may be asked to go into the galleries while the members would come together in the middle of the meeting place.[102] They would then ask the congregation's approbation of the choice of pastor. If the members

---

[97] They were sometimes called the "usual interrogatories" (Rippon, *Register*, 480).

[98] In a Presbyterian ceremony they would ask: 1) Do you feel that you are called of God to the ministry? 2) Do you hold the Old Testament and the New Testament to be the only Word of God and necessary for salvation? 3) Do you promise to execute your charge faithfully according to Scripture? (Horton Davies, *The Worship of the English Puritans* [Westminster: Dacre Press, 1948], 228-229).

[99] Copson, *Ordinations at Bridlington*, 146. Richard Machin, ordained by George Braithwaite, was asked if he were "in full membership with the church."

[100] Rippon, *Register*, 345. The three questions asked by George Braithwaite recorded in the Bridlington Church Book, June 1737, were: Question 1 "For w[ha]t cause has ye Church desired our Company and Presence here at ys time?" Answer "That ye may be witnesses to ye Churches Act in Calling out & setting apart our Br Mr Richard Machin to ye Office of pastor in ye Church." Question 2 "Is Mr Richd Machin a member in full Fellowship & Communion with ye Church?" Answer "Yes he is." Question 3 "If ye Church is free & desirous to constitute and appoint Mr Rich'd Machin to ye solemn office of Pastor over 'em, on his Compliance with their Call & Act, they are desired to signifie it by lifting up of their hands" (Copson, *Ordinations at Bridlington*, 147). For a detailed description of an account see, *Three Discourses Addressed to the Congregation at Maze-Pond, Southwark, on their Public Declaration of having chosen Mr. James Dore their pastor.* March 25th, 1784 (Cambridge, 1784), 18-22.

[101] Rippon, *Register*, 123, 347.

[102] Thomas Crosby, *The History of the English Baptists* (London: John Robinson Bookseller, 1740), IV, 184-185.

acknowledged in the positive, they would raise their right hands.[103] A second request may be taken for asking for votes in the negative.[104] They would then ask for the steps the pastor took in relation to his call and public acceptance.[105] He would then give a brief account of his conversion, his call to ministry, and the providence which led him to that particular church.[106] Then the pastor elect would publicly acknowledge and accept the call.[107] This was a verbal acceptance accompanied with the raising of his right hand.[108] Following his acceptance, he would often express his love and appreciation to the people of the church and describe the great privilege it was to serve them. Caleb Evans, who had pastored at the Broadmead church in Bristol for eight years prior to his ordination, vowed to continue serving them "diligently, faithfully and fervently."[109] He closed this part of the ceremony with a statement recognizing his own insufficiency and complete and total dependence on God for any success in the ministry.[110]

If everything appeared orderly, that is, according to the rule of Scripture, the church and the visiting pastors would accept his acknowledgement and proceed to receive his confession of faith after a prayer.[111] The confession was given verbally, sometimes memoriter, but usually read, in a series of articles that articulated an orthodox Calvinistic theology that was usually also expressly Baptistic and evangelical, especially in the latter part of the eighteenth century.[112]

Statement of Faith

It was important that a candidate for ordination give his statement of faith publicly to allow the other ministers present to examine his beliefs, pray for his endowment with God's Spirit, and exhort both him and the other church members to walk faithfully together in obedience and love.[113]

---

[103] Clarke, *Introductory Discourse*, 9. Evans, *Introductory Discourse*, 6.

[104] Crosby, *History of the English Baptists*, IV, 185.

[105] Clarke, *Introductory Discourse*, 10.

[106] Rippon, *Register*, 190.

[107] Clarke, *Introductory Discourse*, 9.

[108] Rippon, *Register*, 345.

[109] Evans, *Introductory Discourse*, 7.

[110] Crosby, *History of the English Baptists*, IV, 186.

[111] Rippon, *Register*, 348.

[112] Rippon, *Register*, 122. Joshua Burton on 8 December 1791 gave an account of his faith in 18 articles (Rippon, *Register*, 521).

[113] Ernest A. Payne, "Baptists and the Ministry," *The Baptist Quarterly* 25 (April 1973): 54.

The public declaration of a precise doctrinal position was particularly important in a rationalistic age when others, like the majority of the General Baptists, had adopted universalistic beliefs and abandoned their essential doctrines. In a covenantal relationship rooted in a received canon of truth, essential agreement on this rule is crucial. This is particularly significant when the relationship is voluntary and there is a profound and mutual commitment to love and unity. Further, the main expectation of the role of the pastor was to faithfully teach biblical truths "once delivered unto the saints" (Jude 3).

Content

They generally described it as a "confession of faith" or as expressing "a declaration of religious sentiments."[114] Sometimes, as in the case of Caleb Evans, the ordinand would begin with a preamble. Caleb Evans felt it necessary to defend the practice of publicly stating a confession of faith. Apparently some had challenged the practice on the basis that it represented an affront to religious freedom.[115] But Evans argues that though it had become "unfashionable" to disclaim any creeds or systematic expositions, even those who denied their value necessarily just replaced another's system with their own.[116] Everyone has a right to choose what they believe. That is why is it so important that the church and pastor, who bind themselves together voluntarily, agree doctrinally.[117] Those lamenting the loss of religious liberty were really only rejecting the glorious truths that the Particular Baptists had inherited from the Reformation.[118] Therefore the minister giving his statement of faith at an ordination sermon was not interfering with rights for private judgment, but rather expressing that right through his declaration.[119] It is quite telling that even though Evans had already ministered among the Baptist congregation at

---

[114] Abraham Booth, *A Confession of Faith Delivered at his Ordination* in *A Charge and Sermon together with an Introductory Discourse and Confession of Faith Delivered at the Ordination of the Rev. Mr. Abraham Booth Feb.16, 1769, in Goodman's Fields* (London, 1769), 11. Thomas Morgan, *Declaration of Religious Sentiments* in John Ryland and Andrew Fuller, *The Difficulties of the Christian Ministry, and the Means of Surmounting them; with the Obedience of Churches to their Pastors Explained and Enforced* (Birmingham: J. Belcher/London: Button and Son, 1802), iii.

[115] Evans, *Introductory Discourse*, 17.

[116] Evans, *Introductory Discourse*, 17.

[117] Evans, *Introductory Discourse*, 13–14. Note similar comments at the beginning of Gill's systematic theology.

[118] Evans, *Introductory Discourse*, 17.

[119] Evans, *Introductory Discourse*, 18.

Broadmead in Bristol for eight years, he still felt it was absolutely necessary, even a privilege, to give his statement of faith.

Common Content Included

Confessions of Faith given at ordination ceremonies seemed to follow a standard pattern, and although different viewpoints are expressed, the general structure was relatively uniform. Most would begin with an avowal of their belief in the being of God which was displayed everywhere in creation.[120] Evidence displayed in the moon and stars, the rich assortment of vegetation, the variety and complexity of different animals, as well as the human body, all pointed back to single cause—God.[121]

Beliefs

Despite this general revelation in creation, the clearest revelation of God was found in the Scriptures.[122] The Word of God, which represents his revelation to man, manifests his moral character, and especially his goodness and love (as seen particularly in the doctrine of the cross), the future hope of resurrection, forgiveness, and the rest of his promises to the church.[123]

In their confession they would sometimes also include a brief apologetic for Scripture as the only Word of God. For example, W. Belsher says:

> From the sublimity and excellency of the doctrines; the grace and glory of the promises; the freeness of the invitations; the purity of the precepts contained in the writings of the Old and New Testament; connected with the holiness and agreement of the inspired writers; the accomplishment of prophecy; the dispersion and preservation of the Jews; the evidence of miracles, and the astonishing influence of scripture doctrines (through divine agency) upon the minds of men, I believe the Bible to be the word of God.[124]

---

[120] W. Belsher, *Declaration of Religious Sentiments* in John Ryland and Samuel Pearce, *The Duty of the Ministers to be Nursing Fathers to the Church; and the Duty of Churches to Regard Ministers as the Gift of Christ* (London, 1796), 9.

[121] Evans, *Introductory Discourse*, 19.

[122] Morgan, *Declaration of Religious Sentiments*, iii.

[123] Belsher, *Declaration of Religious Sentiments*, 10.

[124] Belsher, *Declaration of Religious Sentiments*, 10, 11. Booth, *Confession of Faith*, 15.

The Word of God consisted of the Old Testament and the New Testament, but excluded the Apocrypha.[125] Because the Bible was God's revelation to man, it was therefore man's duty to submit to it, and to humbly obey all its precepts.[126] The Bible was believed to be an inestimable gift from the Creator and received as the only rule for their faith and practice.[127]

The Trinitarianism of the Nicene Creed was generally acknowledged as orthodox until the time of the Enlightenment in the eighteenth century. In an age where Unitarianism was flourishing again under the leadership of men like Joseph Priestly, a reassertion of the orthodox doctrine of the Trinity was vital. John Gill believed this doctrine was the "foundation of revelation; and of the economy of man's salvation; it is what enters into every truth of the gospel, and without which no truth can be truly understood, nor rightly explained."[128] In their understanding of the doctrine of the Trinity, the Particular Baptists followed the standard Reformed understanding of the Trinity as a unity in essence in three Persons.[129] Scripture reveals that there is one true living God infinite in holiness, and in the unity of the Godhead there are three divine Persons: the Father and the Son and the Holy Ghost.[130]

Another core belief of the Baptists was that Scripture teaches the doctrine of original sin where all mankind is born in a state of alienation from God.[131] God created man in his own image and he placed a tree in the Garden of Eden, the tree of the knowledge of good and evil, as a test of the obedience or disobedience for men and women.[132] His creatures failed the test and willfully transgressed by eating the forbidden fruit. Adam, as the federal head of all mankind, caused his posterity to be born in guilt, depravity, and ruin.[133]

Particular Baptist theology of the eighteenth century emphasized the atonement of Christ as a central doctrine. They were Calvinists believing that

---

[125] Evans, *Introductory Discourse*, 20. Booth, *Confession of Faith*, 14.

[126] Evans, *Introductory Discourse*, 20–21. Booth, *Confession of Faith*, 14–17.

[127] Booth, *Confession of Faith*, 17.

[128] John Gill, *The Form of Sound Words to be Held Fast. A Charge Delivered at the Ordination of the Rev. Mr. John Reynolds* in his *A Collection of Sermons and Tracts* (London: George Keith, 1773), II, 53.

[129] Belsher, *Declaration of Religious Sentiments*, 11; Morgan, *Declaration of Religious Sentiments*, iv.

[130] Evans, *Introductory Discourse*, 21. Booth, *Confession of Faith*, 17.

[131] Morgan, *Declaration of Religious Sentiments*, iv.

[132] Evans, *Introductory Discourse*, 23.

[133] Evans, *Introductory Discourse*, 23. Booth, *Confession of Faith*, 18.

God sovereignly elects a people to salvation according to his eternal decrees.[134] Everything that happens in the world is a result of divine decree and that, "He worketh all things after the counsel of his will" (Ephesians 1:11). They believed that God effectually calls and justifies his elect. Justification was understood as "a complete acquittal from imputed and contracted guilt, a deliverance from the destructive and condemning power of sin."[135] Christians are justified by Christ's imputed righteousness which is received by faith.[136] They also taught that saints could not lose their salvation and that God would keep them in a state of saving grace. They also believed that those who are chosen are sanctified by the Spirit,[137] and that the Law was good and just and so it was their duty to obey it.[138]

The Son of God became incarnate and left a perfect pattern of obedience. Through his blood there is full redemption for the sinner, but people must first exercise repentance and faith.[139] It is therefore a Christian's duty to try and convince people of the truth of the gospel, that mankind is only justified by faith, through the imputation of the perfect righteousness of Jesus Christ. They reiterated over and over again that good works do not save.[140] They believed in the absolute necessity of regeneration.[141] And that only Christ secures salvation by satisfying the demands of divine justice. The Son of God became incarnate and lived a life of perfect obedience to the divine will,[142] then died on the cross to become a vicarious atoning sacrifice for the sins of his chosen people.[143] On the third day he rose again and the justice of God was fully satisfied.[144]

The two ordinances of Baptism and the Lord's Supper were instituted by Christ for the edification of his church.[145] Baptism is by immersion in the name

---

[134] Morgan, *Declaration of Religious Sentiments*, iv.

[135] Belsher, *Declaration of Religious Sentiments*, 14.

[136] Belsher, *Declaration of Religious Sentiments*, 14.

[137] Booth, *Confession of Faith*, 22.

[138] Morgan, *Declaration of Religious Sentiments*, iv.

[139] Morgan, *Declaration of Religious Sentiments*, v.

[140] Morgan, *Declaration of Religious Sentiments*, v.

[141] Evans, *Introductory Discourse*, 30. Caleb Evans's statement of faith identifies him as an evangelical Calvinist. He said, like Fuller, in 1767, "I receive therefore this glorious heart cheering doctrine as well worthy of all acceptation" (Norman S. Moon, "Caleb Evans, Founder of the Bristol Education Society," *The Baptist Quarterly* 24 [October 1971]: 176).

[142] Evans, *Introductory Discourse*, 29.

[143] Evans, *Introductory Discourse*, 29.

[144] Booth, *Confession of Faith*, 20.

[145] Booth, *Confession of Faith*, 22.

of the Father, Son, and Holy Spirit and represents an emblem of the death, burial, and resurrection of Jesus, as the representative of his people.[146] It is only administered on profession of repentance and faith.[147]

The Lord's Supper is a remembrance of the love, sufferings, and death of Jesus Christ.[148] Booth describes it as:

> an ordinance where, "by receiving the elements of bread and wine, according to the appointment of Christ, we shew forth his death. And is designed, ... to impress our minds with the lively sense of the evil of sin, the sufferings of Jesus for it,—the benefits derived to us through those sufferings,—together with the union and communion which we have with him, and one with another."[149]

At death all people's physical bodies disintegrate, but their immortal spirit returns to God.[150] The souls of believers immediately go into glory, and the wicked are immediately transmitted into the abodes of darkness and despair until the judgment day.[151] There will be a resurrection from the dead of both the just and the unjust.[152] God will judge in righteousness according to Jesus Christ, separating the righteous from the wicked.[153] The righteous are awarded eternal life and infinite happiness while the wicked are sent away to everlasting death and eternal torment.[154]

Abraham Booth concludes his confession by declaring that his statement of faith truly reflects what he believes and that he is determined to faithfully preach these doctrines to the people. Yet at the same time, he humbly acknowledges that he is fallible and must always keep his mind open to divine truth.[155] He then expresses his duty and determination to love other

---

[146] Booth, *Confession of Faith*, 22–23.
[147] Morgan, *Declaration of Religious Sentiments*, iv.
[148] Belsher, *Declaration of Religious Sentiments*, 15.
[149] Booth, *Confession of Faith*, 23.
[150] Booth, *Confession of Faith*, 23.
[151] Booth, *Confession of Faith*, 23.
[152] Booth, *Confession of Faith*, 23.
[153] Booth, *Confession of Faith*, 23, 24.
[154] Booth, *Confession of Faith*, 24.
[155] Booth, *Confession of Faith*, 24.

Christians, even despite their denominational affiliation.[156] Finally, he concludes in doxological expression of his utter dependence on God's help.[157]

Joseph Kinghorn at his ordination on 20 May 1780 ends his Confession of Faith as follows:

> Such are the general views of Christianity which I have endeavoured to lay open to the people here, as appearing to me to be the will of God. Should I be hereafter favoured with a clearer insight into his holy will, I hope I shall not hide from them what shall appear as his counsel, but shall look on myself as bound to declare it, being sensible that anything attended with Scripture evidence is not only important, but best calculated to promote the end which I trust I earnestly desire,—the eternal salvation of souls.[158]

There was an implicit understanding that it was not enough just to say the words, but that they must also be believed and acted upon. Therefore the ordinand often sought to assure the church that these truths had been internalized, and, even beyond that, affectionately cherished in their hearts.

Ordination Prayer— "Laying on of Hands"

In order to understand the solemn rite of "laying on hands," it is helpful to consider its main participants. First there was God's role in ordination. He was the one who constituted the office of elder and gave the qualifications and abilities to the pastor. He destines, equips, and chooses men for the office.[159] But before the pastor is chosen by the congregation it must first be demonstrated that he has been prepared by God for the work.[160]

Next there is the role of the church in ordination.[161] In Acts 6 when the people chose their officers, they had them go before the apostles to ordain them.[162] Although Acts 6 seems to refer to the election of deacons, it was also regarded as the pattern for the election of elders. Joseph Stennett argues,

[156] Booth, *Confession of Faith*, 25.
[157] Booth, *Confession of Faith*, 25.
[158] Wolever, *Life of Kinghorn*, 177.
[159] Stennett, *Sermon III*, 107.
[160] Stennett, *Sermon III*, 108.
[161] Important texts are Acts 6:3, 5, 6—chose deacons, call them, desire for them to minister among them (Stennett, *Sermon III*, 107).
[162] Stennett, *Sermon III*, 108.

"And if the deacons are to be chosen of the church, there is a parity of reason that elders should be chosen too; nay, there seems to be a greater reason for it, that the consent of the people should be had to whom they must commit their souls."[163] The deacons were responsible for temporal affairs and the elders were responsible for people's spiritual needs. If in Acts 6 they were encouraged to choose officers to be stewards of their money, why not in like manner, choose stewards of their souls?[164] Yet, the ministerial candidate was not completely passive in the process. His role was to devote himself to the ministry, not by compulsion, but for love for God and concern for the spiritual well-being of his people.[165] So it was vital that he joyfully and willingly give his consent also.[166]

Finally, there was the role played by the visiting ministers who performed the prayer with imposition of hands. Only they had the right to do this,[167] but their authority to do so was given by the church.[168] The church had complete power over the selection of her officers. As mentioned, most believed that the imposition of hands was an indispensable part of the service.[169] The main points they wished to stress in response to opposition to the practice was that it neither conveys extraordinary gifts nor additional qualifications to the person ordained;[170] rather, it represented a solemn, simple, but significant rite setting a man apart to a particular office.[171]

The main purpose of the ordination prayer was to entreat the divine blessing on relationship between the church and the pastor.[172] They believed that without God's presence and helping power the pastor was doomed to failure. Also, the pastor was uniquely connected with the local church he was ordained

---

163 Stennett, *Sermon III*, 108.

164 Stennett, *Sermon III*, 107.

165 Stennett, *Sermon III*, 107.

166 Stennett, *Sermon III*, 110. 1 Peter 5:2.

167 Rippon, *Register*, 354. Sutcliff, *Introductory Address*, 6.

168 Fall, Sr., *Charge of God*, vii: "we have no Right or Authority to solemnize the Ordination of your intended Pastor, but what we *receive* from *you* as a *Church.*"

169 Stennett, *Sermon III*, 111–112; Rippon, *Register*, 345.

170 Sutcliff, *Introductory Address*, 8.

171 Sutcliff, *Introductory Address*, 7.

172 Rippon, *Register*, 481.

in.[173] However, under certain circumstances it was acceptable for him to leave for another pastorate.[174]

Charge to the Pastor

The third major address, and the most prominent in an eighteenth-century Particular Baptist ordination service, was the charge to the pastor. The main purpose of the charge was to describe the motivations, character, qualifications, duties, and purposes of ministers of the gospel.[175] The office of pastor was highly exalted in the sight of God, but that did not mean there would be no hardship. The new pastor was warned of the various trials he would likely face, but he was also given counsel on how to overcome them.[176] In general, the charge contained advice on how to faithfully and diligently fulfill the stewardship of the office for the benefit of the Church and to the glory of God. A much more detailed analysis of the theological content of the charge is described in the next chapter.

ADDRESS TO THE CHURCH

The final sermon of the proceedings, usually following prayer and singing, contained an address to the church. The main purpose of this discourse was to examine the church members' responsibilities to the pastor in the context of

---

[173] Wallin, *Charge Delivered*, 35. "The constitution of CHRIST's Church, and the custom of the saints in the Apostles' days manifestly shew, that whatever occasional call the Pastors of churches may have to minister elsewhere, their stated and constant labours are required among those who are committed to their charge. It is part of the character of a gospel minister that he labours *among them* over whom he is placed: And herein lieth much of the *labour* and *honour* of his work" (Benjamin Wallin, *The Obligations of a People to their Faithful Minister. Represented in a Discourse Preached at the Ordination of the Revd. Mr. Samuel Burford, September 4, 1755* [London: George Keith, 1755], 6).

[174] "I would by no means flatter or countenance the instability frequently seen: he that will shift from place to place, without consent or advice, ... Nevertheless, there may be a *just* and *cogent* reason for a change; the circumstances of a minister, and likewise those of the church, through a variety of events, may speak for his moving" (Wallin, *Charge Delivered*, 45). "It is said that in the eighteenth century a man would often remain in the same pastorate for a considerable period, even for life. Rippon's lists show that this was sometimes the case, but also that a brief pastorate was not uncommon" (Nuttall, *Baptist Ministers*, 384-385).

[175] John Gill, *The Doctrine of the Cherubim Opened and Explained. A Sermon at the Ordination of the Reverend Mr. John Davis, at Waltham-Abbey. Preached August 15, 1764* in his *A Collection of Sermons and Tracts* (London, 1773), II, 30-31.

[176] Sutcliff, *Introductory Address*, 11, 14.

their voluntary relationship.[177] The address also considered the individual member's responsibilities to one another.

The Church's Responsibility

Following the pattern of Jesus, the church must be characterized by love if it is to fulfil its mandate. It is necessary that they love their pastor and treat him with kindness and affection.[178] Their esteem for the pastor was not based primarily on the fact that he was a worthy individual, but rather it reflected the high regard they held for the office of elder. God's servant was worthy of such respect because he had been chosen by God as a leader over them for their good. If God had honoured him, so should his church. Pastors should be encouraged in the work as long as they remained faithful to the Scriptures.[179] They were considered rulers in the church, but not tyrants, and so they had no power to impose laws on the church that are not found in Scripture. They were to govern and guide the congregation for the good of people's souls.[180]

Since it is the nature of love to hide infirmities and weakness, it is important to overlook a pastor's individual flaws. Conversations about him should be positive,[181] always speaking respectfully of him, especially to their families.[182] Also, the congregation should not receive an accusation against him without clear evidence.[183] The only stipulation for these rules was that he had to reflect the gospel through his speech and life. If he continued to declare

177 Benjamin Wallin, *The Obligations of a People to their Faithful Minister. Represented in a Discourse Preached at the Ordination of the Revd. Mr. Samuel Burford, September 4, 1755* (London: George Keith, 1755), 8.

178 Hugh Evans, *A Sermon, etc.* in Caleb Evans and his *A Charge and Sermon; Delivered at the Ordination of the Rev. Thomas Dunscombe, At Coate, Oxon, August 4th, 1773* (Bristol: W. Pine, T. Cadell, M. Ward, 1773), 23.

179 Samuel Pearce, *The Duty of Churches to Regard Ministers as the Gift of Christ* in John Ryland and his, *The Duty of Ministers to be Nursing Fathers to the Church; and the Duty of Churches to Regard Ministers as the Gift of Christ* (London: Button/Worcester: Baskerfield/Birmingham: Belcher/Bristol: James, 1796), 46.

180 William Crabtree, *The Regard which the Churches of Christ Owe to Their Ministers. A Sermon, Preached at the Ordination of The Rev. Joshua Wood, of Halifax, August 6, 1760* in Isaac Mann, *Memoirs of the Late Rev. Wm. Crabtree* (London: Button and Son, 1815), 64.

181 Crabtree, "Regard which the Churches of Christ Owe" in Mann, *Memoirs*, 73.

182 Evans, *Sermon*, 34.

183 John Tommas, *The duties incumbent on church members, and the manner in which they should be performed, represented and inforced* [*sic*] in *A Charge and Sermon, Together with an Introductory Discourse, and Confession of Faith, Delivered at the Ordination of the Rev. Mr. Caleb Evans, August 18, 1767, in Broad-Mead, Bristol* (Bristol: Broadmead Baptist Church, 1767), 86.

the whole counsel of God, preaching Christ alone as saviour, the church was under obligation to treat him with the utmost affection.[184]

This love was to be sincere, motivated by a genuine desire for the pastor's prosperity, and given freely and cheerfully.[185] But true love is always necessarily practical and therefore must be demonstrated tangibly. Consequently, the church was encouraged to constantly look for ways to strengthen and encourage their leaders. For example, if a pastor was struggling with grief and sorrow, they must show him compassion.[186] One of the best ways to encourage the pastor was to regularly attend church meetings,[187] and, especially, the ordinance of the Lord's Supper. Irregular attendance hindered his work by showing a poor example to others.[188] It is particularly discouraging for the pastor, who labours over a sermon designed for the good of the church as a whole, to find members not in attendance. Paying attention to his sermons was another means of encouraging the pastor. The congregation was warned not to be inattentive, smile, whisper, or look about at others during the service.[189]

The need for regular attendance, and attentive listening, was partially based on a utilitarian belief that the church had an obligation to make conscientious use of their pastors.[190] As he was given a stewardship to preach the Word, the church was given the stewardship to listen to the Word. It was the members' duty to be taught by him through his public preaching and his private visitation, learning to humbly accept his counsel, exhortations, and rebukes. It was assumed that these admonitions were given in love and so they were to be received as a blessing and not as a personal attack.[191] Of course, to hear the Word implied that they would apply this truth to their lives.[192] Members should always be transparent about their spiritual condition, sharing their

---

[184] Crabtree, "Regard which the Churches of Christ Owe" in Mann, *Memoirs*, 73.

[185] Tommas, *Duties incumbent*, 80.

[186] Crabtree, "Regard which the Churches of Christ Owe" in Mann, *Memoirs*.

[187] Tommas, *Duties incumbent*, 83; Evans, *Sermon*, 31; Crabtree, "Regard which the Churches of Christ Owe" in Mann, *Memoirs*, 83.

[188] Isaac Mann, *Memoirs of the Late Rev. Wm. Crabtree* (London: Button and Son, 1815), 52.

[189] Mann, *Memoirs of the Late Rev. Wm. Crabtree*, 54.

[190] N. Clark, *Three Discourses Addressed to the Congregation at Maze-Pond, Southwark, on their Public Declaration of having chosen Mr. James Dore their pastor. March 25th, 1784* (Cambridge: J. Archdeacon, 1784), 97.

[191] Tommas, *Duties incumbent*, 82.

[192] Evans, *Sermon*, 31.

struggles and blessings with the pastor.[193] In turn, the church was obligated to lovingly offer their pastor advice when necessity called for it.[194]

Because the pastor was to be wholly committed to the welfare of the church and not distracted by worldly affairs, it was the church's responsibility to make provision for his earthly needs. His primary responsibility was to serve Christ in the Church and he must be freed as much as possible from all temporal concerns.[195] Beyond his basic needs, the church should, to the best of their ability, ensure the pastor and his family are comfortable.[196] They must try and make his ministry joyful, believing that his joy would become theirs.[197]

The church also had an obligation to protect their pastor's time. Two of his primary duties included visiting members and preparing quality sermons,[198] so it was important to guard against those who would try and steal his time just to chat.[199] He must be given the time to do what he had been called to do and so members should leave him to his work, especially guarding his mornings and Saturdays as it "is a little short of cruelty to interrupt him then."[200]

Perhaps most importantly, the church should regularly pray for him.[201] This was considered the supreme demonstration of love for him for they all believed that he could do nothing good without divine assistance.[202] More specifically the church should pray that he would resist temptation, have power in proclamation, have help in the study of Scripture, clear thoughts in formulating ideas, warmth and pleasure in meditation, liberty and boldness in speaking, strength to resist the world and its temptations, and the ability to maintain a good character.[203] But this love was not confined to ethereal needs only, as the church is also encouraged to pray for his physical health and the material welfare of his family.[204] Prayer for the pastor was not just restricted to Sunday

---

[193] Clark, *Three Discourses*, 99.

[194] Crabtree, "Regard which the Churches of Christ Owe" in Mann, *Memoirs*, 82. See 1 Corinthians 13:9; Acts 18:26.

[195] Evans, *Sermon*, 28.

[196] Tommas, *Duties incumbent*, 86; Clark, *Three Discourses*, 96; Evans, *Sermon*, 28.

[197] Evans, *Sermon*, 25.

[198] Crabtree, "Regard which the Churches of Christ Owe" in Mann, *Memoirs*, 96.

[199] Pearce, *Duty of Churches*, 52.

[200] Pearce, *Duty of Churches*, 52.

[201] Tommas, *Duties incumbent*, 79.

[202] Crabtree, "Regard which the Churches of Christ Owe" in Mann, *Memoirs*, 90.

[203] Crabtree, "Regard which the Churches of Christ Owe" in Mann, *Memoirs*, 93.

[204] Clark, *Three Discourses*, 99.

mornings, but should be practiced in private prayers, family devotions, and other church-meetings.[205] If a church refused to pray for their pastor, they hurt not only him, but also themselves.[206]

The address also usually included arguments encouraging the people of the church to implement these admonitions in their church life. Since God had placed the pastor over the church as a ruler, it was a member's duty to submit to him. He was given as a free gift from God and placed there for the church's edification;[207] and the Lord has so ordained it that as his success goes, so goes the church.[208] Since their honour and reputation depend on his success in the office, the church must strive to do everything in their power to help him accomplish his duties effectively.[209]

Yet the church not only has responsibilities to the pastor, they also are accountable to one another. Just as they have an obligation to love their pastor, they also must love one another. As opportunity arises, they must strive to care for one another and bear each other's burdens—both spiritual and temporal.[210] They must freely interact with one another, sharing each other's triumphs and defeats while constantly praying for each other's needs.[211] Peace is essential for a gospel church, but it takes effort. They must struggle for peace and avoid contention, seeking to build each other up in "knowledge, faith, purity, and usefulness" (Romans 14:19).[212]

The ordination proceedings usually ended with the singing of a Psalm or hymn followed by a prayer or benediction.

If the ordination ceremony was not completed in one service in the morning, an afternoon or evening service would sometimes follow. In 1790 at the ordination of Nathan Smith at Barnoldswick, Yorkshire, the church met again at 3:00 pm to hear the address to the church.[213] There is another example of an evening service beginning at 5:45 pm at a deacon's ordination at Salop Baptist Church in 1796. William Steadman opened in prayer, and then hands were

---

[205] Crabtree, "Regard which the Churches of Christ Owe" in Mann, *Memoirs*, 92.

[206] Crabtree, "Regard which the Churches of Christ Owe" in Mann, *Memoirs*, 93; Pearce, *Duty of Churches*, 49.

[207] Crabtree, "Regard which the Churches of Christ Owe" in Mann, *Memoirs*, 97, 102.

[208] Evans, *Sermon*, 35, 36.

[209] Crabtree, "Regard which the Churches of Christ Owe" in Mann, *Memoirs*, 107, 108.

[210] Tommas, *Duties incumbent*, 87.

[211] Tommas, *Duties incumbent*, 88.

[212] Tommas, *Duties incumbent*, 89.

[213] Rippon, *Register*, 518.

laid on a Brother Evans. Samuel Pearce preached from 2 Corinthians 4:7 and a Brother Harrington closed in prayer.[214] At the ordination of Thomas Berry in 1796 the church met again in the evening at 7:00 pm. Brother Sharp gave an Address to the Church from 1 Thessalonians 5:13. There was no address to the church in the morning service which began at 10:30 am.[215] At William Carey's ordination in 1791, Samuel Pearce preached from Galatians 6:14 "in the evening."[216]

These services were shorter in length than the morning service. Usually they opened with prayer and singing, then a sermon was preached. Typically this was an address to the church if one was not given in the morning service, but, as in the case of William Carey, it might be a special sermon to encourage both the church and the newly ordained pastor or missionary.[217] Sometimes, if deacons were being ordained, they may also have included an ordination prayer and the laying on of hands. After the service they would close in singing and prayer. We have an example given in the *Register* of a service ending at 9:00 pm.[218]

Conclusion

These ordination services were central to the spiritual life of these early Baptists and as such reveal important clues to understanding their pastoral theological priorities. The charge which contained the pastoral advice of a more senior minister is central to understanding what was important to them concerning the ministry. The next chapter will define and describe the contours of their theological content as seen primarily in the charge.

---

214 Rippon, *Register*, 483.
215 Rippon, *Register*, 482.
216 Rippon, *Register*, 519. See also Rippon, *Register*, 117, 192,
217 Rippon, *Register*, 483, 519.
218 Rippon, *Register*, 190.

4
Pastoral Theology of Particular Baptists Ordination Sermons

The following chapter will describe the main theological priorities of the Particular Baptists of the long-eighteenth century. More specifically the elder's qualifications and duties will be considered. The purpose is to discover the essence of their pastoral theological priorities as seen in their ordination sermons.

Ordination Themes from Sermons

In an ordination service, consistent themes emerge from the pastoral addresses that show the priorities of Particular Baptist ministry. These essential characteristics help to define how they viewed the ideal of pastoral ministry—highlighting those qualities and concerns that they felt were indispensable to the successful execution of the office.

As we have noted, for the Particular Baptists of the eighteenth century the Bible was the supreme authority of all matters of faith and practice. The importance of the doctrine of Scripture is evidenced in *The Second London Confession*. Based on verses such as 2 Timothy 3:15, 16, 17 the Confession begins:

> The Holy Scripture is the only sufficient, certain, and infallible rule of all saving Knowledge, Faith, and Obedience; Although the light of Nature, and the works of Creation and Providence do so far manifest the goodness, wisdom and power of God, as to leave men inexcusable; yet are they not sufficient to give that knowledge of God and his will, which is necessary unto salvation. Therefore it pleased the Lord at sundry times, and in divers manners, to reveal himself, and to declare that his will unto his Church; and afterward for the better preserving, and propagating of the Truth, and for the more sure Establishment and Comfort of the Church against the corruption of the flesh, and the malice of Satan, and of the World, to commit the same wholly unto writing; which

> maketh the Holy Scriptures to be most necessary, those former ways of God's revealing his will unto his people being now ceased.[1]

Particular Baptists understood the Holy Scriptures to comprise the canonical books of the Old and New Testament, explicitly excluding the Apocryphal books.[2] These canonical books were completely authoritative in the life of the church because they were convinced that an infallible God was their author. Therefore it was the duty and wisdom of men and women to believe it, reverently esteem it, and obey it.[3] Naturally the Bible was the final appeal for all controversy over the opinions of ancient writers, or special new revelations.[4]

The integral relationship between God and the salvific necessity of the Word is emphasized throughout the first chapter of the Confession.[5] Not only are the Scriptures central to salvation, their positive influence affects everything necessary for mankind's relationship to God.[6] But it is not the words of Scripture alone which provide saving understanding, but the accompanying illumination of the Holy Spirit is also necessary.[7] Nevertheless Scripture is plain and clear in meaning and all things concerning salvation are accessible to both the learned and unlearned alike.[8] The most reliable way to get at the intended meaning is to allow Scripture to interpret Scripture.[9]

At the heart of an ordination service was a desire to remain faithful to the precepts of the Word of God. So, for example, in the introductory discourse at

---

[1] Lumpkin, *Confessions*, 248–249.

[2] Lumpkin, *Confessions*, 249.

[3] Lumpkin, *Confessions*, 250. "The Authority of the Holy Scripture for which it ought to be believed dependeth not upon the testimony of any man, or Church; but wholly upon God (who is truth itself) the Author thereof; therefore it is to be received, because it is the Word of God."

[4] Lumpkin, *Confessions*, 252. See Article 10.

[5] For example, "the full discovery of it makes of the only way of mans [*sic*] salvation" (Lumpkin, *Confessions*, 250). See also article seven: "All things in Scripture are not alike plain in themselves, nor alike clear unto all; yet those things which are necessary to be known, believed, and observed for Salvation, are so clearly propounded, and opened in some place of Scripture or other, that not only the learned, but the unlearned, in a due use of ordinary means, may attain to a sufficient understanding of them" (Lumpkin, *Confessions*, 251).

[6] "The whole Counsel of God concerning all things necessary for his own Glory, Man's Salvation, Faith and Life, is either expressly set down or necessarily contained in the *Holy Scripture*; unto which nothing at any time is to be added, whether by new Revelation of the *Spirit* or traditions of men" (Lumpkin, *Confessions*, 250).

[7] "Nevertheless we acknowledge the inward illumination of the Spirit of God, to be necessary for the saving understanding of such things as are revealed in the Word" (Lumpkin, *Confessions*, 250).

[8] Lumpkin, *Confessions*, 251.

[9] Lumpkin, *Confessions*, 252.

Thomas Morgan's (1776–1857)[10] ordination in 1802, John Sutcliff begins, as does the *Confession*, by emphasizing the primacy of the Bible as the "all-sufficient and only guide in matters of religion."[11] The Bible is not only authoritative in the formation of Baptist faith, but it also must regulate all Baptist practice.[12] An orthodox belief in the Word of God represented a beginning point for Particular Baptists of the eighteenth century, but it was not enough just to believe these fundamentals in a hypothetical or intellectual sense. A Christian, and especially a pastor, must also manifest them as a reality in his daily life by living out the truths he professed. The grandest truth of all was to love God supremely, resulting in a corresponding love to all mankind.[13] The most significant manifestation of love for a pastor to the church, in line with the Baptists objectives for the office of elder, was to speak the truth in love—to faithfully exposit the Scriptures.

As we have seen, it was important for Baptists to demonstrate that they were not a seditious body but were committed to obeying the laws of the nation. Yet at the same time, they were bound in conscience to the Word of God, and servants of a superior authority. They had one master, Jesus Christ, to whom they were ultimately bound. The state had no legislative authority in the church, just as the church had no legislative authority in the state. This rule of self-governance gave Baptist churches the right to choose their own officers in elders and deacons.[14] This fundamental right was almost always expressed at some time during an ordination service.

For Particular Baptists, the offices of elder and deacon in a local church were central to God's salvific plan for his elect. In fact the office of elder was believed to be the most worthy office a man could hold on earth.[15] The church was a divine institution where elders functioned as stewards of a trust given by God. Their high view of God as the infallible judge served to further magnify the worth of the office.[16] The minister was likened to an ambassador of Christ,

---

[10] He succeeded Samuel Pearce at Canon-street Birmingham.

[11] Sutcliff, *Introductory Address*, 1.

[12] Sutcliff, *Introductory Address*, 2.

[13] Ryland, *Difficulties of the Christian Ministry*, 19.

[14] Sutcliff, *Introductory Address*, 3–4.

[15] Daniel Turner, *A Charge, etc.* in his and Caleb Evans, *A Charge and Sermon, Delivered at the Ordination of the Rev. Mr. Job David, October 7, 1773, at Frome, Somersetshire* (Bristol: W. Pine, T. Cadell, M. Ward/London: J. Buckland, [1773]), 15.

[16] Clark, *Three Discourses*, 99.

whose job it was to reconcile God's kingdom to a hostile world.[17] It is important to point out however, that they placed more value in the office itself than her officers. Despite the importance of the eldership to them, they also recognized that most people would not recognize the prestige of the office.[18]

The grace of God was a prerequisite for success in ministry.[19] God not only raised up men for ministry, he also qualified them. Without this divine qualification a man could not effectively fulfill the duties of the office. The Lord also supplied him with strength, wisdom, and encouragement, even directing the congregation to accept his ministry.[20]

The Baptists were very concerned that no unqualified men enter the ministry, out of fear it might hinder the advance of the glory of God in the world.[21] Success in ministry was understood as the magnification of the glory of God.[22] In a charge by Daniel Turner to Job David at his ordination on 7 October 1773, at Frome, Somersetshire, Turner admonishes David to, "constantly endeavor to do all with a single eye to the glory of God, and to keep self intirely [*sic*] out of sight."[23] God was glorified in different ways, but the chief means was through the salvation of sinners. John Ryland explains the connection between the glory of God and the salvation of sinners as follows:

> Gospel ministers are called to subserve God's grand and gracious purpose of glorifying all his perfections, in the Salvation of sinners; by restoring them to the enjoyment of his favour, through the Mediation of his only—begotten Son; and bringing them again, by the effectual agency of the blessed Spirit, into a state of voluntary subjection to his will, and genuine conformity to his image: that thus they may glorify and enjoy him, truly on earth, and perfectly and eternally in Heaven. This was God's wise and merciful design, in instituting the gospel ministry;

---

[17] Turner, *Charge*, 15.

[18] Caleb Evans, *A Charge, etc.* in his and Hugh Evans, *A Charge and Sermon; Delivered at the Ordination of the Rev. Thomas Dunscombe, At Coate, Oxon, August 4th, 1773* (Bristol: W. Pine, T. Cadell, M. Ward, 1773), 3.

[19] John Gill, *The Work of a Gospel-Minister recommended to Consideration. A Charge delivered at the Ordinations of the Reverend Mr. John Gill, Mr. James Larwill, Mr. Isaac Gould, Mr. Bonner Stone, and Mr. Walter Richards. Sermon XXXVIII* in his *A Collection of Sermons and Tracts* (London: George Keith, 1773), II, 22.

[20] Osborn, *Introductory Address*, 8.

[21] Stennett, *Sermon III*, 108.

[22] Evans, *Charge*, 17.

[23] Turner, *Charge*, 14.

> and this must be the design with which we discharge all our professional services.[24]

God would be glorified through the salvation of sinners and a chief means he used to accomplish this was through "gospel ministry." This meant that elders stood at the centre of God's plan to glorify his name through the redemption of sinners.

But before a minister could be used effectively by God, he must first be conscious of his own weakness.[25] The magnification of the glory of God did not find its source in natural abilities, reasoning power, eloquence, learning, or diligence, but in the supernatural empowerment of the Holy Spirit in the conversion of souls.[26] As a servant of God, the pastor was ordained as a means for the furthering of the spiritual kingdom of God on earth, and this could only be accomplished by the grace of God. Humility would lead to a greater dependence on the grace of God and true humility and dependence were best demonstrated by frequent prayer.

Ministers were to function as stewards of the mysteries of Christ and the pastoral office was a charge, or trust, committed to them by God (1 Corinthians 4:1).[27] A trust is an interest held by one person for the benefit of another, and so as stewards, their cardinal responsibilities were diligence and faithfulness.[28] The trust they were given was the gospel, a revelation of divine mercy and grace in Jesus Christ, which was considered a treasure of inestimable worth. Again it becomes apparent that undergirding their theology of ministry was this persistent Christological emphasis. Although their primary responsibility was for the state of the flock, they were required by the law of Christ to do good to all men; and they took this responsibility seriously.

The responsibility of such an important office creates the need for a concomitant authority. They did not believe the authority of the pastor originated

---

[24] Ryland, *Difficulties of the Christian Ministry*, 30.

[25] John Ryland, *The Difficulties and Supports of a Gospel Minister* in his and James Hinton, *The Difficulties and Supports of a Gospel Minister; and The Duties incumbent on a Christian Church* (Bristol: Harris and Bryan, 1801), 28. He based this assertion on the verse in 2 Corinthians 12:10: "Therefore, I take pleasure in infirmities, in reproaches, in necessities, in persecutions, in distresses for Christ's sake: for when I am weak, then am I strong."

[26] Ryland, *Difficulties and Supports*, 22.

[27] Stennett, *Sermon III*, 98.

[28] John Brine, *The Solemn Charge of a Christian Minister considered. A Sermon Preach'd at the Ordination of the Rev^d^ Mr John Ryland, on the 26th of July, 1750* (Lonon: John Ward, [1750]), 5.

with man, but that it ultimately came from God. Yet, even though pastors are responsible to God, and placed by him as leaders over his church, they are not to, "lord it over his heritage," but to gently teach and shepherd the flock. As leaders their job was to follow the Master's direction as laid out in his Word.[29] The trust was not given primarily for the minister's personal well-being, but for the edification of the entire church,[30] and so he had a responsibility, "to beseech poor sinners, in Christ's stead, to be reconciled to God, and to build up his people in knowledge, faith, holiness, and comfort unto eternal life."[31]

With diligence and faithfulness as the key criteria, as stewards a minister must serve as one who would give account for his ministry when Christ returned.[32] He was responsible to a higher power—an impartial judge. If any person in his charge was to perish everlastingly due to pastoral neglect and carelessness, he was considered responsible.[33] The pastor was not forced to enter the work of the ministry, but did so voluntarily out of love for Christ and a compassion for souls,[34] and since he accepts the free invitation of the church to proclaim Christ through ministering the Word and Ordinances, he must give himself wholly and unreservedly to the task.[35]

A phrase that appears over and over again throughout extant Particular Baptist Ordination sermons is found in 2 Corinthians 2:16: "Who is sufficient for these things?"[36] Both personal experience and the Word of God had taught seasoned pastors delivering the charge to these newly ordained pastors that difficulties in the ministry were inevitable, and so when they discussed the nature of the office it was important for them to highlight the reality of these difficulties. Throughout the history of Christianity, leaders in particular had

---

[29] Robert Hall, *God's Approbation The Study of Faithful Ministers. A Sermon delivered at the Ordination of the Rev. George Moreton, Pastor of the Baptist Church at Kettering. Nov. 20th 1771* in *The Complete Works of the Late Rev. Robert Hall, Arnsby, Leicestershire. Consisting of Sermons, Essays, and Miscellaneous Pieces. Collected and Arranged by J.W. Morris, with a Prefatory Memoir of the Author* (London: Published by W. Simpkin and R. Marshall, Stationers' Hall Court, 1828), 205.

[30] Clark, *Three Discourses*, 56.

[31] Evans, *Charge*, 17.

[32] Brine, *Solemn Charge*, 5.

[33] Turner, *Charge*, 19, 20.

[34] Ryland, *Duty of Ministers*, 19.

[35] Gill, *Work of a Gospel-Minister*, in his *Sermons and Tracts*, II, 15–16.

[36] For example, see Fall, Sr., *Charge of God*, 17; Hall, *God's Approbation The Study of Faithful Ministers*, in *Complete Works*, 233; Evans, *Charge*, 17.

faced various discouragements, they argued, and so why should it be any different now?[37] Opposition both external and internal was to be expected.

Some difficulties would arise due to the inherent nature of the office. The pastor himself has the impediment of indwelling sin. He was not always consistent, impartial, and wise in his actions and he struggled with a variety of imperfections making him vulnerable to the world's seduction and comforts.[38] Yet his goal was to convert souls to Christ and show the way of eternal life against the opposition of many who do not want to believe his message: proclaiming condemnation under the wrath of God.[39] The preaching of such a message was sure to inspire detestation in some.

Another discouragement was false teachers who try to draw some away from truth by teaching their own gospel and not that of Christ.[40] Finally, John Gill warned ordinands that productive ministers can also expect Satanic attack to hinder their good work in a variety of forms.[41]

Although discouragements were inevitable, pastors were also encouraged to expect God's comfort and support amidst all difficulties.[42] The greatest comfort a minister had was the promise of Christ's gracious presence offering his protection, assistance, and ultimately his reward.[43] As mentioned, when overwhelmed with the pressures of the ministry, coupled with innate human inadequacies, a minister might be tempted to think "Who is sufficient for these things"? The answer given was, "His grace is sufficient for you."[44] These Particular Baptists believed that for those God had called, he gave abilities to do the job effectively.[45] Ultimately the pastor does not rely on his

---

[37] Ryland, *Difficulties of the Christian Ministry*, 11. Acts 20:24.

[38] Ryland, *Difficulties of the Christian Ministry*, 12.

[39] Robert Hall, *On the Discouragements and Supports of the Christian Minister: A Discourse, Delivered to the Rev. James Robertson, at his Ordination over the Independent Church at Stretton, Warwickshire. Published 1812. The Works of the Rev. Robert Hall, A.M. with A Memoir of his Life by Dr. Gregory; Reminiscences, by John Greene, ESQ.: and his Character as a Preacher, by the Rev. John Foster. Published under the Superintendence of Olinthus Gregory, LL.D.. F.R.A.S., Professor of Mathematics in the Royal Military Academy; and Joseph Belcher, D.D. In Four Volumes. Vol. I.* (New York: Harper and Brothers, 1849), 136. This is an interesting example because it is an instance of a Baptist minister preaching at the ordination of an Independent minister.

[40] Ryland, *Difficulties of the Christian Ministry*, 13.

[41] Gill, *Work of a Gospel-Minister*, in his *Sermons and Tracts*, II, 27.

[42] Turner, *A Charge*, 17.

[43] Gill, *Work of a Gospel-Minister*, in his *Sermons and Tracts*, II, 27.

[44] Evans, *Charge*, 18; 2 Corinthians 12:9.

[45] Evans, *Charge*, 17.

inherent abilities, but believes "he can do all things through Christ who strengthens" (Philippians 4:13).[46]

Although God constantly supplies help to the minister, there is no excuse for him to neglect the means of grace appropriated through a disciplined and holy life. He must therefore strive to develop personal traits such as purity of character, long-suffering, and kindness, while continually making every effort to increase in experimental and practical knowledge of God.[47] To do this he must be filled with the Holy Spirit, enabling him to care for others with an unfeigned love.[48]

Church's Call

Another necessary step in the appointment of a gospel minister, secondary to the call of God, was the acknowledgment of the church in the free choice of the people. God qualifies the minister for office, but the church has a responsibility to recognize this calling. A typical example from an early Particular Baptist ordination sermon explains the theological relationship between the Lord's call and the church's recognition of a pastor.

Near the beginning of the "Long Eighteenth Century,"[49] Nehemiah Coxe[50] preached an ordination sermon to a Particular Baptist congregation in London at Petty France, for the appointment of an elder and some deacons.[51] In the exposition of his text found in Titus 1:5: "For this cause left I thee in Crete, that thou shouldest set in order the things that are wanting, and ordain elders in every city, as I had appointed thee." Coxe emphasized the necessity of the implementation of a God-ordained leadership to manage the affairs of a local church as reflected in the example of the primitive church. His basic hermeneutic supposed the requisite of a biblical continuity between the practices

---

[46] Evans, *Charge*, 18.

[47] Ryland, *Difficulties of the Christian Ministry*, 15, 16.

[48] Ryland, *Difficulties of the Christian Ministry*, 20, 21, 22.

[49] The Long Eighteenth Century is sometimes calculated from 1688 to 1832. For example, Frank O'Gorman, *The Long Eighteenth Century British Political and Social History 1688–1832* (Oxford: Oxford University Press, 1997).

[50] Nehemiah Coxe was ordained an Elder at Petty France on 21 September 1675. T.E. Dowley, "A London Congregation during the Great Persecution Petty France Particular Baptist Church, 1641–1688," *The Baptist Quarterly* 29 (January 1978): 234. On Coxe see Crosby, *History of English Baptists*, 265.

[51] Nehemiah Coxe, *A Sermon Preached at the Ordinatoin of an Elder and Deacons in a Baptized Congregation in London* (London: Tho. Fabian, 1681). This sermon is considered to be the "earliest recorded public ordination by dissenters after the Restoration" (Dowley, *Petty France*, 236).

of the early church with his contemporary context. So the implementation of leadership in local churches was not based purely on pragmatic necessity, but as an appropriate response to the requirements of God as seen in Scripture.

Yet at the same time, Coxe recognized a certain discontinuity between the ancient and existing ecclesiastical milieu. He recognized that the apostles were "extraordinary officers"—they were men with a unique historical ministry in that they had "an immediate and extraordinary call to their office, by God and our Lord Jesus Christ."[52] Whereas the apostles received their call directly from Christ, contemporary Baptist ministers, whom he labeled "ordinary officers," were called to the office by the local church, though their authority ultimately did not come from men but from God.[53] With the "extraordinary" call of the apostles came special gifts and abilities as seen primarily through a unique existential guidance of the Holy Spirit; however these extraordinary officers with their attendant authority and gifting had ceased with the completion of the New Testament canon. Now Scripture alone mediated by the Holy Spirit provided guidance and direction to the continuing church throughout the ages. The authoritative principle for the continuing church as opposed to direct existential revelation was:

> all Church—Offices and Affairs are to be regulated and guided by the ordinary and standing Rule of the Scriptures: And every particular Congregation hath not only right, but is in duty bound to dispose herself in that Order, and under that Rule and Government, which Christ hath appointed in his Testament.[54]

As Titus was admonished by Paul to "set things in order that are lacking," so it was the duty of the Particular Baptists to follow suit. This was accomplished through the appointment of officers to local churches in the form of elders and deacons. The motivation for order in the church was opposed to formal litigious niceties characterized by contentment with form; rather the goal was to implement the appointed office of Christ in conformity to his will as seen in Scripture. Christ was the head of the church and as such all church officers received their power and authority from him, for "There is no such thing as Authority in or over the Church, but what is derived from Christ, who

[52] Coxe, *Sermon Preached*, 6.
[53] Coxe, *Sermon Preached*, 6.
[54] Coxe, *Sermon Preached*, 8.

hath all Power in Heaven and Earth committed to him."[55] For Coxe, this Christological prominence is the underpinning of all his practical theology, providing a key to understanding the motives, desires, and inevitable outgrowth of an eighteenth-century Particular Baptist ordination service.

With these general principles in mind, Coxe understands Acts 6 as a description of the first ordination service in the history of the church conducted by "ordinary" ministers. More specifically Coxe believes that Acts 6 provides an example of setting things in order through the appointment of deacons in the Jerusalem Church.[56] As the church membership increased, the need for ordained leaders became necessary to maintain order. The main functions of the elder—preaching and prayer—were being neglected. Therefore they looked for men full of the Holy Spirit and wisdom to tend to the needs of the poor and effectively administer the church's material resources.

Elders were called "ordinary officers" of the church because they did not have the same supernatural powers as the apostles. Because the office of elder is concerned primarily with the spiritual health of the church as opposed to the temporal health, it was considered greater than the office of deacon.

For Coxe, Ephesians 4:11–13 provides as example of both the continuity and discontinuity of the apostolic office. Some of the offices and gifts in Ephesians 4:11 have ceased, but others must continue until Christ returns to perfect his church.[57] Apostles, prophets, and evangelists were necessary in apostolic times because they laid the foundation for the nascent church. But pastors and teachers are necessary for carrying on the work of building the church until Christ returns. The other officers became defunct with the firm establishment of the church.

The terms, "elders" and "overseers" are parallel in meaning. The elder's duty is to provide oversight to the church, as a shepherd does his flock. He must guard their souls as one who will give account. Likewise the church has duties and responsibilities towards their pastor because they are in community. But no church can make a man a minister that Christ has not qualified, "for the validity of all the church's acts depends upon, and is determined by, their conformity to the rule of Christ's Holy Will and Testament."[58] So a

---

[55] Coxe, *Sermon Preached*, 7.
[56] Coxe, *Sermon Preached*, 8.
[57] Coxe, *Sermon Preached*, 16.
[58] Coxe, *Sermon Preached*, 16.

minister must be convinced of the call of ministry in his own life, in addition to the call of the church, after having authenticated this call through a public demonstration of his abilities.[59]

Characteristics of Ministers

There is a possibility for confusion when describing the qualifications and duties of an eighteenth-century Particular Baptist elder. There is a subtle distinction between intrinsic and extrinsic elements of an elder's qualifications and duties that can easily overlap and appear redundant. Some of the qualities of elder reflect more the essential being, nature, or constitution of the man, whereas, other characteristics emphasize a more extraneous quality. For example, the extrinsic qualification of "not addicted to much wine" may be a practical manifestation of the more intrinsic quality of "temperateness." Both qualities are essentially ontological, but one, the extrinsic, leans more towards the functional, or practical, yet it is still distinguishable from a duty. Adding to this possible confusion is the fact that duties, though primarily functional, are still also grounded in the ontological (being). What one does is connected to who one is. Yet duties are distinguished from the natural or outer extrinsic characteristics (i.e. aptitude for learning) and are even farther removed from the more "being orientated," or intrinsic characteristics (i.e. zeal for the glory of God), by a primarily operational, as opposed to ontological, characteristic. From an eighteenth-century Particular Baptist theological perspective, actions manifested as duties reflect intrinsic characteristics. Therefore, in describing qualifications there is often a subtle semantic layering affecting these descriptions of pastoral characteristics, which really only reflect different points of a continuum, but which at times may seem repetitive.

The church recognized the call of God on an elder based on evidence of certain qualifications manifest in him. These scripturally defined qualifications, found mainly in the biblical texts 1 Timothy 3:1–7 and Titus 1:5–7, reveal the essential moral standards that the church required.[60] For those ordinands

[59] Gill, *Work of a Gospel-Minister*, in his *Sermons and Tracts*, II, 24.

[60] William Staughton summarizes the Qualifications for Elders as follows. The sign of the necessary qualifications are primarily: not displayed by a passion for souls alone, or by the assertions of relatives and friends, nor is success in ministry a sign. These qualities are all too subjective. Things that are supposed to disqualify but do not, include a deep persuasion of a man's entire unworthiness, great fear at the prospect of service, the neglect or contempt of those who profess, or an appearance of no immediate success. Godliness is requisite (holiness of heart and purity of

that emerged from within the ranks of the local church, their character was already well known, but if a man came from outside the church, he usually brought with him recommendations of other Particular Baptist pastors who could attest to his character. As mentioned, the steps of his calling were publicly reviewed at his ordination to ensure orderliness according to Scripture.

The qualifications and duties of a newly ordained pastor were expounded by a visiting elder during the charge. The most important preliminary characteristic for the office of elder was evidence that his heart had been renewed by grace so that he both knew and felt the gospel.[61] "Knowing the Gospel," referred to an understanding and adherence of biblical precepts expressed through a Reformed, Baptistic orthodoxy as articulated, for example, in Baptist confessions of faith, while "feeling the Gospel" implied an emotional attachment to those truths. They were looking for signs that he had become a new creature in Christ no longer governed by the old nature. This did not mean he was perfect or free from the influence of sin, but that his life was generally consistent with the gospel.[62] Further, he was not to be a new Christian but settled and mature in the faith.[63] For example, he should be publicly known as a man who was generally well balanced and who had an even temper,[64] and characterized by liberality and hospitality, not hesitating to entertain strangers.[65] No longer was he self-willed, greedy, or covetous, seeking his own gain; rather he was concerned solely for the glory of God and his church.[66] As a man who did all things in love, displaying tenderness and compassion, he was always empathetic with those in distress.[67] He was also to be a lover of peace[68] who no longer walked with wicked men, preferring instead the company of godly people.[69]

---

life), he must be converted, knowledge is requisite—he must be growing in the Word, he must have an aptness to teach and a readiness to communicate, and he must have a divine call (Roger Hayden, "What are the Qualifications of a Gospel Minister?" *The Baptist Quarterly* 19 [October 1962]: 352–357).

[61] Osborn, *Introductory Address*, 6.

[62] Coxe, *Sermon Preached*, 19.

[63] Stennett, *Sermon III*, 102.

[64] Gill, *Duty of a Pastor*, 6; Coxe, *Sermon Preached*, 20.

[65] Stennett, *Sermon III*, 100.

[66] Osborn, *Introductory Address*, 7; Coxe, *Sermon Preached*, 20.

[67] Gill, *Doctrine of the Cherubim Opened* in his *Sermons and Tracts*, II, 48; Ryland, *Duty of Ministers*, 30.

[68] Coxe, *Sermon Preached*, 10.

[69] Stennett, *Sermon III*, 11.

As indicated, the key qualities of a steward are faithfulness and diligence, and the quality of faithfulness was emphasized as an "indispensable qualification."[70] Faithfulness requires perseverance, even amidst trial, so the visiting elder often gave encouragements or "motives" to the ordinand to resist the lure of the world and its trials, and to remain faithful to the end.[71] James Fall lists several of these encouragements, which are frequently repeated in other ordination sermons. First, a minister must be faithful because it was the command of God. All Christians, and especially his ministers, have a fundamental obligation to obey God. Second, the minister's time and strength are not his own and so his primary obligation is to the Lord and his work. Third, the Lord is worthy of honour and the minister primarily honours the Lord through his fidelity to the Scriptures. Finally, a minister should be faithful because of the importance of the work. The ministry fulfills a high calling, proclaiming the glory of God in the salvation of sinners,[72] and so the time he invests is well worth all his efforts and will be amply rewarded in eternity.

Diligently Strive to Improve Gifts

Some of the gifts Jesus Christ gave to ministers to qualify them for the office of elder (Ephesians 4:11) may be taken away or declined if under-utilized or misused.[73] For Scriptural support for this assertion, John Gill appeals to Matthew 25:28–29: "Take therefore the talent from him, and give it unto him which hath ten talents. For unto every one that hath shall be given, and he shall have abundance: but from him that hath not shall be taken away even that which he hath."[74] The consequences of neglecting ministerial gifts could be devastating, as potentially, "All his light and knowledge, his abilities and usefulness, shall be taken from him" (Zechariah 11:17).[75] Two common temptations to neglect gifts included persecution and discouragement from an apparent lack of success in ministry.

---

[70] Ryland, *Duty of Ministers*, 27; Gill, *Work of a Gospel-Minister*, in his *Sermons and Tracts*, II, 24; Brine, *Solemn Charge*, 4; Hall, *God's Approbation The Study of Faithful Ministers*, in *Complete Works*, 223; Stennett, *Charge Delievered*, 54.

[71] Wallin, *Charge Delivered*, 43–45.

[72] Fall, Sr., *Charge of God*, 16.

[73] Gill *Work of a Gospel-Minister*, in his *Sermons and Tracts*, II, 117; Gill, *Duty of a Pastor*, 3.

[74] Gill, *Duty of a Pastor*, 3.

[75] Gill, *Duty of a Pastor*, 4.

Since the pastor who neglected his gifts harmed not only himself but the whole church, he had a duty not only to use his gifts, but to diligently strive to improve them.[76] In a charge to Thomas Dunscombe, Caleb Evans exhorts him to allow no distractions in the ministry:

> The grand object of your life now, my brother, should be the fulfilment [*sic*] of the ministry you have received in the Lord. You are a Christian minister, and as such, your principal concern should be to make full proof of your ministry. See to it then, that you attend ... to all your duties habitually. ... Guard against everything which might hinder you in your main work and business.[77]

A Baptist minister was to embrace every proper opportunity to use his gifts,[78] which required great self-discipline and industriousness.[79] Knowing this, he must be prepared for a great physical and mental exertion.[80] In fact a common metaphor for a minister of God was a workman. He was a labourer sent by God to plow fallow ground—to convince sinners of their need of repentance.[81] He was also to be characterized by exceptional courage, not fearing men, but intrepid, constant, immovable, and persistent, persevering in this end despite all obstacles.[82]

In order to accomplish this he must be careful to avoid certain things that may hinder diligence. The biggest enemy of diligence was squandering time.[83] A pastor must be careful not to be distracted by worldly affairs, but must focus

---

[76] Stennett, *Charge Delivered*, 49-50.

[77] Evans, *Charge*, 14. This was based on such verses as 2 Timothy 2:15: "Study to shew thyself approved unto God, a workman that needeth not to be ashamed, rightly dividing the word of truth" and 2 Timothy 4:2: "Preach the word; be instant in season, out of season; reprove, rebuke, exhort with all longsuffering and doctrine."

[78] Turner, *Charge*, 5.

[79] Hall, *God's Approbation The Study of Faithful Ministers*, in *Complete Works*, 204, 205; Gill, *Doctrine of the Cherubim Opened* in his *Sermons and Tracts*, II, 48.

[80] Stennett, *Charge Delivered*, 58.

[81] Hall, *God's Approbation The Study of Faithful Ministers*, in *Complete Works*, 205; Wallin, *Obligations of a People to their Faithful Minister*, 4.

[82] William Steadman, *The Qualifications Necessary for the Discharge of the Duties of the Christian Ministry. A Pastoral Charge, Addressed to Mr. George Sample, on his Ordination over the Baptist Church, Assembling at West-Gate, Newcastle upon Tyne, October, 21, 1818* (London: Button and Son, 1819), 7-8; Gill, *Doctrine of the Cherubim Opened* in his *Sermons and Tracts*, II, 48; Hall, *God's Approbation The Study of Faithful Ministers*, in *Complete Works*, 225; John Brine, *Diligence in Study Recommended to Ministers. In a Sermon, Preached at the Ordination of the Reverend Mr. Richard Rist, in Harlow, Essex. December 15, 1756* (London: John Ward, 1757), 26.

[83] Ryland, *Difficulties and Supports*, 10.

on the tasks of meditation, prayer, and reading Scripture and the writings of "good men."[84] He must also avoid "trifling recreations" as he is not in the ministry for his own comfort, but for service to God and his church.[85] Even in the discharge of duties such as visiting individuals in the congregation, he must be careful not trifle away time through idle chatter, but rather focus on the task of spiritual edification.[86]

The gifts that the pastor was required to "stir up within," or improve, included both natural and spiritual gifts.[87] Since a key function of an elder was teaching (1 Timothy 3:2), one of the chief ways to improve talents was through an improvement of his knowledge of Scripture. They believed in two aspects of knowledge: human and divine. Human, or natural knowledge, included information derived from academic disciplines such as the liberal arts, biblical languages, history, logic, apologetics, and even extra-biblical writings of Christians.[88] But as useful as these were as a supplement to studying the Scriptures, they were less important than divine knowledge. Divine knowledge was the "knowledge of God and his will, of Christ and the way of salvation by him" and was acquired mainly through prayer, Bible study, and meditation on Scripture.[89]

Knowledge must also be experimental, or practical, as well as intellectual, or it is of no use.[90] Experimental knowledge is felt as well as believed and it begins with an acquaintance with the true God.[91] It is absolutely essential that a minister have intimate knowledge of correct biblical doctrine to defend the faith, but he must also be able to discern more subjective phenomenon. For example, he must be able to discern the schemes of the Devil and understand how the Holy Spirit encourages the church.[92] Practical knowledge is the manifestation of intellectual knowledge coupled with the work of the Spirit of God,

---

[84] "The writings of good men" referred to the works of faithful, orthodox, expositors of the Scriptures (Gill, *Duty of a Pastor*, 5).

[85] Brine, *Diligence in Study*, 5.

[86] Gill, *Duty of a Pastor*, 5; Brine, *Diligence in Study*, 6.

[87] Evans, *Charge*, 16.

[88] Gill, *Work of a Gospel-Minister*, in his *Sermons and Tracts*, II, 22.

[89] Stennett, *Charge Delivered*, 50, 51.

[90] Stennett, *Charge Delivered*, 51.

[91] Ryland, *Duty of Ministers*, 25; Abraham Booth, *Pastoral Cautions: An Address to the Late Mr. Thomas Hopkins, when Ordained Pastor of the Church of Christ, in Eagle Street, Red Lion Square, July 13, 1785* in *The Works of Abraham Booth* (London: Button and Sons, Paternoster-row, 1813), III, 142.

[92] Brine, *Diligence in Study*, 8.

which allows an understanding of biblical truth with the accompanying ability to effectively live out and express this biblical truth to others. Since this knowledge must be shared, the art of sanctified persuasion was essential to the pastoral office.

This knowledge must also manifest itself in a pastor's personal life as a self-evident reality. "Example," it was believed, was often a better teacher than "precept."[93] Therefore it is essential that a pastor constantly guard his own heart (Acts 20:28) so that his moral and civil behaviour was consistent with the message he preached.[94] It was believed that this absence of hypocrisy brought power to preaching and authenticated his ministry.[95]

Discretion was believed to be another indispensable quality for a pastor/elder. He must not only abstain from evil, but avoid all appearance of evil,[96] especially in the way he managed his temporal affairs.[97] Wisdom and prudence were also absolutely necessary. He had an obligation to speak out against sin, but it must be done in love. Although a pastor may risk offence with anyone rather than God in this matter, he must do it in love not anger.[98] John Ryland says, "Imprudence is one of the greatest enemies to the pastoral office: and, excepting a gracious heart, no qualification is more necessary, for a Minister, than prudence."[99] He must be careful that he maintains a good reputation in the community at large.[100]

Another important qualification for an elder was an attitude of cheerfulness. A pastor is called to serve and should perform his functions willingly and happily, recognizing that God was always present to strengthen him.[101] Part of his responsibility was to comfort people and lead them to closer relationship with God; and he could not effectively do this with a dour disposition.

As mentioned, a chief means for improving a minister's gifts was the attentive reading of Scripture. Although natural knowledge is helpful, it is secondary and should not distract the pastor from studying the Bible.[102] His chief

---

[93] Stennett, *Charge Delivered*, 39.
[94] Wallin, *Charge Delivered*, 41.
[95] Turner, *Charge*, 11.
[96] Ryland, *Duty of Ministers*, 26.
[97] Stennett, *Charge Delivered*, 57.
[98] Ryland, *Duty of Ministers*, 26.
[99] Ryland, *Duty of Ministers*, 26.
[100] Stennett, *Sermon III*, 103.
[101] Stennett, *Charge Delivered*, 62, 64.
[102] Brine, *Diligence in Study*, 6.

work was to know and communicate scriptural truth. Since an important element in effective communication was knowledge of people, he must also make himself a student of human nature.[103] Further, it was not enough to just study Scripture, men, and other writings, but he must meditate on them.[104] Meditation involved prolonged thought on a subject until the truth was internalized.

Gifts were also improved through prayer, both private and corporate,[105] as God's assistance was vital for ministerial success. Caleb Evans concurs with this assessment, advising Thomas Dunscombe to "Give attendance to reading, meditation, and, above all, to fervent prayer."[106]

It was understood that the main reason a pastor would accept a charge was out of love to God and his gospel,[107] as a pastor's religion was to be radically God-centred, doing everything focused on the glory of God.[108] He must deny himself as a humble servant of God and mortify his innate desire for fame, power, possessions, gratification of the flesh, and all selfish ambition.[109] He absolutely could not love money and must detest unjust gain.[110] To be successful he must constantly guard against these things and trust in a wise and good God to supply his happiness.[111] A common example of the dangers of this can be seen in their regular warning to avoid showing preference to wealthy people.[112] They were to maintain a disinterested zeal and impartial love for the glory of God.

This self-denial was demonstrated by a lifestyle characterized by moderation.[113] For example, they were to control the amount of alcohol they drank,[114] as a pastor must always be sober and in control of his passions.[115] Despite this emphasis on controlling the passions and desires, they also guarded against an

---

[103] Hall, *God's Approbation The Study of Faithful Ministers*, in *Complete Works*, 229, 230.

[104] Hall, *God's Approbation The Study of Faithful Ministers*, in *Complete Works*, 225.

[105] Hall, *God's Approbation The Study of Faithful Ministers*, in *Complete Works*, 225.

[106] Evans, *Charge*, 16.

[107] Ryland, *Difficulties and Supports*, 10.

[108] Clark, *Three Discourses*, 14.

[109] Turner, *Charge*, 15.

[110] Stennett, *Sermon III*, 99.

[111] Turner, *Charge*, 15.

[112] Booth, *Pastoral Cautions*, in *Works*, III, 170.

[113] Coxe, *Sermon Preached*, 20.

[114] Coxe, *Sermon Preached*, 20. "Not given to much wine" (1 Timothy 3:3): At times, drunkenness was a major problem in eighteenth-century society in England (G.M. Trevelyan, *The Eighteenth Century* [Harmondsworth: Penguin Books Ltd, 1964], 46; Roy Porter, *English Society in the Eighteenth Century* [Harmondsworth: Penguin Books, Ltd, 1982], 235).

[115] Stennett, *Sermon III*, 99. "Not a Striker" (1 Timothy 3:3).

extreme form of asceticism where they might damage their physical health. Often the presiding pastor would advise new pastors to take care of their health, families etc., in addition to guarding their souls.[116] They were concerned for the whole man, avoiding a dualistic separation of the corporeal and the ethereal.

In regard to marriage and the family, he must be the husband of one wife, which these Particular Baptists generally understood as a prohibition against polygamy. They could not be divorced and remarried.[117] Nor, generally, could they be polygamous before their conversion, as this forfeited the right to become an elder.[118] The husband was also admonished to protect and care for his wife as she represented a co-minister with him.[119] Also their children were required to be faithful to the gospel, not necessarily as believers, but instructed in the Christian faith, sober, orderly, and living submissive lives to the authority of their parents and the church.[120]

DUTIES AS ELDER

Essentially the pastor of an eighteenth-century Particular Baptist church functioned as a ruler.[121] He would maintain discipline over the church, and would direct and encourage Christians to live faithfully to the Scriptures.[122] He was not to be a tyrant, lording it over the church, but a shepherd, gently guiding, protecting, and feeding God's flock.[123] This biblical metaphor of a shepherd was often used to describe the elder's main duty. The flock, which represents the church, was depending on the shepherd to feed them good food, which they understood metaphorically as biblical doctrine.[124] To preach the Word of God was often referred to as the "principle [*sic*] business" of the pastor.[125] He was a type of mediator between God and the people, who offered prayers, petitions, confessions, and public praise on behalf of the church.[126] Also, pastors

---

[116] Brine, *Diligence in Study*, 11; Gill, *Duty of a Pastor*, 2.
[117] Coxe, *Sermon Preached*, 19.
[118] Stennett, *Sermon III*, 97.
[119] Booth, *Pastoral Cautions*, in *Works*, III, 153.
[120] Coxe, *Sermon Preached*, 20; Stennett, *Sermon III*, 97.
[121] Stennett, *Charge Delivered*, 48.
[122] Wallin, *Obligations of a People to their Faithful Minister*, 6–8.
[123] Fall Sr., *Charge of God*, 2–3.
[124] Fall Sr., *Charge of God*, 3, 4, 5.
[125] Gill, *Work of a Gospel-Minister*, in his *Sermons and Tracts*, II, 18.
[126] Stennett, *Sermon III*, 90.

represented God as a mouth piece to his people.[127] The pastor comforts and warns men, speaking in God's name, through the preaching of the Word.[128]

Preaching

The central purpose of Particular Baptist worship was the magnification of the glory of God through preaching the Word.[129] They felt that it was a dangerous, but an ever-present temptation, for a pastor to try and exalt himself above the Lord; to preach "self" rather than Christ. This exaltation occurred when he sought the praise of his people—when there was a desire to please the hearers by preaching what they wanted to hear, rather than faithfully proclaiming the Scriptures. So a common warning to ordinands in the charge was to guard against the fear of man.[130] They were admonished not to be afraid to share all the truths of the gospel even if they were offensive to some in the congregation.[131] Further, they were warned to not try and appeal to a certain theological party to gain favor.[132] Finally, they were cautioned against trying to discover and teach new things in Scripture that God may not have intended so as to entertain the congregation. If a pastor wished comfort and success in the work of the ministry, he had to aim to try and please God as the one who would reward him.[133]

The goal was to "excite people" to the gospel, of which Christ was the main substance.[134] They were to labour for the salvation of souls by warning people of the wrath to come.[135] The goal of preaching was to rebuke sin, comfort in affliction, and encourage in perseverance.[136] In a nutshell the goal was to evangelize and to try and persuade men to be born again and live a holy life submitted to God.[137]

---

[127] Coxe, *Sermon Preached*, 22.

[128] Coxe, *Sermon Preached*, 23.

[129] Clark, *Three Discourses*, 79.

[130] Gill, *Work of a Gospel-Minister*, in his *Sermons and Tracts*, II, 18; Gill, *Form of Sound Words*, in his *Sermons and Tracts*, II, 63.

[131] Clark, *Three Discourses*, 60.

[132] Clark, *Three Discourses*, 66.

[133] Clark, *Three Discourses*, 83, 84.

[134] Gill, *Work of a Gospel-Minister*, in his *Sermons and Tracts*, II, 18, 19.

[135] Coxe, *Sermon Preached*, 14.

[136] Coxe, *Sermon Preached*, 14.

[137] Coxe, *Sermon Preached*, 15.

Content of Preaching

The elder must take great pains to ensure that he was preaching the pure Word of God in its entirety, since there was a constant temptation to add to the sentiments of Scripture through the inclusion of his own ideas. The goal was to not make the words of the Bible advance a pastor's own agenda, but to teach the truths contained in the Scripture, allowing its intended meaning to emerge. This included not only the words of the Bible, but also their sentiments or ethos.[138] He must studiously guard against the temptation to water down, or let his own prejudices determine, the content, but teach all essential biblical doctrines fully explicating all their import. As we have seen, this meant that the preacher must boldly proclaim doctrines that may be offensive to the congregation, without softening their implications. The pastor was not to make hard truths more palatable to the prejudices of the hearers, but to transform those prejudices through faithfully adhering to what was written. These principles of preaching are succinctly summarized by Robert Hall Jr. in his charge to J.K. Hall,[139] where he advises his nephew to:

> Preach the word purely and fully; mix nothing with it that does not belong to it, or may not evidently be inferred from its language. State every doctrine and opinion as near to the mind of the Spirit as you can ascertain. The doctrines of the word you will bring forth in their full import, without concealing them, or endeavouring to melt them down and mould them so as to suit the prejudiced and indolent depravity of the human heart. The gospel is not suited, and cannot be made to suit, the corrupt dispositions and inclinations of the carnal "mind;" but the faithful preaching of it is calculated to oppose and to overcome those evil prejudices so far as to excite men to attend to the doctrines it contains and the blessings it proposes. It is your duty, not to bring down the gospel into a conformity with them, but to change them into a conformity with the gospel.[140]

---

[138] Robert Hall, *The Substance of a Charge, Delivered at the Ordination of the Rev. J.K. Hall, at Kettering, November 8, 1815 [From the notes of the Rev. S. Hillyard, of Bedford]* in *The Works of the Rev. Robert Hall, A.M.*, ed. Olinthus Gregory and Joseph Belcher (New York: Harper & Brothers, 1858), II, 476.

[139] John Keen Hall followed Fuller as Pastor at the Baptist Church in Kettering.

[140] Brian Stanley, *The History of the Baptist Missionary Society 1792-1992* (Edinburgh: T&T Clark, 1992), 32; Hall, *Substance of a Charge*, 476.

There were theological tests to determine whether or not certain doctrines qualified as the "pure word." According to John Brine, the test for a true doctrine is if

> it exalts the Glory of the Grace of God, as the sole and entire Cause of Salvation: If it humbles the Creature, and excludes all Boasting: If it provides for the Honour of the Law and Justice of God: If it is a solid and sure Ground of strong Consolation to the Saints.[141]

Purpose of Preaching

The purpose of preaching was to display the holiness, righteousness, and justice of God.[142] This was achieved through preaching the "whole counsel of God"[143] in order to exhibit the entirety of his revealed character. They wished to guard against partiality in proclamation, so they attempted not to neglect the complete range of biblical doctrine and teaching.[144] Despite this desire, of course some doctrines were highlighted more than others, but even these truths were those which they felt the Bible itself emphasized. In terms of specific doctrines, Particular Baptists tended to stress salvation by Christ, the doctrines of pardon by his blood, justification by his righteousness, and atonement and satisfaction by his sacrifice.[145] Their theology was profoundly Christological because they felt that Jesus was the centre of all religion and life in both the Old Testament and the New Testament.[146] This was not a contradiction to their aphorism of proclaiming "the whole counsel of God," because they saw Christ as central to the meaning and purpose of Scripture. This is well illustrated with Nehemiah Coxe's admonition to a new pastor:

> His [Christ's] Glory must be the Mark aimed at by all your Labours, and his Grace the principal Subject of all your Discourses; It is not a Philosophick Harangue that will save the Souls of Men, but the preaching of Christ Crucified; His Gospel is the Power of God unto Salvation to them that believe; and his Holy Name is the Ointment that perfumes all Religious Exercises; Therefore I will not only say, Let there be Aliquid

---

141 Brine, *Solemn Charge*, 6.

142 Fall Sr., *Charge of God*, 17.

143 From Acts 20:27: "For I have not shunned to declare unto you all the counsel of God."

144 Wallin, *Charge Delivered*, 36.

145 Ryland, *Duty of Ministers*, 20.

146 Turner, *A Charge*, 8.

> Christi, something of Christ in every Sermon, but let Christ be the beginning, middle, and end of your Discourses; for in him are hid all the Treasures of Wisdom and Knowledge; in him is the Fountain and Headspring of all true Comfort and Holiness.[147]

For Particular Baptists, the sum and substance of the whole counsel of God was Christ in his person, offices, and grace.[148] Since Christ was the centre of all Scripture, he should be preached in every sermon.[149]

As Calvinists, this Christological prominence emerged soteriologically in the regular proclamation of the so called "doctrines of grace."[150] But among most Particular Baptists, this emphasis on the doctrines of grace generally encouraged, rather than discouraged, evangelistic preaching, especially in the latter part of the century. Their God was sovereign in salvation, and although God chose his elect before they were even born, this did not inhibit the church's responsibility to proclaim the gospel to the world. Even the so-called father of High Calvinism, John Gill, regularly encouraged pastors to preach the gospel for the salvation of sinners.[151] Particular Baptists maintained this emphasis on the doctrines of grace despite the constant danger of being labeled

---

[147] Coxe, *Sermon Preached*, 26.

[148] Gill, *Work of a Gospel-Minister*, in his *Sermons and Tracts*, II, 18.

[149] Gill, *Work of a Gospel-Minister*, in his *Sermons and Tracts*, II, 18; Stennett, *Charge Delivered*, 42.

[150] Brine, *Solemn Charge*, 7–17.

[151] "Care should also be taken by a minister of the gospel, that his doctrine be the doctrine of Christ; that is, such as Christ himself preached, which he has delivered out by revelation to others, and of which he is the sum and substance. *We Preach Christ crucified, to the Jews a stumbling-block, and to the Greeks foolishness.* This doctrine is most likely to be useful for the conversion of sinners" (Gill, *Duty of a Pastor*, 8). "What can, or does, more strongly encourage ministers to take heed to themselves, to their doctrine, and abide therein, than this? That they may be useful in the conversion, and so in the salvation of precious and immortal souls, which are of more worth than a world: *He that converteth a sinner from the error of his way, shall save a soul from death, and shall hide a multitude of sin*" (Gill, *Duty of a Pastor*, 13). Rathel argues that Gill should be considered a High Calvinist because based on his belief in eternal justification, he rejected duty faith. David Mark Rathel, "John Gill and the charge of hyper-Calvinism: assessing contemporary arguments in defense of Gill in light of Gill's doctrine of eternal justification" *The Journal of Andrew Fuller* Studies 1 (September 2020), 11–29.

"Arminian" on the one hand and "Antinomian" on the other.[152] In summary, their goal was to preach nothing but the crucified Christ.[153]

Preaching the whole counsel of God involved more than just teaching a wide range of biblical doctrine. It also included the sentiments of Scripture. For example, some teaching was more instructional or propositional in nature, whereas other teaching might emphasize morality. For these Particular Baptists, the commitment to Scripture extended even to the ethos of the text, that is, the spirit as well as the letter. They sought to incorporate scriptural attitudes in their teaching, recognizing that even their well-intentioned prejudices could contaminate the intended purposes of the Bible. There was a particular danger of teaching just aspects of morality without the undergirding doctrine which supported it.[154] So they strove to explain the theology emerging from Scriptures and then to clearly delineate its practical implications. In the words of Robert Hall, a common rule was to "preach the doctrines practically, and preach practice doctrinally."[155] The concern was not to just state truth, but to win hearts to God and guide people into a life of holiness.[156] The most important goal, the conversion of sinners, must be kept in mind at all times, as their goal was not primarily to make Baptists.[157]

Method of Preaching

The foundational principle of preaching was a commitment to handle the Word of God with reverence because its content was considered sacred.[158] The pastor was to speak the truth in love without compromising veracity out of a fear of men. Therefore there could be no partiality when teaching biblical doctrines. They were neither to neglect the poor or ignorant nor to favour the rich.[159]

---

[152] Olin C. Robison, "The Particular Baptists in England 1760–1820" (PhD diss., Oxford University, 1963), 41; Ryland, *Difficulties and Supports*, 14.

[153] Coxe, *Sermon Preached*, 146; Evans, *Charge*, 5; Turner, *Charge*, 6; Gill, *Duty of a Pastor*, 8. 1 Corinthians 2:2: "For I determined not to know anything among you, save Jesus Christ, and him crucified."

[154] Hall, *Substance of a Charge*, 477; Brine, *Solemn Charge*, 21.

[155] Hall, *Substance of a Charge*, 478.

[156] Ryland, *Difficulties and Supports*, 12.

[157] Steadman, *Qualifications Necessary*, 27.

[158] Coxe, *Sermon Preached*, 14.

[159] Hall, *Substance of a Charge*, 481.

Further, although they were to speak the truth in love, this was not considered a license to engage in controversy for controversy sake. The pastor must strive to avoid unproductive quarrelling while contending for the faith.[160] This did not mean that he should not reprove those in error or sin through solid reasoning from Scripture.[161] The purpose of such reproof was to magnify the glory of God and the reputation of the gospel as holy; and it was done for the good of the church.[162] The pastor must therefore be careful to avoid bringing his own personal grievances into the pulpit.[163]

Sermons were to be delivered with plainness and simplicity of style as their sole purpose was to effectively communicate the Word of God. There was a tendency to want to entertain the audience, rather than teach them—to give them what they wanted, rather than what they needed—and this must be resisted. It seems that the emphasis on simplicity and plainness was at least partly a reaction to a widespread trend in the eighteenth-century for ministers to deliver eloquent discourses designed to impress congregations with their erudition and elocution. This was accomplished primarily through a display of reasoning powers or beautiful words.[164] Particular Baptists believed that this sort of preaching was a product of intellectual pride, and so in opposition to this they taught that a preacher must have the "mind of Christ" teaching the truth of the text with an attitude of humility and holiness.[165] They were to seek growth in their congregations, but not through entertainment, or by relaxing standards for church membership through invitations to those who are not Christians, or accepting those practicing sin, or by trying to entice others away from their churches.[166] Rather, they were to increase through the real conversion of sinners.[167] They were convinced that God rewarded faithfulness, but not human ingenuity.[168]

So their style of preaching was described as "judicious, methodical, scriptural, plain, and experimental," adapted to the state and conditions of the

---

160 Turner, *Charge*, 6.
161 Brine, *Solemn Charge*, 22.
162 Fall Sr., *Charge of God*, 13.
163 Steadman, *Qualifications Necessary*, 23.
164 Evans, *Charge*, 4.
165 Hall, *Substance of a Charge,* 481; Coxe, *Sermon Preached*, 14.
166 Wallin, *Charge Delivered*, 42.
167 Stennett, *Sermon III*, 125; Wallin, *Charge Delivered*, 41.
168 Stennett, *Sermon III*, 126.

people, and delivered with boldness and earnestness.[169] Preaching was considered an extremely practical event, so speech was to be clear and natural, effectively communicating to all kinds of different hearers.[170] Pastors were admonished to strive to speak to the level of those with the least capacity for understanding[171] as they recognized that people had different natural capacities for understanding.[172]

Although the style and delivery was to be simple, this did not imply that sermonic content was simplistic. They emphasized over and over again the importance and necessity of thoughtful study. When composing a sermon they wanted to make sure that the sermon was not superficial, but was the result of hard dedicated study worthy of the subject matter.[173] As clear communication was a primary aim, they emphasized specificity with the avoidance of generalities.[174]

As they wished to reflect the sentiments as well as the teachings of Scriptures, they stressed that the delivery of the sermon, though plain and simple, should be solemn and void of distracting gestures and tones.[175] Yet preaching was not the same as a passionless lecture, because they were to earnestly contend for souls.[176] It seems that although most pastors allowed for different methods and styles, most preferred preaching extempore without notes, as it reflected their desire for spontaneity in worship.[177]

Simplicity required the pastor to try and prove one main principle, flowing out of his doctrine that answered all possible objections that might arise in the hearer's minds.[178] He was to rebuke sin mainly by teaching the Law, explaining it, and clearly describing what it threatened.[179] The pastor must regularly warn men of the deep need for repentance, living faith, and persevering obedience.[180] Also he was to exhort his congregation and comfort those under conviction of sin with the promises of the gospel, showing that with God salvation

---

169 Wallin, *Charge Delivered*, 38.

170 Hall, *God's Approbation The Study of Faithful Ministers*, in *Complete Works*, 232.

171 Hall, *God's Approbation The Study of Faithful Ministers*, in *Complete Works*, 232.

172 Steadman, *Qualifications Necessary*, 20.

173 Evans, *Charge*, 8.

174 Hall, *Substance of a Charge*, 478.

175 Evans, *Charge*, 9.

176 Evans, *Charge*, 9.

177 Evans, *Charge*, 9; Robison, *Particular Baptists*, 208, 229.

178 Brine, *Solemn Charge*, 23.

179 Brine, *Solemn Charge*, 24.

180 Hall, *Substance of a Charge*, 479.

is possible.[181] Also, he must comfort those who were experiencing different trials, encouraging them to persevere, and demonstrate sympathy with his people in all their temptations and afflictions. For this he needed wisdom, experience, and sound judgment.[182] He was expected to be especially sympathetic with those beginning to inquire after salvation.[183] Also he was expected to exhort men not to sin, to read Scripture, and to pray. They wanted their congregations to truly love others from the heart.[184]

In terms of the frequency of preaching, the main text they referred to was 2 Timothy 4:2, which commands preachers to "Preach the word; be instant in season, out of season; reprove, rebuke, exhort with all longsuffering and doctrine." Essentially, they were to preach whenever they had opportunity, overcoming all difficulties and opposition.[185] This was part of the mandate to faithfully discharge their stewardship. A pastor was expected to be faithful with the gifts God has given them and minister with all his strength as opportunity allowed.

Administer the Ordinances

The second key duty of a pastor was to administer the ordinances.[186] For the Particular Baptists of the eighteenth-century there were two ordinances: Baptism and the Lord's Supper.[187] It was the responsibility of the pastor to teach the nature, use, and ends of the ordinances, which were instituted by Christ. They were to administer the ordinance in his name. Although there was difference of opinion in the matter, generally only the pastor was to administer Baptism and the Lord's Supper.[188] The important thing was to try and

---

[181] Brine, *Solemn Charge*, 26.

[182] Fall Sr., *Charge of God*, 13.

[183] Hall, *Substance of a Charge*, 480.

[184] Gill, *Form of Sound Words*, in his *Sermons and Tracts*, II, 63; Brine, *Solemn Charge*, 33.

[185] Turner, *Charge*, 5.

[186] Stennett, *Charge Delivered*, 47.

[187] We explored the essence of the doctrinal underpinnings of these ordinances earlier, during the discussion of confessions of faith.

[188] Gill, *Work of a Gospel-Minister*, in his *Sermons and Tracts*, II, 20; Davies, *English Puritans*, 223; "All agreed that the pastor was the proper person to administer the Supper, when he was available; but prolonged lack of pastors, because of 'inter-regnums' or imprisonment, saw differing points of view emerge. However, all agreed that the proper authorization of the local church was necessary, even when ordination was not made a pre-requisite" (E.P. Winter, "Who may Administer the Lord's Supper," *The Baptist Quarterly* 16 [July, 1955]: 132). The 1677 Confession of Faith said the Lord's Supper should be administered by "those only, who are qualified and a called according to the commission of Christ" (Winter, *Administer Lord's Supper*, 131). "Baptists

conform to the pattern of Scripture, which they referred to as "orderliness."[189] Baptism denoted dying to sin and living righteously and the Lord's Supper stood for union with Christ and an utter dependence on him.[190] It was a very solemn but joyous act.[191]

Public Prayer

Another important duty of the pastor was to lead public prayer. They were not to give "preaching prayers" but to extemporaneously and earnestly petition God on behalf of his people. Caleb Evans sums up the essentials of a pastor's prayer to Thomas Dunscombe:

> In the discharge of this part of your office, you are sensible, my brother, that it is particularly desirable to preserve a temper of mind strictly devotional; to be methodical, and yet not formal; pathetic but not extravagant; copious, but not tedious; and to suit your prayers to different occasions, and to different frames and circumstances both of yourself and your hearers. Endeavour always to pray with the Spirit, and with the understanding also. Avoid formality and a sameness in your public prayers, and never think the excellency of a prayer consists in the length of it.[192]

Effective public prayer was considered to be as much as a gift as the ability to preach well. Robison says, "With preaching, hymn singing, and reading of the Scripture, prayer was one of the major elements in Baptist worship, the simple and spontaneous expression of the converted to their Lord."[193] The pastor, of course, was also expected as a duty to pray privately for the individuals in his charge.[194] Hall quotes Abraham Booth as saying, "He that does not pray oftener for his people than with them, neglects an important part of his duty."[195]

---

have always agreed that it is the function of the pastor to administer the ordinances. They have not agreed on the question of whether it is exclusively his function so to do. In contrast to the 17th and 18th century practice, the more recent tendency has been to recognize the right of laymen to administer the sacraments if authorized by the church concerned" (R.L. Child, "Baptists and Ordination," *The Baptist Quarterly* 14 [April 52]: 249).

[189] Evans, *Charge*, 12.

[190] Turner, *Charge*, 9.

[191] Stennett, *Charge Delivered*, 47.

[192] Evans, *Charge*, 10.

[193] Robison, *Particular Baptists*, 249.

[194] Stennett, *Sermon III*, 124.

[195] Hall, *Substance of a Charge*, 479.

Church Discipline

In Titus 1:5, Paul tells Titus that, "For this cause left I thee in Crete, that thou shouldest set in order the things that are wanting, and ordain elders in every city, as I had appointed thee." The reason Paul left Crete, according to Nehemiah Coxe, was to set in order the things that were disorderly. This was accomplished through the ordination of elders. To "set in order" referred to:

> the settlement and disposing of things relating to the Offices and Government in the House of God, and the Order of their Communion in the Church who were Members of it, in a full and exact agreement with the Rule of Christ's Appointment; which the Apostle had to time to bring to perfection during his stay with them.[196]

Further this "order" was connected with the edification and beauty of the church, which, to these early Baptists, was essential if the church was to be conformed to the will of Christ.[197] They believed that Christ's will for the purity, peace, and prosperity of the church was maintained through this order, and any neglect of discipline would result in the disruption of harmony and unity.[198] This Christological basis is the foundation of the importance of church discipline to Particular Baptists.

Conformity to Christ's will in the church required order and, as an elder was God's overseer, following the apostolic pattern as seen in the written Word, it was ultimately his responsibility to zealously ensure that church discipline was practiced when necessary.[199] The power of discipline properly belonged to Christ as the head of the church, but it was to be executed through the elder with the consent of the church.[200] He was required to diligently watch over the state of his flock as he was responsible to know their spiritual condition as a duty of eldership.[201] This watchfulness began with the admission of new members, as he was to guide the church in impartially determining a potential member's fitness for church membership.[202] It was important to take great care when a person joined membership by ensuring that they were

[196] Coxe, *Sermon Preached*, 4–5.
[197] Coxe, *Sermon Preached*, 5.
[198] Wallin, *Charge Delivered*, 40.
[199] Coxe, *Sermon Preached*, 3; Gill, *Work of a Gospel-Minister*, in his *Sermons and Tracts*, II, 20.
[200] Gill, *Work of a Gospel-Minister*, in his *Sermons and Tracts*, II, 20.
[201] Coxe, *Sermon Preached*, 28.
[202] Wallin, *Charge Delivered*, 40.

believers who were committed to covenant with the local church and assume the expected responsibilities of membership willingly.[203]

If discipline became necessary it was the Elder's duty to ensure that the church gathered for judgment.[204] They followed the scriptural rules in enacting church discipline where the offended brother was to first tell the offender of his fault, and then try to convince him to repent. If he failed, then he took one or two more members with him, but if the offender remained stubborn, he was to bring it to the church.[205] But those who sinned openly, visibly disgracing the church, they were to be publicly rebuked so that others may fear and not follow their example.[206] In the implementation of discipline the church was encouraged to exercise wisdom, prudence, gentleness, tenderness, diligence, and impartiality. The pastor was to authoritatively rebuke those needing discipline, but not lord it over them as dictator.[207]

Discipline normally took the form of censure, suspension from the Lord's Table, and exclusion from the church. Censure was the most lenient form of discipline, dealing with sins that were impulsive or considered less serious than other sins.[208] This may include things like absence from worship and was meant primarily as a reprimand or as an admonishment for those guilty of error. If this did not elicit repentance then the member may be suspended from the Lord's Table, thereby disrupting fellowship with the church. Finally, the definitive disciplinary action was expulsion from the church. This was a last resort after many attempts to seek repentance from the offender. The excluded person however, if they repented, could be restored back into fellowship, and indeed this was the goal. The purpose for expulsion was not only to glorify God by keeping his church pure, but also it was an act of love meant to persuade a wayward sinner back into fellowship with God and his church, through humble submission and repentance.[209] Discipline issues included such things as heresy, apostasy, and immorality.[210]

---

[203] Stennett, *Sermon III*, 91; Evans, *Charge*, 12.

[204] Wallin, *Charge Delivered*, 40.

[205] Gill, *Work of a Gospel-Minister*, in his *Sermons and Tracts*, II, 21. See Matthew 18:15–17.

[206] Stennett, *Sermon III*, 90; 1 Timothy 5:20; Gill, *Work of a Gospel-Minister*, in his *Sermons and Tracts*, II, 21; 2 Thessalonians 3:6.

[207] Evans, *Charge*, 12; Stennett, *Sermon III*, 91.

[208] Robison, *Particular Baptists*, 328.

[209] Evans, *Charge*, 13.

[210] Stennett, *Sermon III*, 91; Evans, *Charge*, 12; Gill, *Work of a Gospel-Minister*, in his *Sermons and Tracts*, II, 21.

Visitation

Verses such as Acts 5:42: "And daily in the temple, and in every house, they ceased not to teach and preach Jesus Christ" and Acts 20:20–21: "And how I kept back nothing that was profitable unto you, but have shewed you, and have taught you publicly, and from house to house," provided the scriptural basis for the pastoral duty of visitation.

As mentioned, it was essential that a pastor know the spiritual state of his flock.[211] If he were always locked away in his study, not intermingling with his people, there was a danger of neglecting his oversight of the flock.[212] He was to make himself accessible to the church so they would feel comfortable in approaching him to share honestly their spiritual state.

Great wisdom and prudence was necessary for pastoral visitation. He was not to be a stranger yet careful not to visit too frequently. Still it was better to visit more frequently in short periods rather than stay for extended periods of time.[213]

The main purpose of visitation was to ascertain, and enhance, the spiritual condition of the person visited. He was to help them by reproof, exhortation, rebuke, and comfort (especially the sick and the afflicted).[214] He would take every opportunity to instruct in the Word and some pastors even catechized children during pastoral visitation.[215]

They were to visit both members and non-members, as non-members provided another opportunity for evangelism.[216] Gill succinctly describes visitation to members in an ordination charge to several pastors:

> Another part of your work, is to visit the several members of the church, as their cases may require, especially when distressed, either in body or mind; then to pray with them, and for them, to speak a word of comfort to them, and to give your best counsel and advice; and this will introduce you into divers families; but take care not to meddle with family-affairs; what you hear in one family report in not in another.[217]

---

[211] Wallin, *Charge Delivered*, 40.

[212] Steadman, *Qualifications Necessary*, 30.

[213] Steadman, *Qualifications Necessary*, 31; Wallin, *Charge Delivered*, 40.

[214] Evans, *Charge*, 13.

[215] Evans, *Charge*, 13.

[216] Gill, *Work of a Gospel-Minister*, in his *Sermons and Tracts*, II, 21.

[217] Gill, *Work of a Gospel-Minister*, in his *Sermons and Tracts*, II, 21.

The aim of these visits was strictly business, and so the ordinands were often reminded to avoid certain dangers that might distract them from their spiritual purposes. Often they were warned to avoid gossiping, levity, and pointless conversation.[218] The pastor must not meddle in people's lives as a busy body, but must know them well enough as to offer sound spiritual advice.

Knowing the spiritual condition of the congregation was also an invaluable tool for effective preaching. By better learning their state, visitation helped the pastor to make his sermons more relevant to the congregation's needs. In the words of William Steadman in his charge to George Sample, knowing his people well allowed the pastor to "adapt his public discourses to their capacities and their wants."[219]

Preside Over Singing

Another duty of an eighteenth-century Particular Baptist minister, albeit mentioned very infrequently in the extant published ordination sermons, was the duty of "presiding and regulating" over congregational singing.[220] Caleb Evans says, "Another branch of worship, which as a minister of Christ it lies upon you to preside over and regulate, is singing psalms and hymns."[221] He admonished Thomas Dunscombe not to think it was too unimportant a task for a minister to be involved in the choosing of "suitable compositions" that would inspire the people's devotion, helping them to set their affections on God.[222]

The selected hymns and Psalms were to complement the subject matter of the sermon by helping to more deeply impress those truths on the congregation's minds. Clearly Evans believed that singing was a useful and effective means of enhancing worship and so he encouraged the church's participation. He said, "If public singing be a duty, let it be attended to accordingly, and attended so that it may answer, not frustrate the animating, enlivening designs of it."[223]

---

[218] Hall, *Substance of a Charge*, 481.

[219] Steadman, *Qualifications Necessary*, 30.

[220] Evans, *Charge*, 11.

[221] Evans, *Charge*, 11.

[222] Evans, *Charge*, 11.

[223] Evans, *Charge*, 11–12. Baptists have often recognized hymn selection as an important part of worship (H.V. Larcombe, "A Minister and His Hymns," *The Baptist Quarterly* 10 [July, 1940]: 154).

Ordination of Deacons

In a Baptist church, the other office besides that of elder was that of deacon. Essentially the term "deacon" meant "to minister"[224] and his duties and responsibilities were clearly outlined in 1 Timothy 3:8–13. In most cases deacons were men, but some like John Brine seemed to believe in the biblical validity of deaconesses.[225]

---

[224] John Brine, *A Sermon preached at an Ordination of Deacons* (London: Aaron Ward, 1735), 10.

[225] "The Apostle bestows this Character on Phebe; I commend unto you Phebe our Sister, which is a Servant, a Deaconess, of the Church which is at Cenchrea (Romans 16:1). I am of Opinion, that there were Deaconesses in the primitive Churches, whose business it was to visit the poor, afflicted, and aged Sisters, and to administer Relief to them; to acquaint the Church with their Necessities, and obtain Help for them. Persons chose to this Work were generally Widows, such who had been married, and behaved in that Station of Life with Chastity, Diligence, and Prudence, who are called Widows indeed (1 Timothy 5:3.). It was required that they should be Sixty Years of Age when appointed by the Church to attend on this Service; let not a Widow be taken into the Number, under Threescore Years old, having been the Wife of one Man (Ver. 9). The excellent and learned ecclesiastical Historian Mr. *Bingham* speaking of them hath these Words: 'There is some mention made of them in Scripture, by which it appears, that their Office was as ancient as the apostolical Age; St. Paul calls Phebe, a Servant of the Church at Cenchrea, Romans 16:1. The original Word is *Diakonov*, answerable to the *Latin* Word *Ministra*; which is the Name given them in *Pliny's Epistle*, which speaks about the Christians. Tertullian and some others, call them *Viduae*, Widows; and their Office, *Viduatus*; because they were commonly chosen out of the Widows of the Church. For the same reason Epiphanius, and the Council of Laodicea, call them elderly *Widows*; because none but such were ordinarily taken into this Office.' Not but that Virgins were sometimes admitted to this Service, as he afterwards observes. And Dr. Cave allows the same, whose Account of them is this: 'Their Original was very early, and of equal standing with the Infancy of the Church; such was Phebe in the Church at Cenchrea, mentioned by St. *Paul*; *such* were those two Servant-Maids spoken of by Pliny in his Letters to the Emperor ... Constantinople, not to mention any more particular Instances. They were either Widows, and then not to be taken into the Service of the Church, under Threescore Years of Age, according to St. Paul's Direction, or else Virgins, who having been educated in order to it, and given Testimony of a chaste and sober Conversation, were set apart at Forty. What the proper Place and Ministry of these Deaconesses was in the ancient Church, though Matthew Blasteres seems to render a little doubtful, yet certainly it principally consisted in such Offices as these; to attend upon the Women at times of public Worship, especially in the Administration of Baptism, that when they were to be divested, in order to their *Immersion*, they might overshadow them, so as nothing of Indecency and Uncomeliness might appear; sometimes they were imployed in instructing the more rude and ignorant sort of Women in the plain and easy Principles of Christianity, and in preparing them for Baptism; otherwhiles in visiting and attending upon Women that were sick, in conveying Messages, Counsels, Consultations, Relief (especially in Times of Persecution, when it was dangerous for the Officers of the Church) to the Martyrs, and them that were in Prison. And these Women, no doubt it was, that Libanius speaks of among the Christians, who were so very ready to be imployed in these Offices of Humanity: 'To these Observations the Words of Clemens Alexandrinus agree; We also know what Things Paul requires of Deaconesses in the first Epistle to Timothy. It has been thought proper by some Congregations of late Years, to appoint faithful Women to such Service among them, as the Primitive Churches did; nor can I apprehend that anything is justly to be excepted against that Practice, since it appears to be apostolical. This

Based on Acts 6:6, deacons were ordained in a similar manner as elders by the imposition of hands.[226] A good illustration of the procedure at a deacon's ordination is found in Crosby's account at the installation of the Rev. Joseph Burroughs:

> After the ordination of Mr. Burroughs, they proceeded to the ordination of two deacons, which was after this manner. Mr. Stinton stood and up said. We must now address our selves again to you, the members of this congregation, that statedly worship God in this place. We were informed by your messengers aforesaid, that you have chosen two persons from amongst yourselves, unto the office of deacons, in this church of Christ, viz. brother Matthew Shelfwell, and brother George Reynolds. It will therefore be necessary, that you should in this, as you have in the other case, declare and confirm your election. All you, therefore, that do approve, and confirm your former choice of brother Matthew Shelfwell, to be a deacon in this church, and desire that he may now be ordained to that service, be pleased to signify it, by the lifting up of your hands. And then the negative. After this the same question was put, both in the affirmative and negative, with respect unto the other; and it appeared, they were both unanimously chosen; and upon being asked, whether they accepted the churches call to this work? and, were willing to take this office upon them? They answered, they were. Then the deacons elect kneeled down, and the ministers laying their right hands upon their heads, ordained them, Mr. Mulliner putting up a prayer to God suitable to this part of the solemnity; and then he went up into the pulpit, and entertained the assembly with a very excellent discourse, on 1 Thes. v. 12, 13. in which, according to the province assigned him, he treated of the duties of the members of a Christian church to their officers, both elders and deacons, after which he prayed, then a psalm of thanksgiving was sung, at the conclusion of which the assembly was dismissed with one of the apostolic benedictions.[227]

---

name is especially given to the Stewards of the Church-Treasure, and those who take care of the Poor; which is one considerable Branch of their Work'" (Brine, *Ordinations of Deacons*, 2–3).

[226] Stennett, *Sermon III*, 81, 112; Coxe, *Sermon Preached*, 8. "From the seventeenth to the early nineteenth century the laying on of hands was general at the appointment of deacons" (Ernest A. Payne, "Baptists and the Laying on of Hands," *The Baptist Quarterly* 15 [January 1954]: 207). See *Second London Confession*: "And of a Deacon that he be chosen by the like suffrage, and set apart by Prayer, and the like Imposition of hands" (Lumpkin, *Confessions*, 287).

[227] Crosby, *English Baptists*, IV, 188–189.

This usually occurred on the same day as the elder's ordination, or in an evening ceremony, or in another ceremony on the day following an elder's ordination.[228]

Deacons were appointed to the office by the church and ordained by the eldership.[229] Like the elders, they were to be faithful stewards in the office entrusted to them by the church by performing their duties diligently. Two qualities that complimented these characteristics of diligence and faithfulness, which were often mentioned as being particularly crucial for a deacon, was discretionary prudence coupled with a heart of compassion. As their main duty was to relieve the poor and to care for the "outward state of the church," empathetic kindness was an essential quality.

There was no standard rule as to the number of deacons a church should have, but it was determined by the need of the church and the availability of qualified officers.[230]

Qualifications

The necessary qualifications for the office of deacon were reflected in the characteristics described in 1 Timothy 3:8–13:

> Likewise must the deacons be grave, not double tongued, not given to much wine, not greedy of filthy lucre; Holding the mystery of the faith in a pure conscience. And let these also first be proved; then let them

[228] Stephen Copson, "Two Ordinations at Bridlington in 1737," *The Baptist Quarterly* 33 (July 1989): 148. This was the case at the ordination of Deacons at Bridlington, 1737: "The Order in Which the Deacons were set apart was as followeth. Lords-day June 5th 1737 being the day next following the forementioned solemnity publick service being over the Auditory dismyssed ye Brethren stay'd and signified their desire (by Br. George Nessfeild the onely acting Deacon of late Years) to the Pastors present the Churches desire of their assistance in the ordination of Br. Robt. Sedgefield, Br. Marmaduke Slumber and Br. Michael Cannome with him the said George Nesfeild to the office of Deacons in the same Church. Upon which Mr. George Braithwaite asked the Church. Q1. Whether they had solemnly called the Sd. Brethren to that Office. It was answered they had after which the said Mr. Braithwaite asked the said Brethren seperately [*sic*] whether they Accepted the said Office to which the Church had called them. They answered they did, then Mr. John Sedgefeild spent some time from Act 6th to display the Office and Duty of a Deacon, after which the said Mr. John Sedgefeild with the Imposition of the Right hand of Every Pastor present on the head of Br. Geo. Braithwaite Br. Robt. Sedgfeild, which was succeeded by Mr. Alvery Jackson praying over Br. Marmaduke Slumber and the whole concluded by Mr. Rich'd Machin's praying over Br. Michael Cannome—the hands of the pastors being on the head of ye Deacons during the time each was prayed over."

[229] Coxe, *Sermon Preached*, 10.

[230] Coxe, *Sermon Preached*, 11.

> use the office of a deacon, being found blameless. Even so must their wives be grave, not slanderers, sober, faithful in all things. Let the deacons be the husbands of one wife, ruling their children and their own houses well. For they that have used the office of a deacon well purchase to themselves a good degree, and great boldness in the faith which is in Christ Jesus.[231]

Generally they were to be honest men whose innocence and holy life were well attested to in the community at large;[232] men of known integrity filled with the Holy Spirit and wisdom (Acts 6:3).[233] For Rees, being "filled with the Holy Spirit" signified "persons of remarkable piety, and who have wisdom and discretion to manage the office well."[234]

They generally interpreted the 1 Timothy qualifications as follows. "Grave" meant that the deacon was not inappropriately humorous, regularly displaying great "levity of mind." He was not to be a flippant person who always teased and joked.[235] Rather deacons were characterized by honest sobriety—"men of probity"—as they were entrusted with the care of the church's wealth.[236]

"Not double tongued" inferred men of great integrity who were not double-minded in their commitment to the gospel ministry. This sincerity was reflected in purity of speech,[237] so they were to be free from any guile or hypocrisy and were to speak and act truthfully.[238] They were not to feign love for the needy, but rather demonstrate sincere affection and compassion. Further they were to act on this love by doing all in their power to supply the poor any relief they could, while at the same time not promising more than they could deliver.[239]

"Not given to much wine" reflected the same temperateness required of an elder. They believed that moderate use of good things was allowable, including drinking wine, but excessive drinking was "absolutely unlawful."[240]

---

[231] 1 Timothy 3:8-13.
[232] Coxe, *Sermon Preached*, 11.
[233] Coxe, *Sermon Preached*, 11.
[234] Stennett, *Sermon III*, 106.
[235] Stennett, *Sermon III*, 103.
[236] Brine, *Ordination of Deacons*, 2.
[237] Stennett, *Sermon III*, 104.
[238] Brine, *Ordination of Deacons*, 2.
[239] Brine, *Ordination of Deacons*, 2.
[240] Brine, *Ordination of Deacons*, 2.

The dangers of drunkenness were particularly concerning for a deacon who was responsible for the church's treasury.

"Not greedy of filthy lucre" suggested a deacon had to be faithful and just in the distribution of the church's resources.[241] He must not be a person prone to covetousness or greed, but generous by nature. Leading by example, his generosity would encourage other members to give generously also.[242]

"Holding the mystery of faith with a pure conscience" meant that they must know and love biblical truth as reflected in their Reformed Baptistic orthodoxy. They must understand the "fundamentals" of the Bible and also practice these truths with a clean conscience.

"Let them first be proved" did not refer to a test after their call as deacon to see if they were fulfilling their mandate properly.[243] Rather, it was antecedent to the call, determining if the person had demonstrated the characteristics required in 1 Timothy.[244] After thorough examination, they were chosen to the office when these qualifications had been demonstrated in their lives.[245]

Regarding the family relations of deacons, there were several stipulations. "Wives must be grave." This simply meant that wives of deacons were to be sober-minded like their husbands.[246] Also, like the elders, deacons were to be "the husband of one wife," meaning that they, "never had the scandal of polygamy upon them."[247] And finally, they must "rule their household well" by teaching their children and servants the Scriptures, reproving them for sin, and encouraging them to pursue the things of God.[248]

Deacons were to be "blameless" men, "no slanderers, sober, faithful in all things." This was important in that they were in a unique position to shame the church and its testimony to Christ in the community by defrauding it.[249]

Duties

Based on Acts 6 the essential duty of a deacon was to serve tables, which was understood as comprising of three main tasks. First, they were responsible for

---

[241] Stennett, *Sermon III*, 104.
[242] Brine, *Ordination of Deacons*, 2.
[243] Coxe, *Sermon Preached*, 12.
[244] Coxe, *Sermon Preached*, 12.
[245] Stennett, *Sermon III*, 104.
[246] Stennett, *Sermon III*, 105.
[247] Stennett, *Sermon III*, 105.
[248] Brine, *Ordination of Deacons*, 6.
[249] Stennett, *Sermon III*, 105.

the table of the Lord. "The Deacons are to provide everything necessary for the Celebration of this Institution, but not at their own private Expense."[250] The Lord's Table was a community affair and the church as a whole was to supply all the resources necessary. The deacon was expected to furnish the table, and to "communicate the Bread and Wine to the several Members of the Society."[251] Second, it was their duty to relieve the poor. They were to distribute the stockpile that the church gathered for this purpose. Deacons collected the money and distributed to those in need of help. They were required to visit members who required assistance to determine the extent and necessity of the need. For example, if it was determined that the person was wasting money or living extravagantly, the deacon was to reprove them. Visitation was also important because sometimes people were too timid to ask the church for help. When visiting various members the deacon had a wonderful opportunity to encourage them. This is why compassion and a kind disposition were essential.[252] Finally, it was a deacon's duty to take care of the minister's table. They were responsible to ensure that the pastor and his family were adequately taken care of.[253] "It belongs to the Deacons to consider, whether the Elder of the Church is agreeably furnished with the Accommodations of Life" and if not to procure a "more liberal Contribution" from the church to provide for his needs.[254]

In the charge addressed to deacons outlining their responsibilities, characteristics, and duties, the preacher, as in the charge to the elder, would encourage them to persevere in their important work. They would remind the deacon that he was called to God's work and as such could expect God's help. When God called a man to the office of deacon, he would give him the necessary abilities to perform the job effectively. The office was difficult, but it was a great honour to be a deacon and provided a unique opportunity to serve the Lord through his church.[255]

CONCLUSION

These key aspects of the themes that emerge from a study of the extant eighteenth-century Particular Baptist ordination sermons provide a general

---

[250] Brine, *Ordination of Deacons*, 10.
[251] Coxe, *Sermon Preached*, 10.
[252] Coxe, *Sermon Preached*, 10.
[253] Brine, *Ordination of Deacons*, 11.
[254] Brine, *Ordination of Deacons*, 11.
[255] Brine, *Ordination of Deacons*, 12–13.

overview of their pastoral priorities. They had high standards for both the qualifications and duties of a pastor. Especially central to the pastor's duties was the need to preach plainly and evangelistically in order to affect the hearts of the hearers. In the next chapter, Fuller's pastoral theology will be explored to help determine his own unique contribution to his tradition and to determine what key theological priorities shaped his understanding of pastoral ministry. Was there a radical discontinuity in Fuller's theology from his Baptist forbears?

5
The Pastoral Theology of Andrew Fuller

Andrew Fuller is recognized as perhaps the most influential figure among the Baptists of the late eighteenth-century. The purpose of this chapter is to discover his particular theological emphasis from his ordination sermons. What was the unique emphasis in Fuller that helped set the theological course for later Baptists? When compared with other Particular Baptists, how much continuity did Fuller share with them? To help to answer these questions Fuller's ideal of the role of the pastor, his duties, and his qualifications will be considered, particularly as demonstrated in the charge and address to the church.

Pastoral Theology in Ordination Sermons

As we begin this investigation of the pastoral theology found in Andrew Fuller's ordination sermons, it is necessary to distinguish between the "ordination service," a "theology of ordination" (as a sub-category of pastoral theology), and a "pastoral theology," which is contained in an ordination sermon.

An ordination service was the actual event where the church and others gathered to recognize the call of the pastor to the ministry as described earlier. Studying the ordination service itself might examine things like the outline of the service, the timeline before ordination, the day/length of the service, and the details of the actual ordination procedure. A "theology of ordination" refers to the biblical basis, or theology, of the ordination ceremony which may or may not be found in ordination sermons. A theology of ordination answers questions like, "why is the ceremony performed?" "Why did the Particular Baptists practice it?" "How did they practice it based on biblical standards?" This is a valuable study and acts as a subset of a pastoral theology of ministry contained in his other sermons. But the purpose of this chapter is to consider the published ordination sermons, and sketches of sermons of Andrew Fuller, originally preached at various ordination services, as a unique corpus of material that sheds a very personal and practical light on the pastoral theological priorities of this prominent eighteenth-century Baptist.

One of the main goals is to show Andrew Fuller's pastoral priorities, emphases, and therefore his unique contributive influence among Particular Baptist practical theology in eighteenth-century ordination sermons, especially in light of the growing evangelistic concern within his denomination. Was he distinguished by a particular theological emphasis?

As we have seen for the Particular Baptists in the eighteenth century, ordination was of central importance because it displayed the heart of a loving God in his divine plan for the redemption of his elect.[1] These God-called elders were given as the primary means to equip the saints for the work of ministry, and to build up the body of Christ until they attained to the unity of the faith and of the knowledge of the Son of God, to mature manhood, to the measure of the stature of the fullness of Christ.[2] The ceremony itself, in this sense, was a public confession of God's love as demonstrated by his enduring plan to redeem the world through the church, by the proclamation of the cross of Christ, as evidenced by the reality of the divine establishment of chosen men to facilitate the fulfillment of that mandate. These leaders represented the gracious provision of God to his beloved church for the successful discharge of the stewardship of the gospel that was entrusted to them. They saw ordination as the scripturally-prescribed establishment of God's call on a man's life to the office of elder or deacon. And so the frequent publishing of these sermons reflected the esteem that Particular Baptists held for the office of elder itself.

This unique corpus of material is extremely valuable for illuminating Fuller's pastoral theological emphasis, for it reveals his understanding of the motivations, character, qualifications, duties, and purposes of ministers of the gospel. The charge to the pastor is of particular importance because, as mentioned, it represented an admonition from one pastor to another pastor on how the office of elder should function effectively and successfully. These sermons embody a uniquely personal and practical exposition of the execution of the pastoral office. More seasoned pastors would share their unique insights and experiences with usually less experienced men with the goal both of encouraging them and also advising them on any potential pitfalls they may face in the ministry. Therefore, they were dealing with very practical issues as opposed to mere theological or academic reflection. This gives us an exclusive look at the issues that really drove Fuller's pastoral convictions in the context of his

---

[1] Andrew Fuller, "Importance of Christian Ministers Considered as the Gift of Christ," in *Complete Works* (London: William Ball, 1837), IV, 506.

[2] Ephesians 4:12–13.

inherited Particular Baptist theology described earlier. It reveals what really mattered to him.

There are thirty-one extant ordination sermons of Fuller, of which, thirteen are charges to an ordinand,[3] nine are addresses to churches,[4] five are single sermons which both address the church and charge the new pastor,[5] two are charges to students (one to students at the Bristol Education Society[6] and the other to the students at Stepney Academical Institution[7]), and the last two represent charges to missionaries for India sent through the Baptist Missionary Society.[8] All of these will be examined to discern clues to Fuller's pastoral theological priorities.

The Significance of the Ministry

It was important to Fuller that his ordinands understand that through the act of delivering the charge, Fuller in no way considered himself superior or

---

[3] Fuller, "The Qualifications and Encouragement of a Faithful Minister Illustrated by the Character and success of Barnabas" in *Complete Works*, IV, 25-39; "The Obedience of Churches to their Pastors Explained and Enforced," IV, 111-119; "Pastors Required to Feed the Flock of Christ," IV, 446-448; "Spiritual Knowledge and Holy Love Necessary for the Gospel Ministry," IV, 448-453; "On an Intimate and Practical Acquaintance with the Word of God," IV, 453-458; "Ministers are Appointed to Root out Evil and to Cultivate that which is Good," IV, 458-461; "Ministers Should be Concerned not to be Despised," IV, 462-465; "Ministers are Fellow-Labourers with God," IV, 465-468; "The Nature of the Gospel and the Manner in which it Ought to be Preached," IV, 469-472; "The Work and Encouragement of the Christian Minister," IV, 472-478; "On Preaching Christ," IV, 478-482; "The Influence of the Presence of Christ on the Mind and Work of a Minister," IV, 483-484; "Habitual Devotedness to the Work of the Ministry," IV, 485-488; "Affectionate Concern of a Minister for the Salvation of his Hearers," IV, 488-491.

[4] Fuller, "Importance of Christian Ministers Considered as the Gift of Christ," IV, 505-507; "Nature and Importance of Christian Love," IV, 507-510; "Christian Churches Fellow-Helpers with their Pastors to the Truth," IV, 510-513; "On Christian Steadfastness," IV, 513-516; "Churches Walking in the Truth—the Joy of Ministers," IV, 517-519; "Churches should Exhibit the Light of the Gospel," IV, 519-523; "On Cultivating a Peaceful Disposition," IV, 523-528; "Christian Churches are God's Building," IV, 528-530.

[5] Fuller, "The Satisfaction Derived from a Consciousness that our Religious Exercises have been Characterized by Godly Simplicity," IV, 531-533; "The Reward of a Faithful Minister," IV, 534-536; "Ministers and Churches Exhorted to Serve One Another in Love," IV, 536-538; "Ministerial and Christian Communion," IV, 539-541; "Ministers and Christians Exhorted to Hold Fast the Gospel," IV, 541-543.

[6] Fuller, "Faith in the Gospel a Necessary Prerequisite to Preaching it" in *Complete Works*, IV, 497-501.

[7] Fuller, "The Young Minister Exhorted to Make Full Proof of his Ministry" in *Complete Works*, IV, 501-505.

[8] Fuller, "The Nature and Encouragements of the Missionary Work" in *Complete Works*, IV, 491-494; "The Christian Ministry a Great Work" in *Complete Works*, IV, 494-497.

authoritative to them.[9] Really, many charges offered a reminder of what the ordinands already knew and had experienced, especially when addressed to more seasoned pastors.[10] This declaration of equality, however, was more than just a token display of humility as Fuller understood all pastors to be subject to the same divine authority. They were co-servants whose humility stemmed from a belief in the impartial love of God coupled with a deep sense of man's unworthiness to minister as a sinner, albeit redeemed, apart from the grace of God. For Fuller this emphasis on a minister's absolute dependence on God is foundational to understanding the qualifications and duties of an eighteenth-century Particular Baptist pastor.[11] He believed that without Christ's sovereign grace there could be no success in the ministry. Fuller wanted his comments to be understood in this vein; not as coming from a superior, but from one also seeking his way, knowing that all his advice and encouragements applied equally to himself.

Fuller considered the work of ministry to be a very significant thing. Ministers are servants of the people, but ultimately they serve the God who commissioned them. So they are not the servants of the people in a sense that implies inferiority, for the people are commanded by God to "obey them that have the rule over you." However, ministers are servants inasmuch as all their time and energy should be devoted to the spiritual advantage of their people—to know, caution, counsel, reprove, instruct, exhort, admonish, encourage, stimulate, pray, and preach to them. The pastor was to work hard to promote their spiritual interests as individuals, and their prosperity as a people.[12] Indeed, the significance of the work of ministry, based on a great love for the cause of God, was the raison d'être of the ordination ceremony itself.[13] The charge was to motivate successful pastoral ministry through counsel, advice, and encouragement based on the experiences of the usually more seasoned pastor giving the charge.[14] The encouragement was needed because of the magnitude of the responsibilities coupled with the inevitable difficulties

---

[9] Fuller, "Qualification and Encouragements" in *Complete Works*, IV, 25; "Intimate and Practical Acquaintance" in *Complete Works*, IV, 454.

[10] Fuller, "Spiritual Knowledge" in *Complete Works*, IV, 448; "Intimate and Practical Acquaintance" in *Complete Works*, IV, 454.

[11] Fuller, "Fellow-Labourers" in *Complete Works*, IV, 465.

[12] Fuller, "Preaching Christ" in *Complete Works*, IV, 482.

[13] Fuller, "Ministry a Great Work" in *Complete Works*, IV, 495.

[14] Fuller, "Qualification and Encouragements" in *Complete Works*, IV, 25.

inherent in the office.[15] Firm rootedness in this grand divine mission would encourage wholeheartedness, diligence, and perseverance throughout the inevitable setbacks and oppositions that accompany all great works of God.[16] But the magnitude of the work, if misunderstood, could create an unsolvable dilemma as the inherent inability of sinful creatures to perform spiritual work presented the minister with an impossible task. The guiding principle to motivate the pastor to give his life to a seemingly impossible task was a foundational reliance on God to help him.[17] It was true that the pastor was not sufficient in himself to do the work, but he could be assured of God's promised help.[18] Rather than encouraging the ordinand along the strain of "all will be well," Fuller did not shrink back from expressing the inevitable and inherent difficulties of the pastorate. He knew it was challenging work, but he also believed that the man God called as an elder would be helped by the One who called him. As a result, in addition to passing along practical advice regarding the ministry, Fuller was also concerned to educate his charge that all great work is accompanied by trials.

Pastoral work involved the salvation of souls, which, though minimized or despised as unimportant by many outside the true church, was of far more importance than any other "temporal deliverances." By, "temporal deliverances" Fuller is thinking of those providences of God which do not directly relate to the salvation of souls. An example may be seen in a military victory or political coup. The reason he emphasized the magnitude of a faithful minister's work was because he believed that every soul was destined to eternal misery or eternal bliss.[19] Therefore, heaven or hell was at stake for every man, woman, and child. Because of the potential offensiveness of this message for some, Fuller knew that there would be conflict from the world, with its ideology that opposed God and his kingdom. The inevitable opposition ultimately came from the Accuser, Satan, whose goal was to resist the work of God and his people at every step. As we shall see, a large part of Fuller's encouragement to pastors was eschatological, rooted in the faith of promised rewards at

[15] Fuller, "Work and Encouragements" in *Complete Works*, IV, 472.
[16] Fuller, "Ministry a Great Work" in *Complete Works*, IV, 495.
[17] Fuller, "Ministry a Great Work" in *Complete Works*, IV, 496.
[18] Fuller, "Ministry a Great Work" in *Complete Works*, IV, 495.
[19] Fuller, "Ministry a Great Work" in *Complete Works*, IV, 495.

judgment.[20] But also in the here and now the minister could count on God's promises to be with his people to support them and strengthen them.[21]

One of Satan's tactics was to divert God's people from their assigned tasks, so it was essential that the Christian leader stay focused on what he was called to do and not be distracted by temporal things. In the eighteenth century there was a pervading fascination among the English of this time with all things political. For Fuller, gospel ministry deserves single-minded devotion not to be interfered with by worldly affairs.[22] For example, it was likely this supercharged political climate coupled with Fuller's own experience with missionary candidate John Fountain that perhaps influenced him to cite excessive political involvement as an example of this form of diversion.[23] This did not mean that the pastor was to have no involvement in the world, as Fuller himself benefited from political involvement firsthand in defense of the Baptist Missionary Society with Parliament,[24] but all such activity must remain subservient to the pastor's primary calling.

As mentioned, the rationale of many ordination sermons was not only to point out the necessary pastoral qualifications, but also to encourage faithfulness and diligence in the newly-ordained pastor's charge. So there were often exhortations, encouragements, and motivations offered for successful stewardship of the entrusted charge. One such motivation was to persuade the new pastor to reflect on the great cost underpinning the Christian ministry as described above.[25] For Fuller the groundwork of the pastoral ministry lay in the sacrifice of the Son of God. Given the doctrinal centrality of Christology among eighteenth-century Baptists, this was tantamount to saying there was no more-expensive sacrifice to be made. Since the death of the Son of God was of inestimable cost, indeed the quintessential expense, so it followed that a sacrifice of this magnitude required a corresponding conscientiousness on the part of the appointed steward. But the main encouragement for the pastor was

---

[20] Fuller, "Hold Fast the Gospel" in *Complete Works*, IV, 543.

[21] Fuller, "Ministry a Great Work" in *Complete Works*, IV, 497.

[22] Fuller, "Ministry a Great Work" in *Complete Works*, IV, 514.

[23] *Letter to John Fountain* 25 March 1796 (Transcribed by Joyce A. Booth from a calendar of Fuller's letters prefaced by the Rev. Ernest A. Payne found in manuscript box [4/5/1]) (Angus Library, Regent's Park College, Oxford). As seen when he felt it necessary to rebuke the missionary John Fountain (1767–1800) who was thought to be jeopardizing the success of the mission because of radical political views that he was propagating in India.

[24] See chapter 1.

[25] Fuller, "Ministry a Great Work" in *Complete Works*, IV, 496.

the assurance of God's divine help in fulfilling his purpose to prosper his church.

The supremacy of the divine sacrifice mirrors the pre-eminence of the concomitant divine purpose for God's steward. So for Fuller the work of the pastor reflects the chief design of God inferring the subservience of all other enterprises to that of the pastor's mandate of evangelism. These other temporal enterprises only serve the grander purpose of God's divine will for the sake of the gospel. It follows that a sovereign God would assist the pastor in this, his chief design, and all opposition was ultimately futile and all so-called setbacks, temporary. The despondent pastor was encouraged to remind himself of this reality and to believe in it with certitude.[26] With the cross at the centre of human history and imputed sin at the root of all mankind's woes, Fuller believed that salvation, with the associated reversal of the effects of the Fall, was the only path to happiness. The work of the Christian minister was therefore not only good for the church, but also represented the only hope for the happiness of all mankind. The joy of both believers and unbelievers alike rested on the success of this "great work," which made the pastor's purpose more universal in nature.[27]

Discontented with just an esoteric teaching and fully expecting actuality in his hearers, Fuller offers some very practical principles necessary to accomplish the work of evangelism, which he called a "great work."[28] A minister, if he is to be successful, must pay close attention to the little things to do a great work. Usually such works are accomplished by a series of seemingly less important labours rather than a single great heroic act. So a minister is called to pray, inquire of God, weep, and be persistent.[29] Conversely, a great work can be hindered or stopped by little things like disagreements between Christians and self-will.[30] These must be anticipated and nipped in the bud as a preventative method.

Fuller was convinced that a key technique for communicating scriptural truths in preaching was through highlighting the lives of biblical characters. He believed that by studying the characteristics and actions of proven saints, those

[26] Fuller, "Ministry a Great Work" in *Complete Works*, IV, 496.
[27] Fuller, "Ministry a Great Work" in *Complete Works*, IV, 496.
[28] Fuller, "Ministry a Great Work" in *Complete Works*, IV, 496.
[29] Fuller, "Ministry a Great Work" in *Complete Works*, IV, 496.
[30] Fuller, "Ministry a Great Work" in *Complete Works*, IV, 496–497.

blessed of God, it encouraged emulation among contemporary observers.[31] He was persuaded that this was an inherently scriptural methodology designed to positively influence Christian living.[32] Especially worthy of imitation were the apostles and prophets,[33] but this does not exclude the value of studying other important figures in church history. Through these positive examples, the pastor's need for improvement is revealed and he will be motivated to be more effective.[34] Biblical models represent the best illustrations for emulation because they are God-inspired examples of certain important truths.[35] Fuller's emphasis on the close connection between the life of a minister and his effectiveness is evident here. We will explore this in more detail as we progress, but we must note here the connection between piety and efficacy in ministry. Fuller cites Barnabas[36] as a model for emulation, who based on his faithfulness and unction in the Spirit, was successful in evangelism. His piety resulted in many people coming to the Lord. Indeed, this was God's usual method in evangelism, to prosper the spiritual labours of godly men.[37] So as there were certain qualities in a minister that would help to prosper his work, there were also qualities that may hinder his work. The starting point for successful ministry was always the minister's own spirituality, so he must take great care to watch his own soul in addition to the souls of his people. In fact, he was particularly susceptible to the neglect of his own soul as he invested in the spiritual welfare of others.

A final great encouragement for the minister to persevere was to look to the end of his ministry while constantly taking stock along the way. He believed that everyone, including the minister, would one day at the eschaton stand before God to give an account for the ministry entrusted to him, where he would receive either rewards or punishment. This reminder was both to serve as a motivator to promote faithfulness and an incentive to look forward to the reward of faithful service.

As mentioned, a primary feature of the ordination service was that it was conducted in the context of community. The ordination was a covenant

---

[31] Fuller, "Qualifications and Encouragements" in *Complete Works*, IV, 26; Fuller, "Intimate and Practical Acquaintance" in *Complete Works*, IV, 454.

[32] Fuller, "Intimate and Practical Acquaintance" in *Complete Works*, IV, 454.

[33] Fuller, "Intimate and Practical Acquaintance" in *Complete Works*, IV, 454.

[34] Fuller, "Qualifications and Encouragements" *Complete Works*, IV, 26.

[35] Fuller, "Qualifications and Encouragements" in *Complete Works*, IV, 26; Fuller, "Preaching Christ" in *Complete Works*, IV, 479.

[36] Acts 4:36–37.

[37] Fuller, "Qualifications and Encouragements" in *Complete Works*, IV, 26.

between the church and the pastor, and therefore each had their own concomitant responsibilities to one another. The charge to the pastor outlined his responsibilities to God, himself, his family, and the church. The address to the church outlined in turn the church's responsibility in covenant to their pastor and to one another. First, we will consider the responsibilities of the pastors as described in the various charges to ordinands.

Fuller's Theology in the Charge

The Pastor as a Shepherd

According to Fuller a genuine love for the church was the foundational and indispensable quality necessary for pastoral success.[38] Therefore, it is not surprising that he seemed to prefer the biblical metaphor of the shepherd, for the biblical shepherd must have an authentic, affectionate concern for the salvation of souls just as a shepherd protects and nurtures his beloved sheep.[39] He saw the pastor as a shepherd after the example of the Great Shepherd Jesus Christ. Christ was very concerned that his sheep be "fed," and the notion of feeding was even closely linked with his death: "Take heed therefore unto yourselves, and to all the flock, over that which the Holy Ghost hath made you overseers, to feed the church of God, which he hath purchased with his own blood."[40] In other words, just as Jesus as a shepherd was motivated primarily by a sacrificial love to give people what they needed to subsist, so the pastor, his under-shepherd, was required to feed the flock of Christ with the Word of God.[41] The pastor was to imitate Christ's example through loving self-sacrifice.[42]

Also, Christ had a form of ownership of his sheep, since they were bought with his blood (Acts 20:28), and they were given to him by God (John 10:29); he was not willing to entrust them to another shepherd that did not love them (John 10:12).[43] Christ only entrusts his flock (the church) with under-shepherds who love the church as he does. This is the source of the pastor's love for his people; he will love them because Christ loves them, and he loves Christ. This is the sign of authentic pastoral ministry; if a minister does not

---

[38] Fuller, "Work and Encouragements" in *Complete Works*, IV, 474.
[39] Fuller, "Affectionate Concern" in *Complete Works*, IV, 488.
[40] Acts 20:28.
[41] Fuller, "Faithful Minister" in *Complete Works*, IV, 535.
[42] Fuller, "Feed the Flock" in *Complete Works*, IV, 446.
[43] Fuller, "Feed the Flock" in *Complete Works*, IV, 447.

love his people, he is a counterfeit and doesn't belong in the office because without love the pastor cannot properly care for them, be vigilant for their well-being, or defend them from all dangers.[44] The genuine shepherd is prepared to literally risk his life for his "sheep." Love for God and the church is the foundation of all the duties of a pastor.

Pastoral Duties

Continuing with the metaphor of a shepherd, the pastor's main duty was to feed his flock. "Feeding" refers not only to giving them the Word of God as food for their souls through preaching, but for Fuller it includes the complete care of the flock, including all the inherent duties and responsibilities of their governance and protection.[45] He is describing the role of the "elder" usually referred to as an "overseer." But a minister can only rule effectively when he is first intimately acquainted with Jesus and his gospel.[46] He is concerned that the young ordinand bear much fruit through all his ministerial duties and in order to accomplish this he needs "a special divine influence."[47] As it shall be observed, this emphasis on effectiveness in the ministry, through divine power, dominates his thought throughout the ordination sermons.

Before a pastor can preach effectively, he must understand some important characteristics of the gospel. Since the gospel by its very nature is often offensive to people, the pastor must determine to be faithful in preaching it accurately.[48] He cannot assume that all his hearers are saved,[49] and so when he preaches subjects that offend people's conscience he must resist the pressure to soften hard truths. Likewise, there is a temptation to tell people what they want to hear so they will approve of him and congratulate him. Ultimately, he must be faithful to the Scriptures regardless of what people think of him. He says, "beware of giving up the authority of God over the heart."[50] By this he means, don't try and minimize someone's sins by comforting them so they may feel better in the short term but be lost in the end. The key to preaching

---

[44] Fuller, "Feed the Flock" in *Complete Works*, IV, 447; Fuller, "Work and Encouragements" in *Complete Works*, IV, 475.

[45] Fuller, "Feed the Flock" in *Complete Works*, IV, 447.

[46] Fuller, "Feed the Flock" in *Complete Works*, IV, 447.

[47] Fuller, "Nature of the Gospel" in *Complete Works*, IV, 469.

[48] Fuller, "Nature of the Gospel" in *Complete Works*, IV, 469.

[49] Fuller, "Affectionate Concern" in *Complete Works*, IV, 489.

[50] Fuller, "Nature of the Gospel" in *Complete Works*, IV, 470.

effectively was the approbation of God himself. No matter what happens to the minister as a result of his preaching, his main objective must be to please God, and if a pastor was ashamed to preach the entire gospel, he was not worthy to hold the office of elder.[51] Therefore, great faith and boldness was required of every minister of God.

The Role of Scripture in the Ministry

For effectiveness in ministry, Fuller, in full unison with his Particular Baptist heritage, felt it absolutely essential that the ordinand build his ministry on the Word of God, as seen in the canonical Scriptures, for they reveal the will of Christ to his people.[52] There is a consistent emphasis in Fuller's thought that a pastor must practice what he preaches before he is equipped to feed people effectively. This consistency in Christian character is learned mainly through the laborious work of disciplined study of the Scriptures.[53] Although Fuller sees value in reading the works of other Christians he respects, he consistently exhorts pastors to "learn your religion from the Bible."[54] Non-biblical sources were only valuable in proportion to the level they reflected the Bible. The pastor must learn to discern the teachings of the Scriptures himself without always relying on someone else's interpretation. He did this by diligently seeking truth in every part of the Bible through reading, meditation, and prayer.[55] The goal of this study was not merely for intellectual knowledge, but also to know Christ more intimately, for it was possible to read Scripture without discerning the mind of Christ, making the exercise all but spiritually valueless. Fuller gives Thomas Paine as an illustration: "Paine read the scriptures to pervert and vilify them. We may be acquainted with the original languages, and be able to criticize texts; and yet not discern the mind of the Spirit."[56] Because study was a religious exercise, prayer and meditation were necessary for understanding, for studying was essentially concerned with a spiritual illumination that must come from God. Such illumination was central to pastoral success. In harmony with his axiom that the goal of ministry was to both enlighten the mind and affect the heart, he was not suggesting a kind of mysticism where

---

[51] Fuller, "Nature of the Gospel" in *Complete Works*, IV, 470.
[52] Fuller, "Intimate and Practical Acquaintance" in *Complete Works*, IV, 454.
[53] Fuller, "Intimate and Practical Acquaintance" in *Complete Works*, IV, 454.
[54] Fuller, "Intimate and Practical Acquaintance" in *Complete Works*, IV, 454.
[55] Fuller, "Intimate and Practical Acquaintance" in *Complete Works*, IV, 455.
[56] Fuller, "Godly Simplicity" in *Complete Works*, IV, 532.

one relies solely on the Spirit's illumination. Rather, he was saying that the intellect must be spiritually conditioned through prayer, not only to see factual truths and doctrine, but also to "see the beauty and feel the force of many parts of scripture."[57] When a minister is in a "carnal" state of mind he cannot be passionate about these truths. A frequent admonition from Fuller is to study the Scriptures as a Christian and not as a minister.[58] In other words he must feed his own soul first before trying to impart spiritual wisdom to others. If a minister doesn't take time to do this, he has nothing of value to offer his people. The pastor's great temptation was to go to the Bible to try and find something to teach the people without letting the same truths impact him first. But to do this was extremely dangerous because an important aspect of the ministry was not just to teach truth, but to model it as well. If the message of his preaching was inconsistent with the minister's character, there would be little spiritual fruit. This close communion with God enlivened a ministry and improved the graces necessary for effective ministry.

Subject of Preaching

The subject matter of preaching, in perfect harmony with Particular Baptist theology, was to preach Christ as the main theme.[59] Christ was considered to be the grand theme of the Christian ministry, and so Fuller says, "This is the work of God, that ye believe on him whom he hath sent ... Preach Christ, or you had better be anything than a preacher. Woe unto me if I preach not the gospel."[60] Fuller believed that Christ should be the main subject of every sermon. He says, "every sermon, more or less, should have some relation to Christ, and bear much on his person and work."[61] The pastor doesn't need to fear running out of material or having boring sermons because Christ's person and work are an unfathomable topic. Every Divine attribute is seen in him; all the Old Testament types pre-figure him, the prophecies point to him, every truth somehow relates to him, and finally even the Law itself is properly understood through him.[62] For Fuller, to preach Christ meant that the pastor must regularly exhibit Christ's divinity and all his glorious attributes, always

[57] Fuller, "Intimate and Practical Acquaintance" in *Complete Works*, IV, 455.
[58] Fuller, "Intimate and Practical Acquaintance" in *Complete Works*, IV, 456.
[59] Fuller, "Faith in the Gospel" in *Complete Works*, IV, 498.
[60] Fuller, "Faith in the Gospel" in *Complete Works*, IV, 498.
[61] Fuller, "Faith in the Gospel" in *Complete Works*, IV, 499.
[62] Fuller, "Preaching Christ" in *Complete Works*, IV, 481.

point to the efficacy of Christ's blood in saving sinners, display his atonement as the only ground for a sinner's hope, resist any hope that good works can save, convince hearers that their natures are corrupt, and dwell on the freeness and all sufficiency of his grace.[63] Only when Christ was properly preached would the pastor see effective results in evangelism. Fuller says, "This is the doctrine that God owns to conversion, to the leading of awakened sinners to peace, and to the comfort of true Christians."[64]

The eminent usefulness of a minister through preaching is accomplished on a practical level through teaching everything in the Bible and not being afraid to teach every truth.[65] Every part of Scripture should be taught proportionately in the way Scripture itself presents it.[66] This way the pastor can avoid the temptation to dwell on his favourite topics to the neglect of other important truths he may not personally find so appealing. Here Fuller distinguishes between doctrinal preaching and practical preaching.[67] Doctrinal preaching included more abstract topics like the Trinity, whereas practical preaching dealt with moral directives. To be effective the minister must, in the words of Fuller, "Preach the law evangelically, and the gospel practically; and God will bless you and make you a blessing."[68] Finally, since the very nature of the gospel is a mystery that needs to be revealed, the minister cannot be satisfied with a superficial knowledge of it. Therefore he must learn to think for himself.[69]

Fuller's concern for the effectiveness of a minister stems from his belief that the gospel was the most important thing you could tell someone because its subject was the salvation of their souls.[70] It is God's only way to eternal life, and if a pastor were to distort the message, he was in danger of losing his own soul.[71] Essentially the gospel is a message of love, and so it must be preached with great warmth.[72] Therefore, he can say "To preach these things with an

---

[63] Fuller, "Preaching Christ" in *Complete Works*, IV, 481–482.
[64] Fuller, "Preaching Christ" in *Complete Works*, IV, 482.
[65] Fuller, "Intimate and Practical Acquaintance" in *Complete Works*, IV, 457.
[66] Fuller, "Intimate and Practical Acquaintance" in *Complete Works*, IV, 457.
[67] Fuller, "Intimate and Practical Acquaintance" in *Complete Works*, IV, 457.
[68] Fuller, "Intimate and Practical Acquaintance" in *Complete Works*, IV, 457.
[69] Fuller, "Nature of the Gospel" in *Complete Works*, IV, 471; Fuller, "Habitual Devotedness" in *Complete Works*, IV, 486
[70] Fuller, "Nature of the Gospel" in *Complete Works*, IV, 471.
[71] Fuller, "Nature of the Gospel" in *Complete Works*, IV, 470.
[72] Fuller, "Nature of the Gospel" in *Complete Works*, IV, 471.

unfeeling heart are not to preach as we ought to preach. Cultivate the affectionate."[73] The minister's delivery must be wholly consistent with the message for it to be effective. As Christ wept for sinners so must the good pastor, and these tears were motivated by love.

Goals of Ministry

This mutual love in a voluntary society was necessary for effective ministry because the two chief goals for a pastor were to enlighten the minds and affect the hearts of the people in his sphere of ministry.[74] Enlightening the mind involved teaching them the entire gospel faithfully as presented in the Scriptures. Fuller says, "I love a sermon well laden with Christian Doctrine."[75] But his goal was not to just impart intellectual understanding.[76] He was concerned that they be emotionally attached to Christ in love as a living person. Truthful and faithful Bible exposition reveals Christ and provides the foundation for this relationship, but as Fuller says, "the union of genuine orthodoxy and affection constitutes true religion."[77]

In order to enlighten others, the pastor himself must be an example of what he teaches. Just as he communicates intellectual knowledge through expositional preaching, the affections, or emotions, likewise are communicated through the pastor's own intense love for Jesus and the gospel.[78] Fuller illustrates a distinction between two main types of ministers in his day. One sort, which he labels "popular preachers," may be applauded by people, but really have little "spiritual light" to give.[79] For Fuller, spiritual light is that intangible yet authentic knowledge from the Holy Spirit that effects real spiritual change in people's hearts. The other type of preacher, gospel ministers, are used by God not to promote themselves, but Christ.

---

[73] Fuller, "Nature of the Gospel" in *Complete Works*, IV, 471; Fuller, "Serve in Love" in *Complete Works*, IV, 537.

[74] Fuller, "Spiritual Knowledge" in *Complete Works*, IV, 448.

[75] Fuller, "Affectionate Concern" in *Complete Works*, IV, 490.

[76] Fuller, "Hold Fast the Gospel" in *Complete Works*, IV, 543. Conversely Fuller recognizes the danger of emphasizing the heart to the exclusion of the head. He says, "People foolishly discard doctrines under the pretence of exalting practice; but holy doctrine is the source and spring of a holy life."

[77] Fuller, "Hold Fast the Gospel" in *Complete Works*, IV, 543.

[78] Fuller, "Spiritual Knowledge" in *Complete Works*, IV, 448.

[79] Fuller, "Spiritual Knowledge" in *Complete Works*, IV, 448.

The first type of minister is merely exercising their natural gifts of speaking without this spiritual light that influences people's hearts away from worldly interests towards godly interests.[80] It is quite possible for a minister to preach with great enthusiasm without having a genuine love for God or the salvation of souls. The other—the ideal servant of God—is characterised by this spiritual light coupled with a holy love for his people in all aspects of his life and ministry—especially in preaching, ruling the church, and visiting the church people.[81]

So, if he must first be transformed in order to be effective in preaching the gospel, it follows that it is essential that the pastor be knowledgeable about the holy character of God. Fuller believed that most people see God as an extension of themselves, thus essentially ignoring his revelation of himself in Scripture.[82] The pastor's job is to educate people on what God is really like. For example, the minister must teach them that God is holy, and that they are sinners and therefore his enemies. Fuller believed that almost all error in the church, including those prevalent in his day such as Socinianism, Arianism, and Antinomianism, stemmed from a misunderstanding of the true nature of God.[83] For the pastor to avoid this common error himself, he is urged to spend much time in communion with God through prayer. Communion with God through private prayer is the best way to know and experience his holy character.[84]

The pastor also must know Christ as the only mediator between God and man.[85] He must know Jesus as a living resurrected person and value this relationship above all others, and in turn pass this knowledge along to his people. This knowledge does not just comprise of facts about his life and work, but also the glory of his character. The pastor must be familiar with, and able to relate to, Christ's works and qualities.

Because his goal is not just to impart facts, the pastor, as shepherd, was required not only to know the Scriptures, but also human nature as created in innocence, as depraved after the Fall, and as sanctified by the Holy Spirit.[86]

---

[80] Fuller, "Spiritual Knowledge" in *Complete Works*, IV, 448.
[81] Fuller, "Spiritual Knowledge" in *Complete Works*, IV, 448.
[82] Fuller, "Spiritual Knowledge" in *Complete Works*, IV, 449.
[83] Fuller, "Spiritual Knowledge" in *Complete Works*, IV, 449.
[84] Fuller, "Spiritual Knowledge" in *Complete Works*, IV, 449.
[85] Fuller, "Spiritual Knowledge" in *Complete Works*, IV, 449.
[86] Fuller, "Spiritual Knowledge" in *Complete Works*, IV, 449–450.

Just as a doctor is required to know the anatomy of a body, the minister must be intimate with the anatomy of the human soul.[87] He will not be able to help men if he is unaware of their spiritual condition, so he must be able to identify the motives that affect their actions. Fuller distinguishes between what he calls "primary" and "criminal" emotions.[88] Primary passions involve things that belong to man's nature and are not in-and-of-themselves evil if used as God intended. But if they are abused, that is, used in excess, they become "criminal" or evil.[89] For example, God has given every person a desire to own things, which is not wicked unless it is cherished to excess and then it becomes idolatry or covetousness.[90] The pastor must follow the Scriptures and appeal to man's created nature and show that all these passions are only satisfied in God. For example, the desire for possessions on earth is dwarfed in light of God's promise of an eternal inheritance. This is the promise and hope toward which the pastor must direct his people.

Further, in order to minister effectively, a pastor must also be aware of the depraved nature of the human condition. One of the characteristics that makes sin so dangerous is its deceptiveness in making bad things seem good. For example, sin makes attitudes resulting in "parsimoniousness," or stinginess, appear as the more noble virtue of frugality.[91] Unless the pastor is aware of the root of sin and the nature of its operation, he will not be able identify these deceptions and so help the people.

Likewise, he must understand human nature as sanctified by the Spirit of God. He is speaking here of recognizing if a person has become a Christian through God's supernatural work. As mentioned, conversion entails the creation of a new man with a new nature, and the pastor must be equipped to recognize these changes. Only then can he help mature the individual as a Christian and identify real from counterfeit converts, as Fuller believed that some who alleged faith were false professors.[92]

The Importance of "Feeling"

Because a central goal was also to affect the heart of his hearers, the minister could not be successful in preaching if his sermons were dry or insincere. As

---

[87] Fuller, "Spiritual Knowledge" in *Complete Works*, IV, 450.
[88] Fuller, "Spiritual Knowledge" in *Complete Works*, IV, 450.
[89] Fuller, "Spiritual Knowledge" in *Complete Works*, IV, 450.
[90] Fuller, "Spiritual Knowledge" in *Complete Works*, IV, 450.
[91] Fuller, "Spiritual Knowledge" in *Complete Works*, IV, 450.
[92] Fuller, "Spiritual Knowledge" in *Complete Works*, IV, 450.

mentioned, he is not merely relating information, but endeavouring to have his church experience the emotion of the truths he proclaims. So he himself must believe it to the point where it in turn affects his emotions and manifests itself as sincerity to his listeners. Biblical truth must warm his heart and create a genuine zeal for scriptural truths. If he is not passionate about the truths in this way, his words are empty, hypocritical, and powerless. Fuller says, "Indeed, without feeling, we shall be incapable of preaching any truth or of inculcating any duty aright."[93] For Fuller the greatest enemy to truth is indifference.[94] This is not something that can be faked and if it is not felt by the preacher it will not be felt by the congregation. If he preaches against sin, he must really feel holy indignation against it.[95] These feelings are not merely an emotion the pastor must drum up to bolster his sermonic delivery, rather they are the result of a genuine love for God and men. Just as Christ wept over lost sinners, so must the pastor. But Fuller still believed that not only is the content of the sermon important, so too is the way it is preached:

> Some have supposed that it is the matter, and not the manner of preaching, that God blesses. But I see no ground for this distinction. I allow that the matter is of the first importance; but the manner is not of small account. For example: the apostle prays that he might make the gospel manifest, "as he ought to speak," Col. iv. 4. And this relates to manner, not to matter. You may preach even the gospel dryly. It must be preached faithfully, firmly, earnestly, affectionately. The apostle so spoke that many believed. Manner is a means of conveying truth. A cold manner disgraces important truth.[96]

The point is not that emotion is inappropriate in the pulpit, but that the emotion is genuine, rooted in love for Christ and the church. Fuller's sole desire was that people should apprehend the gospel, and to accomplish this, the minister must preach with a correspondingly integral passion. Accordingly, he pleads:

> How would you feel in throwing out a rope to a drowning man, or in lighting a fire in a wilderness to attract the attention of one who was dear

[93] Fuller, "Spiritual Knowledge" in *Complete Works*, IV, 451. See also Fuller, "Godly Simplicity" in *Complete Works*, IV, 531.

[94] Fuller, "Hold Fast the Gospel" in *Complete Works*, IV, 543.

[95] Fuller, "Spiritual Knowledge" in *Complete Works*, IV, 451.

[96] Fuller, "Affectionate Concern" in *Complete Works*, IV, 490.

> to you, and who was lost? How did Aaron feel during the plague, when he stood between the dead and the living? O my brother, enter into these feelings. Realize them. Let them inspire you with holy, affectionate zeal. Souls are perishing around you; and though you cannot "make an atonement for the people's sins," yet you can publish one, made by our great High Priest; and, receiving and exhibiting this atonement, you may hope to save yourself and them that hear you.

For he adds, "a spiritual, diligent minister is commonly a fruitful one, and a blessing to his people."[97]

Doctrine and Christlikeness

The pastor's task in enlightening minds and affecting hearts was also accomplished through discouraging evil and promoting good in the church. Every minister faces certain dangers, or evils, that can prevent or even destroy his work of building up the body of Christ.[98] In order to avoid this he must consciously guard against potential errors in his doctrine. An essential part of his preaching ministry involved overturning all heresies through sound scriptural argumentation.[99] Since love was the predominant motive and foundation for ministry, it was a pastor's duty to vigorously oppose anything that could damage God's holy character or damage his church. For Fuller an attack against biblical doctrine was an attack on the character of God himself, revealing again this Particular Baptist axiom that the Bible was the inspired Word of God. For example he encouraged the ordinand to diligently defend important Particular Baptist doctrines, like the atonement of Christ.[100] In order to maintain this purity of belief, regular church discipline must be applied according to the standard of Scripture. There was no room for partiality here, even if the member being disciplined was rich and influential in the church.[101] The pastor, while constantly battling false doctrines that impugn God's character and destroy the souls of his people, must also proactively seek to build the church by encouraging truth. In disseminating biblical truth, the pastor does the most to build the church through unity.

[97] Fuller, "Habitual Devotedness" in *Complete Works*, IV, 488.
[98] Fuller, "Oppose Evil" in *Complete Works*, IV, 459.
[99] Fuller, "Oppose Evil" in *Complete Works*, IV, 458.
[100] Fuller, "Oppose Evil" in *Complete Works*, IV, 459.
[101] Fuller, "Oppose Evil" in *Complete Works*, IV, 459.

Christian unity is comprised of three main factors. First, each member must strive for individual purity in their personal Christian life.[102] The people of a church must be united in their commitment to individual holiness. Second, they must be mutually committed to apostolic doctrine.[103] There will always be some difference of understanding, but they must all agree on the essentials. Essentials include things like those outlined in their statement of faith, especially concerning the atonement and person of Christ. Third, each member must serve in the church humbly according to their individual gifting.[104] Each should use their gifts for the edification of the whole church or else there will be disorder and growth will be hindered. These are the main things that promote fellowship and unity in a church.

In regards to cultivating love and unity in the local church, Fuller again stresses the importance of careful attention to the pastor's own spiritual state:[105] "While you root out and pull down, and build and plant in God's house and vineyard, do not overlook your own. Personal religion is of the utmost importance to a minister."[106] He must be united with Christ in holiness because God's help was connected to his spirituality. God's help was absolutely essential for success because the pastor was co-labouring with God in ministry.

By the term "co-labourer" Fuller understands pastors as both subordinate and co-operative with God in the work of the ministry.[107] The pastor shares with God in the same goal and the same cause, which is essentially to glorify Christ, abase the sinner, alarm the wicked, and comfort the believer.[108] Fuller says in this regard, "our constant message must be—It shall be well with the righteous, but it shall be ill with the wicked."[109] Fuller envisions the nature of ministry as a labour. It requires hard work and so if an ordinand enters ministry with the idea of an easy idle life, he will be sorely disappointed. His main work was to labour in the Word of God and doctrine, to devote himself to the continuous study of Scripture. The pastor is to be characterized as a "perpetual

[102] Fuller, "Oppose Evil" in *Complete Works*, IV, 460.
[103] Fuller, "Oppose Evil" in *Complete Works*, IV, 461.
[104] Fuller, "Oppose Evil" in *Complete Works*, IV, 461.
[105] Fuller, "Ministerial and Christian Communion" in *Complete Works*, IV, 538.
[106] Fuller, "Oppose Evil" in *Complete Works*, IV, 461.
[107] Fuller, "Fellow-Labourers" in *Complete Works*, IV, 465.
[108] Fuller, "Fellow-Labourers" in *Complete Works*, IV, 467.
[109] Fuller, "Fellow-Labourers" in *Complete Works*, IV, 467.

gospel student," always searching and learning.[110] Fuller likens studying the Scriptures to mining.[111] One must work hard to extract the gems so that he can transfer the treasures to others. Of course, consistently, this is again not just the accumulation of facts about God, but the goal is to apprehend the mind of Christ, to feel the things that Christ felt, and to absorb scriptural sentiments along with the facts.[112]

Once the pastor has mined the Bible to achieve intimate communion with Christ the goal is then to instruct the people. He does this by applying the Scriptures to their particular situation in life. Whatever circumstances the people are facing he must apply scriptural wisdom, so they might learn to love Christ more. In order to do this effectively, the minister must also study his people. By observing them in the daily experiences of life, he can better understand their situation and can more effectively encourage them in Christlikeness.[113]

Fuller recognizes the reality of the opposition of spiritual warfare and so for encouragement to the ordinand he reminds him that because he is a co-labourer with God, he can also expect divine support, blessing, assistance, and sympathy. Further, he can one day anticipate a great reward for all his faithful labours.[114]

The pastor will never experience success in ministry if he is not concerned for a mutual love between the church and her pastor. He has been given a very important stewardship and as a steward he is a servant of God, entrusted with his church, so he must be faithful with that trust.[115] When Jesus returns he will ask the minister if he warned his sheep about eternal destruction; if not, their blood will be on his head.[116] As a result, it was very important that this warning be useful.

Piety and Effectiveness

In every example of extant ordination charges by Fuller, there is an emphasis, to varying degrees, on a direct connection between the character, or spiritual maturity, of the pastor and his effectiveness in the ministry. Effectiveness, or

[110] Fuller, "Fellow-Labourers" in *Complete Works*, IV, 466.
[111] Fuller, "Fellow-Labourers" in *Complete Works*, IV, 465.
[112] Fuller, "Fellow-Labourers" in *Complete Works*, IV, 465.
[113] Fuller, "Fellow-Labourers" in *Complete Works*, IV, 466.
[114] Fuller, "Fellow-Labourers" in *Complete Works*, IV, 468.
[115] Fuller, "Work and Encouragements" in *Complete Works*, IV, 473.
[116] Fuller, "Work and Encouragements" in *Complete Works*, IV, 474.

success, was not measured strictly in terms of numerical growth, but rather more by the spiritual character of the individuals comprising the church. Fuller instructs the ordinand therefore to "labour to build up your people ... That is not always the best ministry that draws the most followers, but that which does the most good. When I see a company of modest, humble, upright, lovely, diligent, holy people, I see the best evidences of a good minister."[117] Ideally these saints would be added to the church as converts through evangelistic efforts.

This connection between piety and success is well illustrated in Fuller's charge at the ordination of the Rev. Robert Fawkner at Thorn, Bedfordshire in 1787, where Fuller describes the qualifications necessary for the successful discharge of the stewardship of the office of pastor. He uses Barnabas from Acts 11:24 as an example to the ordinand to emulate, as he is paradigmatic of the characteristics of a man that is blessed by God.[118] Fuller then goes on to describe his character in detail as one who loved God and his people, and was particularly tender and affectionate as a preeminent quality of his ministry. Indeed Barnabas' particular strength was even reflected in the meaning of his name, "son of consolation."[119] For Fuller, these personal characteristics were indicative of spiritual maturity. He observes three main things about Barnabas that the ordinand must emulate in order to achieve similar results in his ministerial efforts, especially in evangelism, so that "more people would be added to the Lord."[120] He must be a good man, a man full of the Holy Spirit, and a man of faith. Piety reflected through these attributes would result in a corresponding success in evangelism.

First, the pastor must be a "good man." This "goodness" necessarily begins at conversion, but it extends beyond regeneration to a maturity in piety, meekness, and kindness.[121] But this piety is not a passive thing; it must be nurtured as a key priority in the minister's life. It begins with a proper valuation of a man's character before God. He must value this goodness above all worldly ambition to achieve personal greatness. For the Christian minister does not judge greatness according to the world, but as God judges, according to the Scriptures. As is consistent with Fuller, this piety is pragmatic and purposeful. The minister is not pious for the sake of piety, but rather in order to

[117] Fuller, "Oppose Evil" in *Complete Works*, IV, 460.
[118] Fuller, *Qualifications and Encouragement*, in *Complete Works*, IV, 26.
[119] Fuller, *Qualifications and Encouragement*, in *Complete Works*, IV, 26.
[120] Fuller, *Qualifications and Encouragement*, in *Complete Works*, IV, 27.
[121] Fuller, "Fellow-Labourers" in *Complete Works*, IV, 467.

increase his effectiveness in ministry. This piety is not just necessary when the pastor is functioning in his office in the church as an elder, but it extends to every aspect of his being as a Christian. He was not to be just a professional minister but a sincere Christian at all times. In order to do this, he was required to discipline himself with certain personal habits. A minister must study the lives of men who have been faithful to the gospel, men that "God has distinguished for gifts, and graces, and usefulness."[122] Second, although these examples are important, most of his time must be spent reading the Scriptures. When he does this, coupled with prayer, his heart will become passionate about what he believes and is teaching.[123] Third, he must learn to read human hearts, both his own and others. The best understanding comes from observing practical life, so the minister must constantly study how the human heart operates. If he just reads about human nature in a book, rather than learning it personally, it would likely be inaccurate.[124] Here again is the repeated emphasis on originality of thought, even in the observation and experience of interpreting day to day life.

It begins with being pious at home.[125] The pastor was to live out his life before his family with integrity, constantly both modeling the gospel through his life and faithfully and consistently teaching the Scriptures to his children. This involved regular family worship and prayer while maintaining of proper discipline in the home. By "proper" Fuller seemed to mean that discipline was neither too indulgent on one hand nor too strict on the other. Further, stressing the pastor's obligation to his family's spiritual welfare, Fuller also regularly warns against the tendency of some pastors to neglect time with the family by visiting others church members just to loiter and gossip.

The pastor must also strive for goodness in his personal devotional life with God. As noted, the pastor must first desire the influence and presence of Christ in his mind and heart, but he must also possess it if he would be successful in the ministry.[126] This influence is hard to describe in words, rather it is only understood as it is experienced, or felt, in the heart of the Christian. When Christ is present through intimate communion, Christians have their wants provided for, they are strengthened, and their work is rendered

[122] Fuller, "Spiritual Knowledge" in *Complete Works*, IV, 452.
[123] Fuller, "Spiritual Knowledge" in *Complete Works*, IV, 452.
[124] Fuller, "Spiritual Knowledge" in *Complete Works*, IV, 452–453.
[125] Fuller, "Qualifications and Encouragement" in *Complete Works*, IV, 27.
[126] Fuller, "Influence of Christ" in *Complete Works*, IV, 483.

productive. In this respect Fuller distinguishes between these special blessings of Christ's presence with the spiritual gifts he gives to all Christians. These gifts do not ensure this special communion with God, in fact without this special influence of the Spirit of God, gifts on their own could even prove to be destructive.[127] Rather, this presence of Christ sanctifies these gifts and makes them spiritually effective. This is the foundation of all effective ministry, and so Fuller says, "If we study, and pray, and preach merely as ministers, we shall make but poor work of it; but if as Christians, we shall prosper."[128] It is foundational because it will affect everything a minister does. The influence of Christ helps a pastor understand and delight in biblical doctrine, it gives him the ability to communicate more effectively, it gives him wisdom in dealing with people, and it helps sustain him during periods of difficulty.[129]

He appropriates the presence of Christ by devoting himself to the study of the Word of God and prayer:[130] "Walking with God in the closet is a grand means, with his blessing, of illuminating our minds and warming our hearts."[131] A warmed heart is a conscious realization of the love and presence of God, and accordingly the minister who feels God's love will never be bored or disinterested when studying the Bible. Likewise, if private prayer is neglected, the minister will lose his passion for the work. As a pastor converses with God it "heightens" his "graces," and better prepares him for spiritual work.[132]

This personal spiritual preparation is necessary for a pastor to bring this correspondingly real and vital spirituality into all his ministrations, especially in his preaching. But it must be genuine zeal, not a phony enthusiasm for God as some of his contemporaries apparently expressed in the pulpit, through their violent gestures and yelling. The minister must really feel the truths he preaches. People will discern his sincerity and it will influence the effectiveness of preaching. If they know he is sincere it gives him a sort of prophetic authority,[133] whereas faking it just creates disgust.[134] The reference to

[127] Fuller, "Influence of Christ" in *Complete Works*, IV, 483.

[128] Fuller, "Influence of Christ" in *Complete Works*, IV, 483–484.

[129] Fuller, "Influence of Christ" in *Complete Works*, IV, 484.

[130] Fuller, "Qualifications and Encouragement" in *Complete Works*, IV, 28.

[131] Fuller, "Spiritual Knowledge" in *Complete Works*, IV, 453.

[132] Fuller, "Qualifications and Encouragement" in *Complete Works*, IV, 29.

[133] Fuller, "Qualifications and Encouragement" in *Complete Works*, IV, 29. Fuller uses the words "divine authority."

[134] Fuller, "Qualifications and Encouragement" in *Complete Works*, IV, 29.

"prophetic authority" means that people will discern if his heart, motives, and message are from God and that he is not just pursuing a personal agenda. This will give weight to his preaching. He must continually test his motives to ensure that he is not preaching just to be heard, but sincerely motivated by love for Christ and the furtherance of his kingdom, as it is possible to preach with selfish motives even in the name of Christ. In regards to the injunction to the biblical command to "preach in season and out of season,"[135] for example, a pastor could manipulate that Scripture as an excuse to be heard by a wider audience as an attempt to promote his own name. As noted, Fuller was more outward looking than some of his Particular Baptist predecessors in the early eighteenth century, and in line with his belief in the so-called "free offer," he was concerned that everyone be persuaded to respond positively to the gospel. He says in regards to responding to the gospel that,

> It is not merely the privilege of believers; for then it would not be for every creature. It is a declaration of what Christ has done and suffered, and of the effects; exhibiting a way in which God can be "just and the justifier of the ungodly." It is not merely to convince of sin, but also to point to the remedy.[136]

Some of his High Calvinist forefathers would stop short of an evangelism that asked people to respond to the biblical crisis of sin.

Finally, this goodness or piety should also be reflected in the pastor's general behaviour. He should strive to be known as a meek and peaceful man who is generous and caring to those inside and outside the church. Reflecting the biblical priority, he should especially care for the poor and afflicted and show them mercy practically and spiritually.[137]

These characteristics are antithetical to selfish ambition, hence the regular emphasis on the necessity of humility in a pastor. The pastor's goal was not to be great in this world. So, although Fuller did not believe that it was wrong for a pastor to be wealthy, the accumulation of riches was not a minister's ultimate objective. He must guard against the temptation to be distracted from his

---

[135] Fuller, "Qualifications and Encouragement" in *Complete Works*, IV, 29. See 2 Timothy 4:2.

[136] Fuller, "Affectionate Concern" in *Complete Works*, IV, 449; Fuller, "Make Full Proof" in *Complete Works*, IV, 503.

[137] Fuller, "Qualifications and Encouragement" in *Complete Works*, IV, 29.

calling in this regard. Rather he had a responsibility as a steward to develop his natural gifts to be used solely for the edification of the church over personal gain and the applause of men.[138] Again, there is an emphasis on the development of character for the pragmatic purpose of ministry.

Fuller also believed that a pious minister should strive to be filled with the Holy Spirit. He is not referring to the "extraordinary" gifts of special power as seen in the apostles in the first century, but rather the normal working of the indwelling of the Holy Spirit common to all Christians.[139] The Spirit works in the Christian to produce certain characteristics like those described in Galatians 5:22–23, such as love, joy, peace, longsuffering, gentleness, goodness, faith, meekness, temperance. This is what defined distinguished spirituality. Fuller believed that when a fruit such as patience (longsuffering) was manifested in a man, it was a "miracle" far superior than a dramatic supernatural event. While the extraordinary gifts as seen in apostolic times displayed God's unique power, his holy nature was revealed through Christians through the fruit of the Spirit.[140] To be "filled" with the Spirit did not refer to quantity as in filling up a cup of water, but rather denotes the influence, or the effects, of the Spirit on the Christian. The Spirit, in this sense, controls the actions of the pastors and it is reflected in his character, which in turn enhances his ministry. This divine influence was often described using the word "unction."[141] Fuller's distinction between extraordinary and ordinary gifts reveals that he followed the majority in his Particular Baptist heritage as a cessationist in regards to the apostolic gifts of the Spirit.[142]

Unction, or this filling of the Holy Spirit, was essential for ministerial success as it allowed the Scriptures to become more easily understood by the pastor. The Spirit authored the Scriptures and so the man filled with the Spirit had the Word, metaphorically, written on his heart.[143] The Holy Spirit within would then help him easily and accurately understand divine truths. And this filling was also important for the people in his charge listening to his sermons. This corporate filling of the Spirit produced unity among Christians by

---

[138] Fuller, "Qualifications and Encouragement" in *Complete Works*, IV, 30.

[139] Fuller, "Qualifications and Encouragement" in *Complete Works*, IV, 30.

[140] Fuller, "Qualifications and Encouragement" in *Complete Works*, IV, 30.

[141] Fuller, "Qualifications and Encouragement" in *Complete Works*, IV, 31.

[142] A cessationist believes that some special endowments of the Spirit, such as *speaking in tongues*, were unique to the apostolic era and so are no longer available today. See for example Coxe, *Sermon Preached*, 6.

[143] Fuller, "Qualifications and Encouragement" in *Complete Works*, IV, 31.

promoting agreement with essential doctrines. Those not filled with the Spirit were unable to perceive the judiciousness of Christian doctrine, so many biblical truths seemed offensive or absurd to them and their natural tendency was therefore to reject them. For the minister, as a sinful man himself, there is always a tendency to soften some key truths, like the imputation of sin. The filling of the Spirit would help him resist this. The minister's success in ministry was contingent upon his dependence on the Spirit, above his own natural gifts, and without the filling of the Spirit there was no chance of success, as he was sure to slip into error.

Another reason the pastor must be filled with the Spirit is to empower his preaching and public prayer by more closely and accurately reflecting the mind of Christ. Fuller is speaking here about the way divine truths are communicated to others. A pastor may communicate true facts while still missing the essential meaning of the text. For example, when scriptural terms such as "holiness" are replaced by words like "morality," the intended sentiment is softened and thereby changed.[144] Fuller believes that this can have a profound spiritual effect on listeners. "Holiness" communicates the separateness of man from God by his sin, where the gap can only be breached through the mercy of God and grace, whereas the term "morality" hints at the ability of man to "fix" his own shortcomings through determined self-effort. Morality is a more vague term that usually reflects the pervading values of a secular culture, whereas a Christian morality is clearly defined in Scripture and directly linked to the person of God and his revealed law. Morality is achievable through self-effort, whereas holiness comes only through grace as a gift of God. Or if the term "believer" was to be replaced by the words "good men," the exclusivity of the gospel through election would be substituted by an indistinct group of relatively moral people who may or may not be saved. Fuller was concerned to remind the novice pastor that language can be used as a subtle form of manipulation that could soften the hard truths of the gospel and repackage them in a less obtrusive manner, but in the process destroy the author's intended meaning. It is interesting that Fuller, as an eighteenth-century man, was well aware of linguistic traps that could affect meaning, reflecting to some degree the contemporary "postmodern preoccupation."[145]

---

[144] Fuller, "Qualifications and Encouragement" in *Complete Works*, IV, 33.

[145] Neil Postman, *Building a Bridge to the 18th Century: How the Past Can Improve Our Future* (Vintage Books: New York, 1999), 74.

Fuller, in encouraging new pastors, is not just concerned that they effectively fulfill a role to the satisfaction of a congregation, he believes that the truths they proclaimed were real and life changing, and they would, if followed, result in the salvation of souls. If he was to be effective it was absolutely necessary that a minister's character reflected these truths he was proclaiming.[146] Otherwise, people would quickly recognize him as a hypocrite and reject his ministry.[147] Therefore unction was necessary to prove that the Holy Spirit was truly at work in the minister and his message.

This filling of the Spirit would not only empower the ministry of the pulpit but also give power to the full range of pastoral duties. For example, if the pastor were to have success in his important duty of visiting his flock, he would need this divine infilling to help discern people's spiritual condition and supply him with the wisdom to rebuke, edify, and encourage as the occasion required. During visitation it was especially important that he manifest the fruits of the Spirit of faithfulness and love.[148] Both a head (doctrine) and heart (the engaged affections) knowledge are necessary for the effective implementation of the important pastoral duty of visitation. Visitation for Fuller represented a "considerable part of the pastoral office."[149] The scriptural basis for this pastoral duty is found in the book of Acts where Paul is appealing to the elders of the church of Ephesus to teach "from house to house" (Acts 20:20). Since this visitation, consistent with Fuller's sanctified pragmatism, was purposeful for the instruction and edification of the saints, the pastor needed the same filling of the Spirit required for effective preaching. That is, the pastor must both "know" and "feel" the truths he was teaching. Fuller recognized that in the name of ministry a pastoral visit could quickly deteriorate and become just a social call that amounts to "religious gossip."[150] Satan is particularly at work here. If this visitation is not spiritually purposeful it becomes a waste of time and an excuse to avoid the discipline of hard study in sermon preparation. The preciousness of time and the accompanying required stewardship was clearly acknowledged by Fuller and consistently demonstrated by his actual work ethic. Pastoral visitation was such an important duty for pastors because it allowed him to better understand the circumstances and spiritual needs of his

---

[146] Fuller, "Spiritual Knowledge" in *Complete Works*, IV, 456.
[147] Fuller, "Qualifications and Encouragement" in *Complete Works*, IV, 33.
[148] Fuller, "Qualifications and Encouragement" in *Complete Works*, IV, 33.
[149] Fuller, "Spiritual Knowledge" in *Complete Works*, IV, 451.
[150] Fuller, "Spiritual Knowledge," in *Complete Works*, IV, 451.

congregation.[151] It created an openness of communication that allowed the pastor to give more candid and personal counsel in a way he could not do from the pulpit. If a pastor's people knew he loved them and truly wished their best for eternity, Fuller believed he could say almost anything to them without their being offended.[152] He consistently emphasized the necessity of genuineness in all of a pastor's ministrations. So he advised the ordinand not to "affect the gentleman in your visits."[153] He was essentially warning not to pretend he was more important than his people because he bore the title of pastor. On the other extreme, the pastor should guard against a causal familiarity where he told rude jokes or where he acted silly.[154]

For Fuller, the key to effective visitation, as with every other duty as a pastor, is a genuine, impartial love for the church. In order to govern effectively in the church a pastor must maintain a position of neutrality among members and be zealous for the glory of God and his truth above all else.[155] It is essential not only that a minister loves his people, but also that they know he loves them. Often major differences in a church could be overcome through frank discussion during home visitation.[156] Fuller also recognized that the pastor could also greatly benefit from home visitation, because as people relate their spiritual condition to him, "it will assist him in his preaching more than a library of expositors."[157] The empowering of the Holy Spirit is essential for effective ministry during home visitation.

Another essential quality necessary for a pastor to be effective in ministry, and in particular, evangelism, is faith. Faith involves three key elements: "having the mind occupied with Divine sentiment; being rooted and grounded in the truth of the gospel, and daily living upon it."[158] The first deals with the pastor's knowledge of doctrine and the Scriptures. He must have worked out his theology and be certain of what he believes and why he believes it. If not, he was particularly susceptible to false teaching or to constantly changing his view on issues.[159] This principle may reflect Fuller's own emphasis on

151 Fuller, "Spiritual Knowledge," in *Complete Works*, IV, 452.
152 Fuller, "Spiritual Knowledge" in *Complete Works*, IV, 452.
153 Fuller, "Not Despised" in *Complete Works*, IV, 464.
154 Fuller, "Not Despised" in *Complete Works*, IV, 464.
155 Fuller, "Spiritual Knowledge" in *Complete Works*, IV, 451.
156 Fuller, "Oppose Evil" in *Complete Works*, IV, 460.
157 Fuller, "Obedience of Churches" in *Complete Works*, IV, 114.
158 Fuller, "Qualifications and Encouragement" in *Complete Works*, IV, 34.
159 Fuller, "Qualifications and Encouragement" in *Complete Works*, IV, 35.

independent thought, which was described earlier. The second aspect of faith helps defend against the pressure of public opinion as the standard of truth rather than the Scriptures. The gospel message sometimes appears to counter the truth of the age, so the pastor first must be settled in his view that it represented the truth. Then he must be convinced of the essential doctrines of the Christian church, like the deity and humanity of Christ.[160] The third key element of faith again deals with the issue of personal integrity. If the pastor studies the Scriptures just to instruct others and not to feed his own soul, he is in danger of not growing in grace. He himself must combine his knowledge of the Scriptures with genuine personal faith. In other words, he must be striving to live out the doctrines he preaches to others. Fuller uses the analogy of a surgeon or a soldier who are so used to the sight of blood that they grow insensitive to it. Likewise, a pastor who studies the Bible just for knowledge and not to feed his own soul is in danger of imparting facts without feeling them. Fuller regularly advises, "read as one (a Christian) converse as one — to be profited, as well as to profit others."[161] He must first live the life of a Christian if he will succeed as a minister.[162]

When looking at the thirteen specific charges of Fuller in his collected works, at least eleven of them explicitly point out the necessity for a pastor to read as a Christian and not as minister in order to first feed his own soul. Fuller was convinced that one of the greatest temptations for the Christian pastor was to read the Scriptures with the goal to edify and teach others while neglecting his own soul. For Fuller this was one of the most dangerous temptations for pastors, to handle truth as a minister and not as a Christian and so edify others but neglect his own spiritual growth. Profession of faith alone was not enough but must be worked out in the pastor's life. Fuller believed that graceless, or wicked, pastors were "generally the most hardened against conviction of any character whatever."[163] Therefore, he must read, and preach, and converse so that he is profited too. Then he will have the Word mixed with faith, and others will profit also. So unless the minister studies the Scriptures primarily to feed his own soul rather than reading in order to teach others, he

---

160 These essentials include the key doctrines as summarized by the pastor in his personal statement of faith delivered at his ordination service.

161 Fuller, "Spiritual Knowledge" in *Complete Works*, IV, 453.

162 Fuller, "Faith in the Gospel" in *Complete Works*, IV, 499.

163 Fuller, "Qualifications and Encouragement" in *Complete Works*, IV, 36.

will have nothing of spiritual value to say to the church.[164] Just as he encourages his own people, the minister must also regularly examine his own spiritual state. Fuller says, "It is certainly possible, after we have preached to others, that we ourselves should be cast away!"[165] It was common to take it for granted that the pastor was a Christian, but he must be careful to nurture his own soul while preparing to feed others.[166]

Results of Piety

The labours of a pious minister would most likely be evidenced through effective evangelism as demonstrated by a growing church. Fuller did not define success in terms of merely numerical growth, which in of itself was of little value to him. He wanted to see the pews filled with committed believers through the conversion of sinners.[167] This is very important because it demonstrates again Fuller's conviction of an integral connection between the piety of the minister and success in ministry. In fact Fuller believed that it was axiomatic that "eminent spirituality in a minister is usually attended with eminent usefulness."[168] In Fuller's observation the most effective pastors did not necessarily have the greatest intellectual gifts, rather they were most often characterised by a "humble and affectionate" character.[169] But for Fuller, because God works sovereignly according to his own purposes, this relationship is not *a priori*.[170] It is not a formula whereby the pastor must do this and then blessings are guaranteed. Still it seemed to Fuller that God often prospered pastors in this regard. Ineffectiveness in ministry was more often due to a lack of piety than a lack of natural gifting and talent. So men with lesser abilities than others often had great success in the ministry above very naturally talented men.

Fuller understands piety in terms of character traits such as humility, watchfulness, godliness, and sobriety.[171] Humility is the proper understanding and response of man in relation to God. Since man is finite and God is infinite, and because the purpose for mankind is the glorification of God, it is necessary for the pastor to assume his proper role and minister accordingly.

---

[164] Fuller, "Spiritual Knowledge" in *Complete Works*, IV, 453.
[165] Fuller, "Preaching Christ" in *Complete Works*, IV, 478.
[166] Fuller, "Preaching Christ" in *Complete Works*, IV, 479.
[167] Fuller, "Qualifications and Encouragement" in *Complete Works*, IV, 36.
[168] Fuller, "Qualifications and Encouragement" in *Complete Works*, IV, 36.
[169] Fuller, "Affectionate Concern" in *Complete Works*, IV, 488.
[170] Fuller, "Qualifications and Encouragement" in *Complete Works*, IV, 36.
[171] Fuller, "Qualifications and Encouragement" in *Complete Works*, IV, 37.

Watchfulness is concerned with the careful appropriation of God's supplied graces that ensure successful Christian living, such as maintaining a consistent and meaningful prayer life with daily Bible study, including a close examination and maintenance of the "heart." For Fuller this was the repentant soul in close communion with God. Godliness concerned walking in obedience to God's commands, the avoidance of habitual sin, and regular repentance and forsaking of all things opposed to God and his Word. And finally, sobriety represented a life or demeanour consistent with the gravity and importance of the gospel.

When a minister reflected God's grace through a pronounced spirituality it would be apparent to all. First, it would increase his love for Christ and his passion for evangelism.[172] The Bible provides evidence that when men obey God with all their heart, it often results in a spiritual revival among the people of God.[173] Second, it would allow him to avoid selfish ambition and focus solely on the glory of God's name.[174] Selfishness would ruin all his work and reveal poor judgment.[175] Then the minister works with God to accomplish his will for the salvation of souls. If he had only his own goals and agenda in mind, God would not walk with him and he could not prosper in his work. And finally, it would allow the pastor to prosper in ministry without increasing pride in his own ability and effort.

Practical Advice on Guarding Character

This connection between the piety of the pastor and his effectiveness in ministry is so central to Fuller's theology that the pastor is obligated to make sure the love of the church is not disrupted through his own character flaws. For Fuller it was axiomatic that "contempt is not a voluntary feeling."[176] Men can dislike someone, but deep in their hearts they cannot despise him for no good reason.[177] Therefore, it follows that if a minister reflects the character of

---

[172] Fuller, "Qualifications and Encouragement" in *Complete Works*, IV, 37.

[173] Fuller, "Qualifications and Encouragement" in *Complete Works*, IV, 37. See for example, 2 Chronicles 31:21: "And in every work that he began in the service of the house of God, and in the law, and in the commandments, to seek his God, he did *it* with all his heart, and prospered" (Emphasis added).

[174] Fuller, "Qualifications and Encouragement" in *Complete Works*, IV, 38.

[175] Fuller, "Feed the Flock" in *Complete Works*, IV, 447.

[176] Fuller, "Not Despised" in *Complete Works*, IV, 462.

[177] Fuller, "Habitual Devotedness" in *Complete Works*, IV, 485.

Christ, as he should, he cannot be despised by his people.[178] In the three main areas of a pastor's life—in the pulpit, the church and in the world—Fuller gave the ordinand some practical advice on promoting love in a local church. In his preaching he must be sincere, not pretending he is someone he really isn't. His goal is not to appear more educated than he really is or use the pulpit for a personal performance.[179] The goal was not to promote himself, but to promote Christ. He was to relate the simple message of the gospel rather than advance his own genius or orthodoxy. This desired simplicity was attained by using common language, avoiding coarse language, and maintaining seriousness. Fuller felt there was no room for joking in order to make people laugh just to entertain them in the pulpit.[180] So in order to avoid perverting the central message of the gospel, he must always be able to support his arguments with biblical support.

Another way that the people can grow to despise a pastor is if he preaches an "unfelt gospel."[181] This makes people doubt his credibility and judge him a hypocrite. And finally, the pastor must ensure that he does not let his fear of certain individuals prevent him from teaching all the doctrine of the Bible. Even if he knows a friend may be offended, he must boldly preach the Word of God. For if he does not, over time people will begin to despise him for his cowardice in proclaiming the Word.[182]

Also, the pastor must also guard his character when presiding over the church as overseer. The pastor as under-shepherd of Christ's church must not be a dominant and controlling dictator always trying to force others to submit to his will and way.[183] Sometimes the pastor must be willing to happily acquiesce to the will of the church in non-essentials if his views are opposed by the majority.[184] Always demanding his own way on everything does not foster love. But this does not mean that he cannot be firm on some important issues. If he is weak and always tries to please the people, he will also be despised over time, and so at times the pastor must take a strong stand on certain issues, but only if he can provide biblical evidence to defend his case.

---

[178] Fuller, "Not Despised" in *Complete Works*, IV, 462.
[179] Fuller, "Not Despised" in *Complete Works*, IV, 462.
[180] Fuller, "Not Despised" in *Complete Works*, IV, 462.
[181] Fuller, "Not Despised" in *Complete Works*, IV, 463.
[182] Fuller, "Not Despised" in *Complete Works*, IV, 463.
[183] Fuller, "Not Despised" in *Complete Works*, IV, 463.
[184] Fuller, "Not Despised" in *Complete Works*, IV, 463.

Fuller's Pastoral Theology in the Address to the Church

As mentioned, the ordination service was a physical outworking of the reality of a spiritual covenant between an elder and the members of a local church. As the charge to the pastor outlined his covenant responsibilities to the people, so the address outlined the church's responsibilities to the pastor. Therefore, through Fuller's addresses to churches we see glimpses into his pastoral theology from the perspective of the "other side" of the covenant.

Mutual Success Based on Mutual Love

Since the relationship between the pastor and the people in Dissenting Churches was completely voluntary, the only bond that could truly unite them for success was love.[185] The importance of ministers to the church was not based on some special quality within the man, for he was a sinner like every other man. The reason the church was to esteem him was because he represented a gift to the church from Christ.[186] The church was to esteem him and love him for Christ's sake. This special blessing from the Lord was another aspect of Christ's mediation between God and man. Although Fuller at times acknowledges that the two main ways that God dwells with men and women in a local church is through the ordinances and ministers, he certainly emphasizes the latter.[187] To the degree that people in a church loved and feared God, they would also love and respect their pastor as Christ's special gift to them.

All the duties of the church to her pastor and to one another were summed up in the words "Christian love."[188] For Fuller, Christian love was not just civility between men, or mere friendship, or respect, or just membership in a social group, or even just benevolence itself.[189] Rather, it was something spiritual, where individuals' hearts were united in Christ.

---

[185] Fuller, "Walking in the Truth" in *Complete Works*, IV, 517.
[186] Fuller, "Ministers the Gift of Christ" in *Complete Works*, IV, 506.
[187] Fuller, "Ministers the Gift of Christ" in *Complete Works*, IV, 506.
[188] Fuller, "Importance of Christian Love" in *Complete Works*, IV, 507.
[189] Fuller, "Importance of Christian Love" in *Complete Works*, IV, 508.

Obedience to the Pastor

Fuller believed that the church had a duty to obey their pastor based on passages in Scripture such as Hebrews 13:17.[190] In fact, the church's success or failure hinged on it. Even in the address to the church there is connection between biblical obedience and effectiveness in the divine cause. But Fuller also prudently recognizes that the whole area of authority must be treated with care because of the potential for abuse. So, consistently with Fuller's theology, the minister was primarily a servant of God who was mandated to not "lord it over" the church (2 Corinthians 1:24). He recognized rather that this necessary obedience of the church was conditional upon certain requirements. First, the pastor must have been freely chosen by the church.[191] This is in accordance with Particular Baptist theological tradition that both insisted on and emphasized the right of the church to choose its own officers. Second, his rule is subject to the rule of Christ.[192] So he must be obeyed as long as he faithfully teaches and preaches scriptural truth. But for Fuller, because the mind and heart are intricately connected, the minister must not only teach correct doctrine, but it is also necessary for him to live out biblical truths. He is responsible to be consistent with his own teaching in his lifestyle, in fact, even in greater measure.[193] Fuller says, "And, when he exhorts and warns you, if he himself should privately pursue a contrary course, he seals his own destruction."[194] When all three of these factors were present, the church was obligated to obey their pastor. This obedience to the pastor was to be manifested in four main areas. First, the members of the church were expected to obey his instruction from the pulpit,[195] and this instruction should not only declare the truth but reflect scriptural sentiments through the delivery, because for Fuller "you may as well have no minister, as one who never makes you feel."[196] The individual church member would not profit much if their sole purpose in listening was just to criticize the sermons; they must come to worship with an attitude

[190] Fuller, "Obedience of Churches" in *Complete Works*, IV, 111. Hebrews 13:17 KJV: "Obey them that have the rule over you, and submit yourselves: for they watch for your souls, as they that must give account, that they may do it with joy, and not with grief: for that is unprofitable for you."

[191] Fuller, "Obedience of Churches" in *Complete Works*, IV, 112.

[192] Fuller, "Obedience of Churches" in *Complete Works*, IV, 113.

[193] Fuller, "Obedience of Churches" in *Complete Works*, IV, 113.

[194] Fuller, "Obedience of Churches" in *Complete Works*, IV, 113.

[195] Fuller, "Obedience of Churches" in *Complete Works*, IV, 114.

[196] Fuller, "Obedience of Churches" in *Complete Works*, IV, 114.

of humility. This spiritual fruit was a prerequisite for blessing. Second, they were to be open and honest in pastoral visitations.[197] Church members were to freely share their personal spiritual concerns with their pastor with a view to helping ministers promote in them the mind of Christ.[198] Third, they were to show him respect in church business meetings.[199] He had the authority to maintain proper decorum because disputes in these settings publicly shamed the name of Christ. Fourth, they were to be humble and receptive if they received a private rebuke for sin.[200] It was not always wise to deal with personal individual sin from the pulpit, so if the pastor approached you it would be to your benefit to listen humbly rather than acting irritable and resentful. Things he may discuss in private include: "spiritual declensions, hesitating on important truths, neglect of religious duties, worldly anxiety, and the early approaches to any evil course."[201]

It is not only out of duty that a church is to submit to the authority of her pastor, but it is always in her best interest to do so. The spiritual condition of the church is vitally connected to the ministry of the pastor because the Lord has placed the pastor over the church as a shepherd to watch over their souls. One day the pastor would have to give an account before the Lord for the stewardship of this ministry. The church had a responsibility to help him fulfill this mandate from God.[202] Since the salvation of the people in the local church was his main business, and because the Lord had wed them together, it was in the church's best interest to cooperate with him, because it was possible that not all placed under his charge would reach heaven. Fuller warns the church in this regard saying, "in short, if you have any regard to your own souls, or the souls of others, obey the counsels of heaven, which are communicated to you through his ministry, and submit yourselves."[203]

The feelings of the people in regards to how they respond to his ministry will also have a direct effect on their own happiness. The people have within their power, through their response to his ministry, the ability to make it a joy or a sorrow. For example, if they respond to his preaching with keen interest,

---

[197] Fuller, "Obedience of Churches" in *Complete Works*, IV, 114.
[198] Fuller, "Obedience of Churches" in *Complete Works*, IV, 114.
[199] Fuller, "Obedience of Churches" in *Complete Works*, IV, 114.
[200] Fuller, "Obedience of Churches" in *Complete Works*, IV, 114–115.
[201] Fuller, "Obedience of Churches" in *Complete Works*, IV, 115.
[202] Fuller, "Christian Steadfastness" in *Complete Works*, IV, 516.
[203] Fuller, "Obedience of Churches" in *Complete Works*, IV, 117.

attentiveness, appreciation, love, and humility it will give him great joy in ministry. This is revealed through regular attendance and arriving early for worship especially attending to his preaching ministry.[204] This kind of attitude will motivate him to pray for them and excite him to preach more effectively. For Fuller, this was because "God works not only by the word preached, but by the effects of it on the spirit of believers."[205] In other words, feeling or emotions are directly connected to the effectiveness of the minister's preaching.

They will also create joy for the minister when they support him in issues of church discipline.[206] When a church stands together in unity it promotes joy, but when there is infighting, quarreling, gossip, and slander it makes the pastor's work a misery. It is vital for a church to be concerned with the pastor's joy, because as mentioned, it will directly increase their own spiritual blessing. So since the church's success rests on a mutual love between the pastor and the church, this affection must be guarded and developed constantly.

This love is nurtured when people are concerned for his temporal welfare, when they provide comfort during his afflictions, and when they are gentle with him. Love is the secret to make everyone happy and successful, but this love must be constantly nurtured because it can easily be disrupted.[207] The reward of the pastor for all his efforts is to see his people grow in spiritual maturity, as seen through their growth in holiness and intimacy with God. So the church also demonstrates love to their pastor when they strive for spirituality in their own lives.[208]

When a church member sees weaknesses and faults in their pastor, they should approach him in love with the goal of tenderly correcting him for his own wellbeing. They should not talk to others without first talking to him[209] and they should not listen to gossip about him without evidence.[210]

Because pastors are sinners, they constantly need the church's prayers.[211] Their main role is to enlighten a dark world with the gospel, so the church is

---

[204] Fuller, "Obedience of Churches" in *Complete Works*, IV, 117; Fuller, "Ministers the Gift of Christ" in *Complete Works*, IV, 507; Fuller, "Importance of Christian Love" in *Complete Works*, IV, 507.

[205] Fuller, "Obedience of Churches" in *Complete Works*, IV, 117.

[206] Fuller, "Obedience of Churches" in *Complete Works*, IV, 118.

[207] Fuller, "Ministers the Gift of Christ" in *Complete Works*, IV, 507.

[208] Fuller, "Churches Fellow Helpers" in *Complete Works*, IV, 512.

[209] Fuller, "Importance of Christian Love" in *Complete Works*, IV, 509.

[210] Fuller, "Exhibit the Light" in *Complete Works*, IV, 520.

[211] Fuller, "Churches Fellow Helpers" in *Complete Works*, IV, 511.

to pray that the pastor first be enlightened.[212] Without this enlightenment they would not be effective in feeding the church with "knowledge and understanding."[213] The more they "feel" their Christian experience, the greater the benefit to the church. Also congregants have a responsibility to teach their children and servants to love their pastor, for they won't profit from his ministry if they do not respect him.[214]

This love for the pastor is only part of their responsibility, as they are also required to work hard at loving one another and rejoice to be with God's people in the house of God.[215] When people are concerned with every member's wellbeing and when they love each other, forgive each other, and pray for one another, they will experience God's approbation with his blessing. This special Christian love for one another and for the pastor must be continually nurtured through self-denial and personal holiness.[216] Peace among the brethren ensures prosperity and harmony.[217] This fruit of the Spirit again results in blessing from the Lord.

The key to maintaining this mutual love and harmony in a church is to walk in the truth of the Scriptures.[218] The most effective way to promote the gospel as a church is to believe and practice the gospel in their lives with integrity. Fuller says, "The great means of promoting religious union among Christians is, not by dispensing with disagreeable truth, but by aspiring to conformity to Christ."[219] They must believe and live under the divine authority of the Bible as their rule for both faith and practice.[220] Doctrines that were especially important included: the total depravity of man, redemption by the blood of Christ, election, efficacious grace, and the perseverance of the saints.[221] The goal of the church is conformity to the image of Christ and when holiness is present, God blesses his people with his presence and dwells in his church to prosper it.[222]

---

[212] Fuller, "Exhibit the Light" in *Complete Works*, IV, 521.
[213] Fuller, "Exhibit the Light" in *Complete Works*, IV, 521.
[214] Fuller, "Churches Fellow Helpers" in *Complete Works*, IV, 512.
[215] Fuller, "Importance of Christian Love" in *Complete Works*, IV, 509.
[216] Fuller, "Walking in the Truth" in *Complete Works*, IV, 517.
[217] Fuller, "Peaceful Disposition" in *Complete Works*, IV, 528.
[218] Fuller, "Exhibit the Light" in *Complete Works*, IV, 522.
[219] Fuller, "Churches God's Building" in *Complete Works*, IV, 530.
[220] Fuller, "Walking in the Truth" in *Complete Works*, IV, 517.
[221] Fuller, "Walking in the Truth" in *Complete Works*, IV, 517-518.
[222] Fuller, "Churches God's Building" in *Complete Works*, IV, 530.

EMINENT SPIRITUALITY EQUALS EMINENT USEFULNESS

In summary, these sermons clearly reveal that every published ordination sermon and sketch of Fuller contains the common, prominent, and central thread of thought captured in the phrase: "eminent spirituality leads to eminent usefulness." Included in this first part of the phrase "eminent spirituality" are the related concepts of the admonition to read and to study as a Christian and not as minister for the purpose of having something spiritual with which to feed the flock;[223] words that described emotions, such as the heart, holy love, affecting the heart, and feeling;[224] descriptives such as intimate communion with Christ, consistent character with the gospel, approbation of God, spiritual influence, enlightening the mind, piety, goodness, faithfulness, love, spiritual light, unction, presence of Christ, and the mind of Christ.[225] All of these concepts that help define eminent spirituality would likely result in great usefulness or effectiveness in ministry.

The preeminent evidence of true spirituality, or piety, in a minister was the reality of a manifest love for God resulting in a corresponding love for souls. And this love, if real, must necessarily be revealed through tangible feelings. These feelings were cultivated through an intimate communion with God, which in turn would produce spiritual fruit in the pastor's life. This communion was enhanced particularly through the study of Scripture, through meditation, and through prayer, which would affect the heart, producing a godly character. For Fuller, piety was a very pragmatic thing in that this spirituality was always purposeful. It involved the impartation of God's power, producing the fruit of the Spirit, to make the minister spiritually effective in all his ministrations, but especially in evangelism. For Fuller, there was a direct connection between the minister's personal holiness and his effectiveness in leading souls to repentance in Christ. Eminent spirituality produces eminent usefulness. In the following chapter it will be necessary to compare the continuity/discontinuity between Fuller and other Particular Baptists with a view to discovering the extent of the transformation of pastoral ministry.

---

[223] For example as seen in Fuller, *Complete Works*, IV, 36, 453, 456, 471, 474, 479, 483–484, 486, 500, 532.

[224] For example as seen in Fuller, *Complete Works*, IV, 29, 112, 450, 463, 466, 456, 471, 483, 490–491, 496, 499, 533, 537, 540, 543.

[225] Fuller, *Complete Works*, IV, 27, 113, 447, 448, 455, 460, 462, 465, 470, 472, 479, 483, 486, 491, 492, 496, 499, 507, 508, 516, 521, 530, 533, 535, 537, 538, 539, 543.

Conclusion

Continuity and Discontinuity

An evaluation of the available published Particular Baptist ordination sermons, beginning in the long eighteenth century with Nehemiah Coxe's sermon of 1681 to George Sample's ordination in 1818, as compared with Andrew Fuller's published ordination sermons of the late eighteenth century, manifests a palpable theological continuity within the larger Particular Baptist ordination history. In order to discover if there was indeed a radical re-conception of the pastoral office by Fuller, his theology must be carefully considered in light of other Particular Baptists. This chapter will compare Fuller's theology with theirs, particularly in light of his theological emphasis of eminent spirituality and eminent usefulness. Also, the earlier part of the eighteenth century, prior to 1770 when the evangelical revival began to affect the Baptists, will be the focus of comparison with Fuller.

Ordination Dynamics

Fuller continued in the Particular Baptist belief in the value of ordination as demonstrated through his wide-spread participation in preaching sermonic charges and addresses to the church. His involvement also extended beyond just those two aspects, as we have seen. For example, he closed with public prayer at times. The evidence that his involvement was significant is reflected in the number of his extant ordination sermons, which probably represent the largest remaining corpus among the eighteenth-century Particular Baptists. He not only followed the general Particular Baptist structure of service but he also shared with them its necessity and importance based on apostolic example and biblical precedent. This reveals continuity with the earlier Particular Baptists' stress on the importance of orderliness, for the ordination service's raison d'être was a biblically prescribed church structure achieved through the proper installation of its officers.

The church is God's primary means for building his kingdom and at the centre of this is the pastor who was given the gifts and graces to help build the church up to maturity. Order then, was a sign of biblical fidelity and essential for the approbation of God and his accompanying blessing on the church. In the earlier Particular Baptist sermons, especially prior to around 1773, there is a regular overt mention in charges on the importance of orderliness in the local church, and this emphasis continued, though generally with less force, until the earlier decades of the nineteenth century. Although Fuller would have wholeheartedly agreed with the truthfulness and importance of the regulative principle of worship, he rarely if at all stressed its importance to his charges beyond the need for church discipline and care in accepting new members. When he did point out the importance of taking care in "laying on of hands" it was mostly in his address to a church.[1] He also shared the same Baptist priorities of simplicity, solemnity, and joy as characteristics of the ceremony itself.

As mentioned, ordination was eminently important in the life of the church because the calling of a faithful pastor was directly connected to the prosperity of the church. As a result, there was a comprehensive agreement among Particular Baptists that no man was sufficient for the office without the approbation of God's supplied grace; but because God established a man in the office, as confirmed by the people in a voluntary society, he also promised divine assistance as a reward for faithfulness and diligence. The vast majority of all Particular Baptist sermons at one time or another pose the question, "Who is sufficient for these things?"

Continuity in the Broader Particular Baptist Theological Tradition

Concerning the broader Particular Baptist tradition, Fuller shared essentially all the same foundational theological concerns and emphases. For example, there was homogeneity in their belief that the Bible was the supreme authority of all life and practice as articulated in the *Second London Confession*. They believed that its teachings were plain and clear and accessible to all men with the help of the Spirit of God, and that it was the foundation to all order and worship in the church, which regulated all Baptist practice. The Bible was also believed to be one of the key means to know God and his will for the church in the world. Fuller shared with other Baptists the importance of reading other biblically faithful secondary sources based on the Bible, however, they were always to be read as uninspired works of men subject to error and prejudice.

[1] Fuller, "Churches Fellow Helpers" in *Complete Works*, IV, 510.

Fuller's unique emphasis in this regard reflected the need for autonomous thinking that was characteristic of his whole life, for he regularly stressed the need to think independently and critically no matter how revered or respected the author was. This allowed Fuller to remain faithful to his tradition while critically evaluating some of its aspects—such as no offers of the gospel to all and sundry—in light of an infallibly authoritative Bible. Fuller also shared the Baptist belief that it was not enough to just know the facts of the Bible, but it was incumbent on every believer to live out these truths.

Another axiomatic truth that Fuller shared as foundational to all ministry was the centrality of the magnification of the glory of God, especially as reflected in a love for God and his people as the motive for all ministry. The glory of God was pre-eminently displayed through his redemptive purposes in Christ. For Fuller, as with the other Baptists, this defined success in ministry. That is also partly why they consistently highlighted the great importance of the work of the pastor at the beginning of the charge. The pastor was given an essential stewardship in the primary mission of God. This love was to be expressed in mutual love for God and one another, and so Fuller shares in common with many of his brethren the image of the shepherd as a favourite metaphor for the function of the pastoral office. They all emphasized that in a voluntary society the grand motive for communion was rooted in a love for God and his people.

Another commonality among Fuller in comparison with all other Particular Baptists was the centrality of Christ and the cross. Universally they taught that Christ was the central theme of all preaching. Without Christ there was no reconciliation with God and no way to enjoy fellowship and communion with him. Christ was the centre of all their thoughts, motives, and actions and they stressed this constantly. They expressed it most often through the phrase "preach Christ and not self," which meant that preaching should further the glory of Christ rather than promote the preacher's personal goals or self-interests.

Character Qualifications of a Minister

In terms of the descriptions of the character and qualifications of a minister, there is also a strong connection between Fuller and his tradition. It was very common in the charge to stress the reality of trials and temptations and to discuss the encouragement of God's promised help and comfort. They also reminded the ordinand that a great reward awaited all ministers who were faithful and diligent in the stewardship that God had entrusted to them. Fuller regularly articulated all these same concerns.

Generally, eighteenth-century Particular Baptists emphasized the need for consistency between the message the pastor preached and the life he lived as a prerequisite for success in ministry. Whereas the ordination sermons at the earlier part of the century stressed the specific New Testament qualifications of elders and deacons in Titus and Timothy by listing and describing each in turn, Fuller generally used broader descriptors such as piety and holiness as the necessary qualities of the elder. He was in complete homogeneity with other Baptists on the importance of only allowing qualified men in the office. Perhaps he used these more general categories for the pragmatic purpose of conserving time, as there is evidence that there was pressure to shorten the length of the services as the century advanced. Many later ordinations reflect this same trend. Also, the earlier idea of the excellence of biblical examples as a more effective teaching tool than mere precept continued in Fuller as an essential teaching for the ordinand.

Another area of continuity between Fuller and his brethren was the distinction between extraordinary and ordinary officers, as the vast majority of Particular Baptists seemed convinced that the unique, supernatural gifts ended with the apostles. They went to great pains to describe continuity between the contemporary office of elder with the early New Testament apostolic precedent, but distinguished some of these gospel-pioneer's powers as uniquely historically bound.

Finally, in the general area of the character of a pastor there was a common stress for the need for a complete devotion to his calling and the avoidance of the evils and distractions of the world. They stressed the importance of temperance and self-denial in every aspect of the pastor's personal and private life.

Duties of a Pastor

The Particular Baptists had clearly defined duties for a pastor with very little variation. They included ruling the church, preaching the Word, public prayer, dispensing the ordinances (Baptism and the Lord's Supper), visiting the people, presiding over singing and public meetings, and participating in other ordination ceremonies if called upon. These duties represented a stewardship from God and so the primary response of the pastor was to be faithful and diligent in fulfilling his charge. Fuller, in the tradition of his fathers, frequently mirrors this concern.

We have seen that Fuller describes the same essential duties as other Particular Baptists, especially preaching the Word and visitation, but does not discuss presiding over singing or participating in ordination services as a prescribed duty. In addition, perhaps somewhat surprisingly, Fuller rarely stresses the ordinances in terms of a specific duty of a minister. While he does mention dispensing them as a pastoral duty, he rarely explicates this duty, choosing instead to stress preaching both publicly and privately. It is surprising because elsewhere in his writings he deals extensively with the centrality of the ordinances, even arguing for closed communion against some of his closest friends at length.[2] Perhaps in the charge he was reticent to bring controversial and potentially distracting issues into the joyful proceedings of the day, knowing there was disparity here among the Baptists. He chose instead to encourage the ordinand in less conflict-ridden areas and withheld such a discussion for another time and place. This would be consistent with Fuller's central concern to avoid controversy when possible in the pulpit and with his stress on prudence in the method, manner, and purpose of specific discourses.

As a ruler or overseer Fuller tended to stress the importance of church discipline and careful membership requirements rather than some earlier Baptists who seemed more concerned to describe a theology of church order in and of itself. In the earlier part of the century the Baptists were closer to the political concerns leading to the Act of Toleration in 1689. These Baptists were concerned to clearly articulate issues of self-governance in the context of a politically tumultuous time. Fuller upheld these same principles, but with the enjoyment of increased freedom, they became less of an emphasis in the latter part of the century. Nonetheless, Fuller uses many of their popular metaphors such as the pastor as a shepherd, gardener, builder, or labourer.

As mentioned, Fuller's greatest emphasis was on the duty of the pastor to preach the Word for the edification of the saints and the salvation of sinners. The primary goal was not to make Baptists but to convert lost souls. Because this was so central to Fuller's emphasis as pastoral duty, a more thorough comparison, particularly with the Particular Baptist thought prior to the evangelical revival, is discussed below.

In regards to doctrine in ministry Fuller agreed with the Baptists' common emphasis that a minister must have firm convictions about what he preached, and so as reflected in their inherited Calvinistic confessions, he regularly called

[2] Fuller, "Ecclesiastical Polity" in *Complete Works*, III, 499, 508.

attention to the importance of the Doctrines of Grace, however, in Fuller it was not stressed to the degree found in the charges of John Brine. Brine would explicate in great detail the High-Calvinist stress on these doctrines, where Fuller would usually briefly define them and highlight their importance. But Fuller, akin to his forbears, often described the importance of doctrine in his sermons, at one time saying, "I love a sermon well laden with Christian Doctrine."[3] He, like Brine and Gill, also discussed the necessity and importance of preaching against false teaching to battle the main challenges to orthodoxy in their day, as seen particularly in Socinianism, Arianism, and Antinomianism.

False doctrine was an enemy to all Particular Baptists, but they went even further than a mere contentment with orthodoxy in teaching that the church must also have the correct sentiments of Scripture as well. Fuller, echoing earlier Baptists, believed that the manner of preaching was as important as the method, and so he insisted that the gospel must be preached with great affection. They were to preach doctrines practically and preach practice doctrinally, for the concern was to win the hearts of the people. Particular Baptists were concerned to teach the truth of the Bible to stir up emotions. For Fuller, "the union of genuine orthodoxy and affection constitutes true religion"[4] and even the earlier doyen of High-Calvinism himself, John Gill, had a very similar concern as discussed below. Regarding the manner of preaching, most Baptists believed in a plain, simple delivery with the goal that all and sundry would comprehend and apply its message to their lives.

Whereas some early Particular Baptists put the importance of public prayer on par with preaching, Fuller only mentions it, and never really develops public prayer as a chief pastoral duty. But as mentioned, he himself did participate in public prayer, as evidenced in the ordination service of Thomas Dunscombe. But his main emphasis in ordination sermons is clearly on private prayer to enhance personal communion with God.

Fuller, in complete unison with other Particular Baptists, often stressed the importance of the pastoral duty of visitation. The main content in his discussions of this pastoral duty very closely mirrors the same emphases of his Baptist brethren, with exhortations to frequently visit church members to know their spiritual state and to privately exhort, encourage, or rebuke as needed.

---

[3] Fuller, "Affectionate Concern" in *Complete Works*, IV, 490.

[4] Fuller, "Hold Fast the Gospel" in *Complete Works*, IV, 543.

In summary, an examination of Fuller's pastoral priorities as expressed in his ordination sermons concerning the character, qualifications, and duties of a pastor, which represents the chief subject matter of the ordination charge, shows a great deal of continuity with his Particular Baptist theological tradition. In these categories it is not likely that a congregant familiar with earlier eighteenth-century ordination sermons would have recognized any major disparity in regard to the general emphasis and content of the proceedings.

One noticeable emphasis in Fuller that is also reflected in other Baptists' ordination sermons at the latter part of the century is his stress summed up in the words "eminent spirituality and eminent usefulness." This must be analysed separately in light of Fuller's significant theological departure from some earlier Particular Baptists who were reluctant to offer the gospel to anyone without a warrant. In other words, was there a significant revamping of Particular Baptist pastoral theology, or was this re-correction a response to a historical abnormality that appeared near the beginning of the century?

Some scholars argue that the evangelical revival beginning in 1730 caused a major transformation within Particular Baptist pastoral theology.[5] They argue that there was an evangelical renewal of pastoral theology within the Particular Baptist church as witnessed in a significant alteration in the pastoral office. So the transformation of Particular Baptists to a more outward looking body, as they embraced evangelicalism in late eighteenth century, had an accompanying effect on their pastoral theology. Fuller's emphasis on conversion and the affections, in addition to a Congregationalist desire for orderliness, shows that this renewal happened inside the church. This is significant to this study because it is often argued that this renewed pastoral theology was expressed primarily through Fuller's preaching ministry described as plain (in style), evangelical (in content), and affectionate (in application), which also reflects the emphasis of evangelicalism in the eighteenth century. The evangelical transformation of the Particular Baptists was articulated mainly through a renewed pastoral theology, and was uniquely expressed through the congregationalism reflected by Andrew Fuller's pastoral theology.

But if it can be shown that, specifically in the area of these evangelical affections, voluntarism, and evangelical priorities like conversionism and

[5] Keith Grant, "Very Affecting and Evangelical: Andrew Fuller (1754-1815) and The Evangelical Renewal of Pastoral Theology" (ThM thesis, Regent College, 2007). This work has recently been published as a book in *Studies of Baptist History and Thought*, Keith S. Grant, *Andrew Fuller and the Evangelical Renewal of Pastoral Theology* (Keynes, UK: Paternoster, 2013).

crucicentrism, Fuller in fact showed significant continuity with his Baptist forbearers prior to around 1770 when the revival began to take hold among the Baptists, then this thesis is somewhat undermined. For even if there was a Baptist recovery of evangelism expressed through free offers of the gospel, this does not necessarily show a radical transformation of the pastoral office as an effect of the Enlightenment.

There is no doubt that Andrew Fuller is at the heart of a renewal of Particular Baptists in the late eighteenth century that impacted one key element of the pastoral office in offering Christ to all and sundry. But did this entail a complete revamping of Particular Baptists' perspective on pastoral ministry? In other words, when older Particular Baptists heard Andrew Fuller's ordination sermons, did what they hear differ significantly from what they heard as younger men and women, or did they hear much that was similar?

CONTINUITY IN THE AFFECTIONS PRIOR TO THE EVANGELICAL AWAKENING

It is instructive to analyse the continuity/discontinuity in pastoral theology between Fuller and his brethren of the earlier part of the century, especially in connection with the defining characteristic of Fuller's pastoral theology of eminent spirituality and eminent usefulness. As shown, much of this emphasis reflects the priorities of the new evangelicalism, especially in regard to language concerning the heart and affections, but also in the resulting evangelical pragmatism. Was Fuller's emphasis on conversions and the heart and holiness a new innovation, or is there evidence of it prior to and even during the dominant era of High-Calvinism?

Fuller and Nehemiah Coxe

Our analysis begins with the earliest extant Particular Baptist sermon at the beginning of the long eighteenth century by the prominent Baptist Nehemiah Coxe, in 1681. A contemporary of Coxe, C.M. du Veil, referred to Coxe as "that great divine, eminent for all a manner of learning."[6] As mentioned earlier he was also believed to have been significant in shaping the *Second London Confession*, to which all later Baptists were bound.

One of the most obvious signs of continuity between Coxe and Fuller is their mutual emphasis on the prominence of Christology as a central theme of

---

[6] Nehemiah Coxe, http://www.ccel.org/ccel/anonymous/bcf.iv.v.ix.html?highlight=nehemiah,coxe#highlight (accessed August 4, 2008).

their preaching. Coxe and Fuller regularly highlight the concept of *Aliquid Christi*, that is, something of Christ, in every sermon. There are also parallels in themes like the minister's need to be holy, to sincerely reflect the gospel he preaches, and to continually cultivate his God-given gifts.

Coxe and Fuller also stress the same basic duties of a pastor. In fact, their emphasis is almost identical, except that Coxe seems to make more of the duty of public prayer than Fuller. Throughout the sermon Coxe, like Fuller, emphasizes the necessity of the pastor to be a consistent example to the flock in both word and deed. He says the pastor must be a man "whose general conduct and demeanour is to the adorning of that doctrine which he possesses himself, and must teach others."[7] To be effective he must practice what he preaches by living a holy life that reflects the truth of the Scriptures. For Coxe, just like Fuller, this effectiveness is not just confined to the positive influence of emulation, but through divine communion, reflected in a piety that empowers his message by enlivening heavenly influences. Coxe says:

> it is no less than the evidence of Divine authority that will work upon the soul, and command the conscience of a man; whether it is by way of comfort, exhortation, or reproof, it is the stamp of heaven upon the things delivered by you that renders them powerful. Let it therefore be your principal care in preaching clearly to open and pertinently apply the Scriptures, that your hearers may bear away this conviction from your sermons, that you may "have the mind of Christ." It is not enough that the things you speak be true, but you must manifest them to be so by strong and convincing proof. Make conscience of giving, what in you lies, the very sense of the Holy Spirit in the Scriptures that you speak about.[8]

Although the power comes primarily from a divine influence on the Word preached, piety enhances a pastor's effectiveness.

For Coxe, although the content is crucial, the manner of preaching also bears directly upon pastoral efficacy. Like Fuller, he despises gesturing and yelling as a means for communicating divine truth, showing he is concerned with the sentiments as well as the precepts of Scripture. It is also interesting that Coxe utilizes some of the same biblical language as Fuller in relation to the importance of pastoral piety as an example to the flock. Coxe says:

---

[7] Coxe, *Sermon Preached*, 142.

[8] Coxe, *Sermon Preached*, 145.

> And all this pains must be enlivened by a holy example; for if a minister does not live under the instruction he gives to others, and appear a burning and shining light in life and conversation, as well as in doctrine, his ill manners will do more hurt, than all his words can ever do good. Examples have the greatest influence upon men.[9]

In Fuller's ordination sermon for the Rev. Robert Fawkner in 1787, he introduces the sermon by talking about the power of example for emulation in the context of the holy biblical example of Barnabas, and in a charge to another young minister Fuller instructs him, "burn with holy ardour" as a "burning and shining light."[10]

For Coxe, like Fuller, the goal of a holy example is evangelism. Concerning the task of preaching he says, "let your care be to deal with the souls and consciences of men, as knowing that it is the salvation of souls which you are to labour after."[11] Note also the prominent concern for their consciences which are connected to their emotions. The task of preaching for Coxe was about more than just dispensing biblical truth, but also reflects a desire to affect the minds and hearts of the hearers, making it purposeful or useful. Coxe says in an address to the church concerning the work of an elder:

> Their work is such, as they can never fill up their callings as they ought, but by the special aid and assistance of the Holy Spirit; the success of all their labours depends upon a Divine blessing and the presence of God with them; and in these things both the glory of Christ, and the comfort and edification of your own souls is nearly concerned; which is sufficient reason for your making conscience of this duty.[12]

In exhorting the people to pray for their pastor, Coxe attaches the need for divine empowering with success or usefulness in pastoral ministry, as seen in the edification of the people. Elsewhere, he connects the usefulness emerging from a divine influence on the pastor directly to success in preaching. For Coxe can say:

> He that will do the souls of his people good, and approve himself as a pastor after God's heart, must feed them with knowledge and

[9] Coxe, *Sermon Preached*, 147.
[10] Fuller, "Spiritual Knowledge" in *Complete Works*, IV, 479.
[11] Coxe, *Sermon Preached*, 145.
[12] Coxe, *Sermon Preached*, 151.

> understanding; and endeavour to maintain a constant zeal and affection in them, by well-informing their judgments, and such an opening of the mind of God from scriptures, and may command their consciences. ... Mistake me not! I know the success and fruit of all the studies and labours of him that preaches the Gospel is from the grace and power of the Holy Spirit; but the assistance of the Spirit is to be expected by us in way of our duty.[13]

Like Coxe, Fuller also emphasizes the goal of preaching, which is to stir people's affections.

So regarding eminent spirituality and eminent usefulness, Coxe also connects personal piety and the accompanying divine influence with usefulness in ministry as particularly expressed through the conversion of souls. It is also interesting that in this regard he frequently uses similar language to Fuller, such as "affection," "burning," "shining," "sense," "divine blessing," and the "mind of Christ." This demonstrates not only a very consistent degree of continuity with Fuller's emphasis on the duties and qualifications of a pastor, but also a substantial continuity with Fuller's main emphasis of eminent spirituality and eminent usefulness.

Fuller and Joseph Stennett

In another very early Particular Baptist ordination sermon by Joseph Stennett in 1705, there is also an emphasis on the pastoral duty to "teach people the mind of God." Like Coxe, Stennett stresses that God will supply the divine grace to be effective in ministry, and that the pastor's own example in piety and consistency is a model for effective preaching. He instructs the ordinand to be a "pattern to the flock that they may learn from your behaviour, as well as your preaching, how to practice the duties of Christian religion."[14] Again it is not just good doctrine that matters but a life that reflects that doctrine as a positive model for the church. The pastor must be "very pious and religious; devoted to prayer, reading and meditation when alone."[15] One of the main goals of the pastor, according to Stennett, is to "seek their increase in number, by the conversion of sinners, in preaching the gospel of Christ."[16] Stennett

---

[13] Coxe, *Sermon Preached*, 155.
[14] Stennett, *Sermon III*, 123.
[15] Stennett, *Sermon III*, 123.
[16] Stennett, *Sermon III*, 124.

seems to carry on with some of Coxe's emphasis where he connects the example of a pastor's ministry with success in the conversion of sinners.

Fuller and John Gill

The other major Particular Baptist figure of the eighteenth century and considered by many to be the father of High-Calvinism himself was John Gill (1697–1771). In his *Sermons and Tracts* there are four published ordination sermons containing charges from the years 1734, 1758, 1764, and 1766.[17] He was so influential among the Baptists, especially in the earlier half of the eighteenth century, that his authority was considered "oracular."[18] If there was a radical discontinuity in pastoral theology among the Particular Baptists between the earlier and latter part of the century, one might expect to find very different expressions of the office between Fuller and John Gill, especially in light of the fact that many nineteenth century Baptists polarized into two main camps designated "Gillites" and "Fullerites," as distinguished by the necessity of offering the gospel to everyone. There is a divide in their view of offering the gospel, which obviously had a bearing on the priorities in evangelism, but often the extent of the continuity between Gill and Fuller is overlooked. In regards to the centrality of the Bible, Christology, and other pastoral qualifications, there was little difference in emphasis between Gill's sermons and Fuller's. But what about in the area of the "heart"? Was there a radical theological separation from Fuller's main emphasis of eminent spirituality and eminent usefulness?

Greg Wills reveals that for Gill the "essence of Christian living was loving Christ" and even labels him primarily as "a theologian of the heart."[19] Wills believes that the main emphases in Gills' theology lay in "his promotion of Calvinism, his defence of believer's baptism, and his insistence on the religion of the heart."[20] It is this last point especially where Gill shows a great affinity to Fuller's own key theological emphasis, although, as discussed, it was also a central concern of Fuller to defend the Doctrines of Grace as well as uphold the ordinances of Baptism and the Lord's Supper.

---

[17] John Gill, *A Collection of Sermons and Tracts: In Two Volumes* (London: Keith, 1773), II.

[18] Gregory A. Wills, "A Fire that Burns Within: The Spirituality of John Gill" in *The Life and Thought of John Gill (1697–1771): A Tercentennial Appreciation*, Michael A.G. Haykin, ed. (Leiden: Brill, 1997), 191.

[19] Wills, *Fire that Burns*, 191.

[20] Wills, *Fire that Burns*, 191.

In Gill's ordination sermons there are regular appeals for evangelical spirituality. Like Fuller, he stresses the absolute necessity for a pastor to cultivate his gifts; for if he is not a good steward of them, they may decline, or even be lost entirely, which would render him ineffective. Like his predecessor Coxe, the goal of Christian preaching is not just to impart facts but to communicate spiritual light. So for example he can say in an ordination sermon from 1734 that if a minister doesn't cultivate his gifts, "all his light and knowledge, his abilities and usefulness, shall be taken from him."[21] Gill not only stresses the diligent use of means to cultivate God-given gifts, he also describes these means in the same way as Fuller, namely as Bible study, reading good men, meditation, and prayer.[22] For both men, who use essentially the same language to describe it, it resulted in "more light and knowledge." Gill often uses similarly affective language when describing the cultivation of these gifts. For example, he says, "Gifts are sometimes like coals of fire, covered and buried in ashes, ... which must be stirred up, or blown off, that they may revive and be re-inflamed, and so communicate more light and heat."[23] Gill, like Fuller, is concerned to reach the affections of his hearers for greater spiritual usefulness. He knows that a man cannot procure or increase these gifts himself, but only God gives "more light and knowledge by use of means."[24] So Gill says, mirroring Fuller's own emphasis and language:

> [I]t is the Lord that gives men an understanding to know them, that opens their hearts, and enlightens their minds by the spirit of wisdom and revelation, in the knowledge of them; for whatever understanding natural men may have of natural things, they have none of spiritual ones; there is none that understandeth, there is none that seeketh after God (Rom. 3:12) ... he gives to his ministers a larger understanding of divine things, and of the scriptures and the truths of them; he opens their understandings, as Christ did his disciples, that they may understand the scriptures; he gives unto them to know the mysteries of the kingdom of heaven, to a greater degree than he does to others; and he enlarges their understandings, and increases their gifts, their light, and knowledge; ... and the Lord will give thee understanding in all things; and so is used as an encouragement to consider well what had been said,

---

21 Gill, *Duty of a Pastor*, 4.

22 These are usually the written works by men who have been proven orthodox and effective in ministry.

23 Gill, *Duty of a Pastor*, 5.

24 Gill, *Duty of a Pastor*, 5.

> and to expect a richer furniture of knowledge, and a larger measure of spiritual light and understanding; and as Christ gives more light to his people, who are made light by him; and there is such a thing as growing in grace, and in the knowledge of Christ, and of all spiritual things, in common Christians; and the path of the just is as the shining light that shines more and more unto the perfect day; so faithful ministers of the word, who are diligent and industrious in their work, may expect, and be assured, that God will give them an enlarged knowledge and understanding of divine truths, and of everything necessary to the due performance of that sacred work they are called unto, and holy office they are invested with. I shall close, as I begun, with the words of my text, Consider what I say, or have been saying; consider the work of the ministry, that it is a work, and a laborious one. ... May the blessing of God rest upon you, and may you have success in your work.[25]

Gill is describing an enlightening of the mind and heart that sounds very much like Fuller's own language. He, like Fuller, is seeking the mind of Christ for greater spiritual light and understanding, which is necessary for the effective performance of his task as a pastor. In other words, so he can be more useful; for in describing the pastor who appropriates these means Gill encourages the ordinand to be, "in frequent prayer, constant meditation, and in daily reading the scriptures, and the writings of good men; which are transmitted to posterity for the benefit and advantage of the churches of Christ."[26] For Gill, this usefulness cultivated through personal spirituality was primarily expressed in terms of giving the gospel to the world. He says, "the commission of gospel-ministers being to go into all the world, and preach the gospel to every creature."[27]

In unison with their Particular Baptist tradition both Gill and Fuller are very similar in their expression of the importance of the minister's own example for success. They stress that personal holiness, after the example of Christ, must apply to all aspects of their lives, public and private. Both warn that if a pastor's example doesn't match his teaching, it may be indicative of his unhappy eternal state, so both warn the ordinands to guard their hearts. Gill, like Fuller, connects a minister's usefulness with his character:

---

[25] Gill, *Work of a Gospel-Minister* in *Sermons and Tracts*, II, 28.
[26] Gill, *Duty of a Pastor*, 5.
[27] Gill, *Doctrine of the Cherubim* in *Sermons and Tracts*, II, 41.

> [E]very Christian ought to adorn the doctrine of God our Saviour, but most especially the preachers of it; their lights should so shine before men, that they seeing their good works, may glorify their father which is in heaven. The name of God, the ways of Christ, and the truths of the gospel, are blasphemed, and spoken evil of, through the scandalous lives of professors, and especially ministers. Nothing is more abominable than that one, whose business it is to instruct and reprove others, is himself notoriously culpable; to such a person and case, the words of the apostle are very applicable, Thou therefore that teachest another, teachest thou not thyself?[28]

Likewise, Fuller repeatedly warns that one of the greatest dangers for a minister is to neglect his own heart, leading to his eventual condemnation.

Although for Gill it was not enough that a minister know the truth on just an intellectual level but also must adorn it through his example, for him doctrine was the chief means to this passionate spirituality. In fact, at times he even relates the orthodoxy of a doctrine to its effect on hearers, saying, "Whatever doctrines are subversive of true piety, or strike at the life and power of godliness, are to be rejected: if any man teach otherwise, and consent not to wholesome words, even the words of our Lord Jesus Christ, and to the doctrine which is according to godliness; he is proud, knowing nothing."[29] But Gill was not content to encourage the ordinand to improve only the content of his preaching, but because he was concerned to affect the hearts of his listeners, he also encouraged the importance of perfecting the manner of preaching. He not only advised the standard Particular Baptist exhortation on plain speaking, but also cautions:

> It is also very advisable that he take heed that he express his doctrine in the best manner, and to the best advantage. He ought to be careful about the manner as well as the matter of his ministry; that he speak plainly, intelligibly, and boldly, the gospel, as it ought to be spoken: Elocution, which is a gift of utterance, a freedom of expression, with propriety of language, is one of the gifts fitting for public usefulness in the work of the ministry; and which may be improved by the use of proper means.[30]

---

28 Gill, *Duty of a Pastor*, 7.
29 Gill, *Duty of a Pastor*, 10.
30 Gill, *Duty of a Pastor*, 10.

This is because the manner is a key element in effectively involving the affections of his listeners, which is the goal of preaching. Gill says, "let controversy, as little as may be, be brought into the pulpit; controversial sermons, when best managed, are generally unedifying ones to the people in common; tend to damp the true spirit of religion and devotion, which it is the design of preaching the word to excite."[31] The goal is to reach people's emotions through the truth preached.

The necessity of divine influence for effectiveness is also a common feature of Gill's ordination sermons. He often uses evangelical language of light, warmth, and fervency in Spirit. He says of pastors:

> [I]t is requisite they should be lively in their ministrations; it is most comfortable to themselves, and best for those to whom they minister, when they are lively in their frames, lively in the exercise of grace, and in the discharge of duty; when they are fervent in spirit, while they are serving the Lord their God; and under a divine influence, they are the savour of life unto life; the instruments and means of quickening dead sinners, and of reviving and refreshing drooping saints; and happy are those that sit under the ministry of the living creatures, regenerate men, the living and lively ministers of the gospel.[32]

The minister would not benefit others unless he himself was under a divine influence. He must first be enlightened before enlightening others. For Gill, pastors needed to have:

> their eyes enlightened, their understandings opened by Christ, as were the disciples; the scriptures are to be diligently searched into, and explored for the rich treasure that is in them; and those that search into them, as for hid treasure, shall find knowledge of great and excellent things; but these escape the sight of all but those who have spiritual eyes to see.[33]

As has been demonstrated, Fuller saw the main goal of the minister as "enlightening the minds and affecting the hearts" of his hearers. Gill also sounds very much like Fuller when describing the necessity of a pastor to love his sheep as a prerequisite for ministry. He says:

---

[31] Gill, *Work of a Gospel-Minister* in *Sermons and Tracts*, II, 18.
[32] Gill, *Doctrine of the Cherubim* in *Sermons and Tracts*, II, 38.
[33] Gill, *Doctrine of the Cherubim* in *Sermons and Tracts* II, 43.

> Feed my lambs, feed my sheep (John 21:15–17), intimating, that such a lover of him was a fit person to feed the flock or church of God; even one whose love is so ardent that the coals thereof are coals of fire, which hath a most vehement flame, that many waters cannot quench; even waters of afflictions, reproaches, persecutions, and sufferings for the sake of Christ and his gospel: and by coals of fire may they he described, because of their burning zeal for the glory of God and the interest of a Redeemer; hence they are called Seraphim, fiery or burning, as before observed; and it is not unusual for ministers of the gospel to be compared to lamps; the apostles are called the lights or lamps of the world; and John the Baptist was a shining and burning light or lamp; and so others have been, holding forth the word of light and life to men: and whereas it is said that it, the fire, went up and down among the living creatures; this is true of the word of God, compared to fire, Jeremiah 20:9 and 23:29, by which the minds of ministers are enlightened, their hearts warmed, and are filled with zeal for God, and become the means of enlightening and warming others; which fire was bright, clear, as the word of God is; and out of the fire went forth lightning; denoting the quick and penetrating efficacy of the word, and the sudden increase of the kingdom and interest of Christ by it, which, like lightning, has been spread from east to west.[34]

Again, it is hard to miss the affective language so characteristic of the evangelical revival, like "warming" and "enlightened minds." Fuller even uses similar biblical metaphors to Gill, like shepherds tending their sheep or farmers breaking up the fallowed ground of men's hearts.[35]

For Gill, this divine influence results in divine empowering in the task. The eminent spirituality of a minister would usually produce eminent effectiveness. He says:

> [T]he ... gospel ... under the divine influence; and which is not the voice, sound and word of man, but of God himself; which appears by its powerful effects on the hearts of saints and sinners, when attended with a divine energy; and indeed it is the Lord God almighty that speaks in ministers, and speaks powerfully by them, 1 Thessalonians 2:13; 2 Corinthians 13:3.[36]

---

[34] Gill, *Doctrine of the Cherubim* in *Sermons and Tracts* II, 44; Fuller, "Feed the Flock" in *Complete Works*, IV, 477.

[35] Gill, *Doctrine of the Cherubim* in *Sermons and Tracts*, II, 44.

[36] Gill, *Doctrine of the Cherubim* in *Sermons and Tracts*, II, 45.

Like Fuller, Gill often gives strong appeal for activism where he can say, for example, that Ezekiel 1:8 and 10:8,

> denotes the activity of gospel-ministers, who have not only the theory and knowledge of things, but are men of practice and business; they have much work to do all around them, on every side preaching the gospel, administering ordinances, visiting their people, praying with them, and giving them counsel and advice, instruction and exhortation, when needful.[37]

Gill also distinguishes between natural and divine knowledge, which allows for a theological rationale for a spirituality of the heart and the head. There is a natural knowledge available to all men and spiritual knowledge requiring divine illumination, so accordingly Gill says, "the ministers of the gospel have need of a large share of knowledge, both of things natural and spiritual; knowledge of themselves, and of their state by nature and by grace, and an experience of the work of the spirit of God upon their hearts."[38] Both Gill and Fuller warn against Satan's attacks on the minister to distort both types of knowledge.

In Gill's ordination sermons there is also a strong and constant emphasis on usefulness, directly connected with the empowering of the Spirit especially towards effectiveness in evangelism. First off, he describes the necessity of holiness in a minister by saying, "Ministers, by taking heed to themselves, may, through a divine blessing, and the influences of the Spirit of God, save themselves from an untoward generation, and be preferred from the pollutions of the world."[39] He gives the specific reason ministers must watch both their life and doctrine:

> What can, or does, more strongly engage ministers to take heed to themselves, to their doctrine, and abide therein, than this? That they may be useful in the conversion, and so in the salvation of precious and immortal souls, which are of more worth than a world: He that converteth a sinner from the error of his way, shall save a soul from death, and shall hide a multitude of sins (Jam. 5:20).[40]

---

[37] Gill, *Doctrine of the Cherubim* in *Sermons and Tracts*, II, 45.
[38] Gill, *Doctrine of the Cherubim* in *Sermons and Tracts*, II, 39.
[39] Gill, *Duty of a Pastor*, 12.
[40] Gill, *Duty of a Pastor*, 13.

Holiness leads to usefulness in the mandate of the pastor primarily expressed through the conversion of souls.

Like Fuller, Gill envisions the pastoral work as that of a labourer. To be successful Gill advises ordinands that, "it requires much reading of the scriptures, frequent prayer; constant meditation, and study to prepare for it; and much study is a weariness to the flesh (Eccl. 12:12): and in the performance of this service, with that zeal, fervour, and affection, which are necessary to it, a man, to use the apostle's phrase, may spend and be spent (2 Cor. 12:15)."[41] The means for the cultivation of the affections is for greater usefulness.

The main difference between Fuller and Gill is not in the primary objective of the spirituality of the heart. The main difference is in the method. Gill was reluctant to offer the gospel to all, his style was more didactic, and he didn't plead with sinners in the same way Fuller did. Rather, Gill believed that it was through teaching doctrine truthfully and carefully that this warm spirituality was achieved. Whereas both Gill and Fuller knew that true spirituality came through the head and heart, at times Gill emphasised a more rational appropriation of holiness. Still their final objective of eminent personal experience of communion with God differed little in form or substance. Both wanted to reach the hearts of their hearers. Also both connected the usefulness of the preacher directly with this personal spirituality. For Gill the divine power of the Word seemed to lay more in the declaration than in the exhortation, though in practice, as Wills observes, "The brevity of Gill's exhortations differed little from the practice of Andrew Fuller (1754–1815), the Northamptonshire pastor and missionary leader who promotes universal invitations. Fuller's sermons exhibited a rhetorical method fully as didactic as Gill's and used as little exhortation."[42]

Fuller and John Brine

The other major figure for the early Baptists was the High-Calvinist John Brine (1703–1765). His main emphasis in the charge usually took the form of detailed doctrinal expositions explicating the necessity of the Doctrines of Grace understood from a High-Calvinist perspective. He like Gill was reticent to offer the gospel to all people.[43] Still even with his emphasis, these doctrines were to

[41] Gill, *Work of a Gospel-Minister* in *Sermons and Tracts*, II, 15.
[42] Wills, *Fire that Burns*, 204.
[43] Wills, *Fire that Burns*, 207.

"be embraced and held with the Heart, as made holy by the Operations of God's Spirit upon it. The Head is not the Seat of evangelical Truths when they are received in a spiritual Manner, but the Soul, the Heart, and Mind."[44] And his ultimate goal was a "warm affection to Christ."[45] He also regularly warned that those who preach the gospel must live the gospel. The things the minister teaches must be mixed with faith and he must live out the truths he preaches.[46]

Fuller and Others Prior to the Revival

In the remaining sermons prior to when the evangelical revival was thought to have significantly affected the Particular Baptists in 1770, there is a great deal of continuity with Fuller's emphasis on eminent spirituality and eminent usefulness. For example, in 1760 at the ordination of Joshua Wood, Isaac Mann describes the nature of the ministry of a pastor to his people to "labour with their affections, to draw them (the people) from the things below, and excite them to things above."[47] And to pray for their pastor for their own maximum benefit, that he might have "much holy warmth and pleasure in his meditation."[48] so he could "enjoy a large measure of the Spirit of God, and of the spirit of prayer and supplication, ... and lay all your cases before his heavenly Father is a pertinent affectionate manner."[49] His spirituality would enhance the spiritual affections making him more useful to the congregation.

In 1767 Samuel Stennett reiterates the standard Baptist teaching that example has a greater influence on the mind than precept and instructs the ordinand to "treat doctrines practically and duties evangelically."[50] He states the goal of preaching is to "labour by all possible means to get at the hearts and feelings of those who hear you."[51] And to accomplish this, the ordinand is encouraged to "enter yourself into the spirit of it, and be not content unless others feel it with you. Speak in the presence of God and as one who remembers he is to give an account. ... In a word, let your preaching be preceeded [*sic*] and followed with your earnest cries to heaven for success."[52] Again the heart is

---

[44] Brine, *Deacons* (1735), 5.
[45] Brine, *Deacons* (1735), 6.
[46] Brine, *Diligence in Study*, 12; Fuller uses a very similar phrase.
[47] Crabtree, "Regard which the Churches of Christ Owe" in Mann, *Memoirs*, 66.
[48] Crabtree, "Regard which the Churches of Christ Owe" in Mann, *Memoirs*, 92.
[49] Crabtree, "Regard which the Churches of Christ Owe" in Mann, *Memoirs*, 93.
[50] Stennett, *Charge Delivered*, 46.
[51] Stennett, *Charge Delivered*, 46.
[52] Stennett, *Charge Delivered*, 47.

the center of successful ministry. Stennett also distinguishes between natural and spiritual knowledge in relation to improving gifts and again connects spirituality with usefulness. He says, "And let me remind you of what I am well persuaded you are sensible, that an exact just and critical knowledge of the scriptures will be of little avail either to your comfort or usefulness, if it be not experimental and practical. Study therefore your own heart."[53] This experimental religion comes through communion with Christ in prayer, reading, and meditation.[54] Again the express purpose is the conversion of souls, for he says, "And above all, as the grand object of preaching is the converting men from their sins, and the saving their souls; so as to deal properly with their understandings, consciences, and passions, on these interesting matters, makes study and preparations, in a dependence upon a superior influence, of very great importance."[55]

Conclusion

As the century progressed to the early nineteenth century, the same basic duties and qualifications were described in these ordination sermons. Fuller's emphasis on eminent spirituality and eminent usefulness was more closely mirrored by his contemporaries as the revival took hold. Especially in sermons from Caleb Evans in the West Counties there was a predominance of evangelical language and exhortations for enhanced ministerial usefulness through personal holiness. But there remained a strong continuity with the Particular Baptists of the earlier part of the century even when compared with those affected by High-Calvinism. This close continuity does not argue in favour of a radical redefinition of pastoral theology transformed by the so-called rise of evangelicalism. The main difference, in terms of renewal, centred on a return to biblical precedent of offering the gospel freely to all. The diversion of this emphasis was connected to the rise of High-Calvinist dogma precipitated by a defence of the orthodoxy from the attacks of a rationalist age. Still Baptist preaching was consistently plain in style, evangelical in content, and affectionate in application.

The increased numerical growth of the Particular Baptists, as seen especially in the latter half of the eighteenth century, cannot be attributed principally to a radical reshaping of their pastoral theology. In fact, it has been

---

[53] Stennett, *Charge Delivered*, 51.
[54] Stennett, *Charge Delivered*, 52.
[55] Stennett, *Charge Delivered*, 59.

demonstrated that there was extensive continuity between the pastoral theology of Fuller and his forefathers like Nehemiah Coxe in the seventeenth century, and even those with High-Calvinist leanings in the early part of the eighteenth century.

Although it may be tempting to try to explain the more outward focus of these Baptists by describing a fundamental change in their essential pastoral theological priorities as the raison d'être behind their numerical growth, it does not fully reflect the reality of contemporary Baptists' ideals, and therefore, hints of anachronism and historical eisegesis. While it is true they were more evangelistically outward looking than many of their High-Calvinist leaning brethren, this was likely more the result of a return to the evangelical priorities of their seventeenth century Baptist forerunners; for as we have seen they also emphasized the priority of the affections in preaching as a necessity for the salvation of souls. The theological anomaly of the High-Calvinist Baptists in the early part of the eighteenth century helped to accentuate this inward, "garden enclosed" mentality, which was precipitated through their reticence concerning the free offer of the gospel, which likely impacted their evangelistic efforts and most probably also their numeric growth. The main elements of Particular Baptist pastoral theology, however, continued with great fidelity throughout the long eighteenth century.

Further, rather than a radical pastoral theological revamping, Fuller's demolition of High-Calvinist dogma was in fact more of a renewal of earlier Baptist evangelical priorities and in this sense was more of a revitalization of pastoral theology within their tradition. It represented a return to the old ways, albeit within the newly evolving context of a nascent shift from Enlightenment to Romantic ideals.

Therefore, rather than a radical redefinition forged by the mysterious and powerful forces of Enlightenment thought, these men were influenced, perhaps more so, by a static theological commitment rooted in biblical authority. Yes, they were men of their age, but they were also men whose central mandate had a passion to reshape contemporary society in light of their biblical worldview, which was fundamentally countercultural. Their evangelism included a concern to establish God's kingdom on earth, which was at conflict with the very emphasis of the times, namely, the authority of human rationalism. They believed that the success of the former objective was contingent on their fidelity to divine revelation. Their sole and absolute authority was the Scriptures, which they were convinced was the God-breathed revelation of a sovereign and transcendent, all-wise being. It is not as though they were immune from all societal influence, but it must be acknowledged that a major aspect of their calling was to resist these very forces by establishing an ideological counterattack with their own almost antithetical philosophical priorities.

Fuller's life and ministry demonstrated, especially through his many polemical publications battling many of the reigning philosophical dogmas of his day like Socinianism, that he understood his times and the theological dangers they posed to his Christian mandate. He spent a significant portion of his time and ministry battling them in print. With so much intellectual and personal moral effort extended to counter these societal pressures, it is hard to believe that he naively inherited its tenets to the point of radical revamping of his calling for the sake of an evangelistic pragmatism. For even though he emphasized, as a central priority, the salvation of souls, this goal was still subservient to the higher Particular Baptist priority to glorify God as the chief end of man. In other words, the means mattered as much, or more so, than the end. If the means used for evangelism did not glorify God, then there would be great internal theological pressure to render that way unacceptable, resulting in abandonment. Since they believed that God had ordained the means, most often by using pious men to preach the Word, any perceived deviation was unlikely to be internally viewed as effective in eternity. Above all, their desire was to be a people conformed to a biblical worldview which inherently sought to resist the pressure of the reigning world view.

Another potential danger of suggesting Fuller as a significant agent of redefinition within the Calvinistic Baptist theological tradition as a result of Enlightenment influence, is that it gives far too much credence to the authority of societal pressures on the church and in that sense is too simplistic. This is because those who argue this imply, or even outwardly declare, that the seeds of pastoral change are more dominant outside the church than within. Throughout its history the church has in fact sometimes successfully resisted the dominant and opposing priorities of contemporary worldviews quite effectively. She does not always substantially change her internal theological nature within a tradition based on these powerful societal forces and can even, in some cases—as during the Great Awakening—in fact, generate substantial biblical influence back in return.

That is not to say that culture had no influence on contemporary eighteenth-century Baptist churches, or that there was no discontinuity whatsoever between these later Baptists and earlier representations. There were certainly varying theological emphases that later Particular Baptists seemed not to share with their theological fathers of the seventeenth century. The fundamental nature and goals of their theological priorities remained essentially the same, albeit perhaps expressed in what they felt were more contemporarily relevant terms, and perhaps with some accentuated emphases on what they thought was now more essential. For as the priorities of a culture change so does the emphatic expression of certain aspects of a fixed theological dogma which is inherently designed to communicate an unchanging message to an ever-changing world.

About the Author

Nigel Wheeler was born in Hailsham, England and emigrated to Canada at the age of six. He is married to his wife Janice and they have five children.

He graduated as Valedictorian at Briercrest Bible College and was elected to membership in the American Association of Bible Colleges Honor Society (Delta Epsilon Chi) and received a Bachelor of Arts in Bible and Theology—Bible Major. He then graduated with high honours from Trinity Western University with a Masters Degree in Theology winning the "Governor General's Gold Medal" for academic excellence at the graduate level, and earned his Ph.D in Theology at the University of Pretoria, S.A. Nigel has taught at both the college and graduate level and is currently Senior Pastor at Lakeview Bible Church in Lethbridge, Alberta, Canada (2007).

He is a visiting professor at Cameroon Baptist Seminary, West Africa; and is the former chaplain for the Toronto Blue Jays, MLB team.

Acknowledgments

I would like to thank the University of Pretoria, as this work is based on research carried out while studying there. I would especially like to thank Professor Graham Duncan, as well as many at Oxford University and the Bristol Baptist College. Thanks also to Michael Haykin for encouraging me to study the life and ministry of Andrew Fuller, and for guiding me through much of this research.

I would like to thank my wife Janice, whose steadfast love and competence made this project happen, and also my children Ali, Jay, Ryan, Katie, and Holly for their sacrifice.

Thanks to our loving church family at Lakeview Bible Church (www.lbclethbridge.org) in Lethbridge, Alberta, Canada. Especially to Arnold and Kathy Thiessen, Theo and Esther Slingerland and Bill and Jackie Oudshoorn. With a deep appreciation and Christian love to my "rope holder," Maurice Indenbosch along with his dear wife Henriette.

Subject Index

Scripture Index

Old Testament

New Testament

Bibliography

Primary Sources

The Baptist Magazine. Vols. 1-57, 1809-65. London: J. Burditt, 1809-10; W. Button, 1809-18; W. Whitemore, 1819; B.J. Holdsworth, 1820-25; Wightman and Cramp, 1826-8; G. Whiteman, 1829-40; Houlston and Stoneman, 1841-56; Pewtress, 1857-63; J. Heaton, 1857-60; Elliot Stock, 1864-5.

"The Baptist Missionary Society Archives: 1792-1914." Angus Library, Regent's Park College, Oxford University. [Available in microfilm.]

Bogue, David and Bennett, James, *History of Dissenters: From the Revolution to the Year 1838.* 3 vols. Stoke-on-Trent, UK: Tentmaker Publications, 2000.

Booth, Abraham. *An Essay on the kingdom of Christ.* 1788. Reprinted, Paris, AK: Baptist Standard Bearer, 1987.

_____. *The Reign of Grace: From Its Rise to its Consummation.* Leeds, UK: Griffith Wright, 1768.

Boswell, James. *Boswell's London Journal, 1762-1763.* Edited by F.A. Pottle. New York: McGraw Hill, 1956.

Bunyan, John. *Grace Abounding to the Chief of Sinners and the Pilgrim's Progress.* Edited by Roger Sharrock. London: Oxford University Press, 1966.

Carey, William. *An Enquiry into the Obligations of Christians to use means for the Conversion of the Heathens.* Facsimile ed. 1792. Reprint, London: Baptist Missionary Society, 1942.

Collins, Hercules. *The Temple Repair'd: Or, An Essay to revive the long-neglected Ordinances, of exercising the Spiritual Gift of Prophecy for the Edification of the Churches; and of ordaining Ministers duly qualified. With proper Directions as to Study and Preaching, for such as are inclined to the Ministry.* London: William and Joseph Marshal, 1702.

Coxe, Nehemiah. *A Sermon Preached at the Ordinatoin of an Elder and Deacons in a Baptized Congregation in London.* London: Tho. Fabian, 1681.

_____. *A discourse of the covenants that God made with men before the law wherein the covenant of circumcision is more largely handled, and the invalidity of the plea for pædobaptism taken from thence discovered / by Nehemiah Coxe.* [London], 1681.

Crosby, Thomas, *The History of the English Baptists, From the Reformation to the Beginning of the Reign of King George I.* 4 vols. London, 1738.

Defoe, Daniel. *A Tour Through the Whole Island of Great Britain.* Harmondsworth, UK: Penguin Books, 1971.

Edwards, Jonathan. *An Humble Attempt to Promote Explicit Agreement and Visible Union of God's People for the Revival of Religion and Advancement of Christ's Kingdom on Earth*. Boston, 1747.

______. *Freedom of the Will.* Edited by Paul Ramsay. New Haven: Yale University Press, 1957.

______. *The Life of David Brainerd.* Edited by Norman Pettit. New Haven: Yale University Press, 1985.

______. *The Works of Jonathan Edwards*. 2 vols. Edited by E. Hickman. 1834. Reprint, Edinburgh, UK: Banner of Truth Trust, 1976.

Fawcett, J., Jr. *An Account of the Life, Ministry and Writings of the Late Rev John Fawcett, D. D.* London: Baldwin, Craddock and Joy, 1818.

Fuller, Andrew. *The Complete Works of the Rev. Andrew Fuller with a Memoir of His Life by Andrew Gunton Fuller*. Edited by Joseph Belcher. 3 vols. 1845. Reprint, Harrisonburg, VA: Sprinkle, 1988.

______. *The Complete Works of the Rev. Andrew Fuller, With a Memoir of his Life by the Rev Andrew Gunton Fuller. A New Edition in Five Volumes.* London: William Ball, 1837.

______. *The Gospel of Christ Worthy of All Acceptation: or the Obligations of Men Fully to Credit, and Cordially to Approve, Whatever God Makes Known. Where in is Considered the Nature of Faith in Christ, and the Duty of Those Where the Gospel Comes in that Matter.* Northampton, UK: T. Dicey, 1785.

______. *Hints to Ministers and Churches*. London: Holdsworth, 1828.

______. *The Last Remains of the Rev. Andrew Fuller: Sermons, Essays, Letters, and Other Miscellaneous Papers, Not Included in His Published Works*. Edited by Joseph Belcher. Philadelphia: American Baptist Publication Society, 1856.

______. *Fuller's Book List.* 1798. Housed at Bristol Baptist College.

______. *Fuller's Common Place Book*. N.d. Housed at Bristol Baptist College.

______. *Fuller's Diary and Spiritual Thoughts.* [1784–1801]. Housed at Bristol Baptist College.

______. *Fuller's Kettering Sermons and Letters*. N.d. Housed at Kettering Baptist Church.

______. *Fuller's Short-hand Sermons.* "Sermon outlines and exegetical notes, Aug, 26th–Dec. 19th, 1813." 1813. Housed at Kettering Baptist Church.

______. *The Letters of Andrew Fuller.* N.d. Transcribed by Ernest Payne and scanned to disc by Nigel Wheeler. Originals and transcriptions in the Angus Library, Regent's Park College, Oxford University.

Fuller, Andrew Gunton. *Men Worth Remembering: Andrew Fuller.* London: Hodder & Stoughton, 1882.

______. *The Principal Works and Remains of the Rev. Andrew Fuller with a Memoir of His Life by His Son.* London: Henry G. Bohn, 1852.

Fuller, Thomas Ekins. *A Memoir of the Life and Writings of Andrew Fuller: By his Grandson, Thomas Ekins Fuller.* London: J. Heaton & Son, 1863.

George Wallis' Diary. "Memoirs, etc., — 1805-1817." 1805-1817. Housed at Kettering Baptist Church.

Gill, John. *A Body of Doctrinal Divinity; Or A System of Evangelical Truths, Deduced from the Sacred Scriptures.* Paris, AR: Baptist Standard Bearer, 1839.

______. *A Collection of Sermons and Tracts: In Two Volumes.* London, 1773.

______. *The Duty of Churches Respecting the Encouragement of Spiritual Gifts. The Circular Letter from the Baptist Ministers and Messengers, Assembled at St. Albans, May 31, and June 1, 2, 1796.* N.p., [1796].

______. *An Exposition of the Old Testament.* Vol. 4. The Baptist Commentary Series. London: Mathews and Leigh, 1810.

Hall, Robert, Sr. *Help to Zion's Travellers.* London: Book Society, 1781.

Hall, Robert. "Reminiscences of the Rev. Robert Hall, A. M." In Olinthus Gregory and Joseph Belcher, eds. *The Works of the Rev. Robert Hall, A. M. with a Memoir of his Life, by Dr. Gregory; Reminiscences, by John Greene, ESQ.; and his Character as a Preacher, by the Rev. John Foster.* 6 vols. New York: Harper and Brothers, 1854.

Haykin, Michael A.G. *The Armies of the Lamb: The Spirituality of Andrew Fuller.* Dundas: Joshua Press, 2001.

Ivimey, Joseph. *A History of the English Baptists: Comprising the Principal Events of the History of Protestant Dissenters, from the Revolution in 1688 till 1760; and of the London Baptist Churches, During that Period.* 4 vols. London: B.J. Holdsworth, 1856.

Keach, Benjamin. *The Glory of a True Church and Its Discipline Display'd: Wherein True Gospel-Church is Described. Together with the Power of the Keys, and who are to be let in, and who are to be shut out.* London: John Robinson, 1697.

Marshman, John C. *The Life and Times of Carey, Marshman, and Ward.* 2 vols. London, 1859.

Martha Wallis' Will. September 6, 1812. Housed at Kettering Baptist Church.

Maurice, Matthias. *A Modern Question Modestly Answer'd.* London: James Buckland, 1737.

Morris, J.W. *Memoirs of the Life and Writings of the Rev. Andrew Fuller*. London: Wightman and Cramp, 1826.

______, ed. *Miscellaneous Pieces on Various Subjects, Being the Last Remains of the Rev. Andrew Fuller. Collected and Arranged, with Occasional Notes, by J. W. Morris: Intended as a Supplement to His Memoirs of the Author*. London: Wightman and Cramp, 1826.

______., ed. *Periodical Accounts Relative to a Society, formed among The Particular Baptists, for Propagating the Gospel among the Heathen*. 3 vols. London, 1800.

Original Minute book of the Church at Kettering. [1768?–1815]. Bound Autograph Manuscript. Housed at Kettering Baptist Church.

Rippon, John. *The Baptist Annual Register: For 1794, 1795, 1796–1797. Including Sketches of the State of Religion Among Different Denominations of Good Men at Home and Abroad*. London: Dilly, Button, Thomas, 1796.

Ryland, John, Jr. *The Work of Faith, the Labour of Love, and the Patience of Hope, Illustrated; in the Life and Death of the Reverend Andrew Fuller*. London: Button and Son, 1816, 1818.

Stuart, Charles. *A Short Memoir of the Late Mr. Andrew Fuller*. London: Britten & Son, 1815.

Ward, William. *A Sketch of the Character of the late Rev. Andrew Fuller, in a Sermon Preached at The Lal Bazar Chapel, Calcutta, on Lord's Day, October 1, 1815*. London: Button & Son, 1817.

White, B.R. *Association Records of the Particular Baptists of England, Wales and Ireland to 1660*. 3 parts. London: Baptist Historical Society, 1971.
Part 1: *South Wales and the Midlands*.
Part 2: *The West Country and Ireland*.
Part 3: *The Abingdon Association*.

Secondary Sources

Ascol, Thomas Kennedy. "The Doctrine of Grace: A Critical Analysis of Federalism in the Theologies of John Gill and Andrew Fuller." PhD diss., Southwestern Baptist Theological Seminary, 1989.

______. "The Pastor as Theologian." *Founders Journal* 43 (2001): 1–10.

Barker-Benfield, G.J. *The Culture of Sensibility: Sex and Society in Eighteenth-Century Britain*. Chicago: University of Chicago Press, 1992.

Bebbington, D. *Evangelicalism in Modern Britain: A History from the 1730s to the 1980s*. Grand Rapids, MI: Baker Book House, 1990.

______. *The Gospel in the World: International Baptist Studies*, Studies in Baptist History and Thought, vol. 1, 1–9. Carlisle, U.K.; Waynesboro, GA: Paternoster, 2002.

Black, J. William. *Reformation Pastors: Richard Baxter and the Ideal of the Reformed Pastor.* Studies in Christian History and Thought. Carlisle, UK; Waynesboro, GA: Paternoster, 2004.

Bogart, Dan. "Turnpike Trusts and the Transportation Revolution in 18th Century England" (http://orion.oac.uci.edu/~dbogart/transportrev_oct13.pdf).

Brackney, William H. *A Genetic History of Baptist Thought: With Special reference to the Baptists in Britain and North America.* Macon, GA: Mercer, 2004.

Bradley, James E., and Richard. A. Muller. *Church History: An Introduction to Research, Reference Works, and Methods.* Grand Rapids, MI: William B. Eerdmans, 1995.

Brewster, Paul. "Andrew Fuller (1754-1815): Model Baptist Pastor-Theologian" PhD thesis, Southeastern Baptist Theological Seminary, 2007.

Briggs, J.H. *The English Baptists of the Eighteenth Century. A History of the English Baptists.* Vol. 3. Edited by B.R. White. London: Baptist Historical Society, 1986.

Brown, Raymond. "Baptist Preaching in Early 18th Century England" *Baptist Quarterly* 31 (January 1985): 4-22.

______. *The English Baptists of the 18th Century.* London: Baptist Historical Society, 1986.

Bunyan, John. *Grace Abounding to the Chief of Sinners.* Middlesex: Penguin, 1987.

Bush, Russ, L., and Tom J. Nettles. *Baptists and the Bible.* Rev ed. Nashville: Broadman & Holman, 1999.

Calvin, John. *Institutes of the Christian Religion.* Edited by John T. McNeill. Translated by Ford Lewis Battles. 2 vols. Philadelphia: Westminster/John Knox Press, 1960.

Carey, Eustace. *Memoir of William Carey, D. D.* Boston: Gould, Kendall and Lincoln, 1836.

Carey, Samuel Pearce. *William Carey: 1761-1834.* London: Hodder and Stoughton, [1923].

______. *William Carey: The Father of Modern Missions.* London: Wakeman Trust, 1993.

Champion, L.G. "Evangelical Calvinism and the Structures of Baptist Church Life." *Baptist Quarterly* 28, no. 5 (January 1980): 196-208.

______. "The Letters of John Newton to John Ryland." *Baptist Quarterly* 27, no. 4 (October 1977): 157-63.

______. "The Theology of John Ryland: Its Sources and Influences." *Baptist Quarterly* 28, no. 1 (January 1979): 17-29.

Child, R.L. "Baptists and Ordination." *Baptist Quarterly* 14 (April 1952): 243-51.

Chun, Chris. "The Greatest Instruction Received from Human Writings: The Legacy of Jonathan Edwards in the Theology of Andrew Fuller." DPhil thesis, University of St. Andrews, 2008.

Copson, Stephen. "Two Ordinations at Bridlington in 1737." *Baptist Quarterly* 33 (July 1989): 146–49.

Cox, F.A. *History of the Baptist Missionary Society, from 1792 to 1842, to which is Added a* Sketch of the General Baptist Mission. 2 vols. London: T. Ward and G. & J. Dyer, 1842.

Clarke, N. "The Meaning and Practice of Ordination." *Baptist Quarterly* 17, no. 5. (January 1958): 197–205.

Clipsham, E.F. "Andrew Fuller and Fullerism: A Study in Evangelical Calvinism." *Baptist Quarterly* 20, no. 3 (1963): 99–114.

______. "Andrew Fuller and Fullerism: A Study in Evangelical Calvinism." *Baptist Quarterly* 20, no. 4 (1963): 146–154.

______. "Andrew Fuller and Fullerism: A Study in Evangelical Calvinism." *Baptist Quarterly* 20, no. 5 (1964): 214–225.

______. "Andrew Fuller and Fullerism: A Study in Evangelical Calvinism." *Baptist Quarterly* 20, no. 6 (1964): 268–276.

______. "Andrew Fuller's Doctrine of Salvation." BD thesis, Oxford University, 1961.

______. "Andrew Fuller and the Baptist Mission." *Foundations* 10, no.1 (January-March 1967): 4–18.

Dallimore, Arnold. *George Whitefield: The Life and Times of the Great Evangelist of the Eighteenth-Century Revival.* 2 vols. Edinburgh, UK: Banner of Truth Trust, 1970, 1980.

Daniel, Curt. "Andrew Fuller and Antinomianism." In Haykin, *'At the Pure Fountain of Thy Word'*, 74–82.

______. "Hyper-Calvinism and John Gill." PhD thesis, Edinburgh University, 1983.

Daniell, David. *William Tyndale: A Biography*. London: Yale University Press, 1994.

Davies, Horton. *The Worship of the English Puritans.* Westminster: Dacre Press, 1948.

Dix, Kenneth. *Strict and Particular: English Strict and Particular Baptists in the Nineteenth Century.* Didcot, UK: Baptist Historical Society, 2001.

______. "Varieties of High Calvinism among Nineteenth-Century Particular Baptists." *Baptist Quarterly* 38 (1999): 56–69.

Doster, G. Reid. "Discipline and Ordination at Berkhamsted General Baptist Church, 1712-1718." *Baptist Quarterly* 27 (July 1977): 128–38.

Dowley, T.E. "A London Congregation during the Great Persecution Petty France Particular Baptist Church, 1641–1688." *Baptist Quarterly* 29 (January 1978): 233–39.

Duncan, Pope Alexander. "Influence of Andrew Fuller on Calvinism." ThD diss., The Southern Baptist Theological Seminary, 1917.

Eddins, John W., Jr. "Andrew Fuller's Theology of Grace." ThD thesis, The Southern Baptist Theological Seminary, 1957.

Ella, George M. "John Gill and the Charge of Hyper-Calvinism." *Baptist Quarterly* 36 (1995): 160–77.

______. *Law and Gospel in the Theology of Andrew Fuller*. Durham, UK: Go, 1996.

______. "Why I am not a Follower of Andrew Fuller." Biographia Evangelica: The Writings of George M. Ella. Accessed January 2, 2021. http://evangelica.de/articles/doctrine/why-i-am-not-a-follower-of-andrew-fuller/.

______. *William Cowper: The Man of God's Stamp: A Bicentenary Evaluation, Vindication and Appreciation*. Dundas, ON: Joshua Press, 2000.

Ellis, Christopher J. *Gathering: A Theology and Spirituality of Worship in Free Church Tradition*. London: SCM Press, 2004.

Elwell, Walter A. ed. *Evangelical Dictionary of Theology*. 3rd ed. Grand Rapids, MI: Baker Book House, 1984.

Elwyn, Thornton. "Particular Baptists of the Northamptonshire Baptist Association as Reflected in the Circular Letters: 1765–1820." *Baptist Quarterly* 36, no. 8 (October 1996): 368–81.

______. "Particular Baptists of the Northamptonshire Baptist Association as Reflected in the Circular Letters: 1765–1820." *Baptist Quarterly* 37, no. 1 (January 1997): 3–19.

Fancutt, Walter. "William Steadman's Hampshire Years." *Baptist Quarterly* 16, no. 8 (October 1956): 366–67.

George, Timothy. *Faithful Witness: The Life and Mission of William Carey*. Birmingham, AL: New Hope, 1991.

______. *Theology of the Reformers*. Nashville, TN: Broadman & Holman, 1988.

George, Timothy, and Davis S. Dockery, eds. *Theologians of the Baptist Tradition*. Nashville, TN: Broadman & Holman, 2001.

Gotch, Davis F. *The History of Non-Conformity in Kettering: The Fuller Church*. Kettering, UK: Hart, 1926.

Grant, Keith. *Andrew Fuller and the Evangelical Renewal of Pastoral Theology*. Keynes, UK: Paternoster, 2013.

______. "Very Affecting and Evangelical: Andrew Fuller (1754–1815) and the Evangelical Renewal of Pastoral Theology." ThM thesis, Regent College, 2007.

Greenall, R.L., ed. *The Kettering Connection: Northamptonshire Baptists and Overseas Missions*. Leicester, UK: Department of Adult Education, University of Leicester, 1993.

Hayden, Roger. *Continuity and Change: Evangelical Calvinism among eighteenth-century Baptist Ministers trained at Bristol Academy, 1690–1791*. Chipping Norton, UK: Nigel Lynn Publishing for the Baptist Historical Society, 2006.

______. *English Baptist Heritage: A Christian Training Programme Course*. The Baptist Union of Great Britain, 1990.

______. "Evangelical Calvinism among Eighteenth-century British Baptists, with Particular Reference to Bernard Foskett, Hugh and Caleb Evans and the Bristol Baptist Academy, 1690–1791." PhD thesis, University of Keele, 1991.

______. "The Particular Baptist Confession 1689 and Baptists Today." *Baptist Quarterly* 32, no. 4 (October 1988), 403–17.

______. "What are the Qualifications of a Gospel Minister?" *Baptist Quarterly* 19, no. 8 (October 1962): 352–54.

Haykin, Michael A.G., ed. *Acorns to Oaks: The Primacy and Practice of Biblical Theology, A Festschrift for Dr. Geoff Adams*. Dundas, ON: Joshua Press, 2003.

______. "Andrew Fuller." *Biographical Dictionary of Evangelicals*, edited by Timothy Larsen. Leicester, UK; Downers Grove, IL: Inter-Varsity Press, 2003.

______. "Andrew Fuller and the Sandemanian Controversy." In Haykin, *'At the Pure Fountain of Thy Word'*, 223–236.

______, ed. *'At the Pure Fountain of Thy Word': Andrew Fuller as an Apologist*. Studies in Baptist History and Thought 6. Carlisle, UK: Paternoster, 2004.

______, ed. *The British Particular Baptists, 1638–1910*. 3 vols. Springfield, MO: Particular Baptist Press, 1998.

______ "'A Habitation of God, Through the Spirit': John Sutcliff (1752–1814) and the Revitalization of the Calvinistic Baptists in the Late Eighteenth Century." *Baptist Quarterly* 34, no. 7 (July 1992): 304–19.

______. "'Hazarding All for God at a Clap': The Spirituality of Baptism among British Calvinistic Baptists." *Baptist Quarterly* 38, no. 4 (October 1999): 185–95.

______. *Kiffen, Knollys, and Keach: Rediscovering our English Baptist Heritage*. Peterborough, Ontario: H&E Publishing, 2019.

______, ed. *The Life and Thought of John Gill (1697–1771): A Tercentennial Appreciation*. Leiden, UK: E. J. Brill, 1997.

______. "On Friendship: John Ryland and Andrew Fuller." *Reformation Today* 140 (1994): 26–30.

______. *One Heart and One Soul: John Sutcliff of Olney, His Friends and His Times.* Durham, UK: Evangelical Press, 1994.

______. "'The Oracles of God': Andrew Fuller and the Scriptures." *Churchman* 103 (1989): 60–76.

______. "Particular Redemption in the Writings of Andrew Fuller." In *The Gospel in the World: International Baptist Studies*, edited by D.W. Bebbington. Studies in Baptist History and Thought 1, 107–28. Carlisle, UK; Waynesboro, GA: Paternoster, 2002.

______. "'Resisting Evil': Civil retaliation, non-resistance, and the interpretation of Matthew 5:39a among eighteenth-century Calvinistic Baptists." *Baptist Quarterly* 36, no. 5 (January 1996): 212–27.

Hindmarsh, D. Bruce. *John Newton and the English Evangelical Tradition.* Grand Rapids, MI: Eerdmans, 1996.

______. "The eschatology of the Calvinistic Baptist John Gill (1697-1771) examined and compared." *Eusebeia: The Bulletin of the Jonathan Edwards Centre for Reformed Spirituality* 5 (2005): 33–66.

Higgs, Lionel F. "The Calling and Ordination of Ministers in the Eighteenth Century." *Baptist Quarterly* 16, no. 6 (April 1956): 277–279.

James, Sharon. "Revival and Renewal in Baptist Life: The contribution of William Steadman (1764-1837)." *Baptist Quarterly* 37, no. 6 (April 1998): 263–282.

Jarvis, Clive. "Growth in English Baptist Churches: With Special Reference to the Northamptonshire Particular Baptist Association (1770-1830)." PhD thesis, University of Glasgow, 2001.

______. "The Myth of High-Calvinism?" In *Recycling the Past or Researching History?*, edited by Philip E. Thompson and Anthony R. Cross. Studies in Baptist History and Thought 11, 231–64. Carlisle, UK; Waynesboro, GA: Paternoster, 2005.

Jordan, M. Dorothea. "John Smyth and Thomas Helwys: The Two First English Preachers of Religious Liberty. Resemblances and Contrasts." *The Baptist Quarterly* 12, no. 6–7 (April–July 1947): 187–95.

Keown, Harlice E. "The Preaching of Andrew Fuller." ThM thesis, The Southern Baptist Theological Seminary, 1957.

Kirkby, Arthur, H. "Andrew Fuller—Evangelical Calvinist." *Baptist Quarterly* 15, no. 5 (January 1954): 195–202.

______. *A Heritage Biography: Andrew Fuller (1754–1815).* London: Independent Press, 1961.

______. "The Theology Of Andrew Fuller and its Relation to Calvinism." PhD thesis, Edinburgh University, 1956.

Langford, Paul. *A Polite and Commercial People, England 1727–1783*. London: Guild, 1989.

Larcombe, H.V. "A Minister and his Hymns" *Baptist Quarterly* 10, no. 3 (July 1940): 154–58.

Larsen, Timothy, ed. *Biographical Dictionary of Evangelicals*. Downers Grove, IL: Inter-Varsity Press, 2003.

Laws, Gilbert. *Andrew Fuller: Pastor, Theologian, Ropeholder*. London: Carey Press, 1942.

Lewis, Donald M., ed. *Dictionary of Evangelical Biography 1730–1860*. 2 vols. Peabody, MA: Hendrickson, 2004.

Lloyd-Jones, David Martyn. "Sandemanianism." In *The Puritans: Their Origins and Successors, Addresses Delivered at the Puritan and Westminster Conferences, 1959–1978,* 170–90. Edinburgh, UK; Carlisle, PA: Banner of Truth, 1987.

Lovegrove, Deryck W. *Established Church, Sectarian People: Itinerancy and the Transformation of English Dissent, 1780–1830*. Cambridge, UK: Cambridge University Press, 1988.

______. "Particular Baptist Itinerant Preachers during the late 18th and early 19th Centuries." *Baptist Quarterly* 28, no. 3 (July 1979): 127–41.

Lumpkin, W.L. *Baptist Confessions of Faith*. Rev. ed. Valley Forge, PA: Judson Press, 1969.

Lundy, Daniel G., ed. *The Ethics of Jesus: The Believer as Salt and Light*. Toronto: Gospel Witness, 1994.

Manley, Ken R. "John Rippon and Baptist Historiography." *Baptist Quarterly* 28, no. 3 (July 1979): 109–25.

______. "The Making of an Evangelical Baptist Leader." *Baptist Quarterly* 26, no. 6 (April 1976): 254–74.

______. "Ordination among Australian Baptists." *Baptist Quarterly* 28, no. 4 (October 1979): 159–83.

______. '*Redeeming Love Proclaim': John Rippon and the Baptists.* Studies in Baptist History and Thought 12. Carlisle, UK; Waynesboro, GA: Paternoster, 2004.

Marsden, George. *Jonathan Edwards: A Life*. New Haven: Yale University Press, 2003.

Marshall, Dorothy. *Eighteenth Century England.* London: Longman, 1962.

McBeth, Harry Leon. *The Baptist Heritage*. Nashville: Broadman, 1987.

McGlothlin, W.J. *Baptist Confessions of Faith*. Philadelphia: American Baptist Publication Society, 1911.

McKibbens, Thomas R., Jr. *The Forgotten Heritage: A Lineage of Great Baptist Preaching*. Macon, GA: Mercer University Press, 1986.

Meyers, John Brown, ed. *The Centenary Volume of the Baptist Missionary Society, 1792–1892*. London: Baptist Missionary Society, 1892.

Moon, Norman S. "Caleb Evans, Founder of the Bristol Education Society." *Baptist Quarterly* 24, no. 4 (October 1971): 175–189.

______. *Education for Ministry: Bristol Baptist College 1679–1979*. Bristol: Bristol Baptist College, 1979.

Moore, William G. "From Biblical Fidelity to Organizational Efficiency: The Gospel Ministry form English Separatism of the Late Sixteenth Century to the Southern Baptist Convention of the Earlier Twentieth Century." PhD thesis, The Southern Baptist Theological Seminary, 2003.

Morden, Peter J. "Andrew Fuller (1754–1815) and the Revival of Eighteenth Century Particular Baptist Life." MPhil thesis, Spurgeon's College, University of Wales, 2000.

______. *Offering Christ to the World: Andrew Fuller and the Revival of Eighteenth Century Particular Baptist Life*. Studies in Baptist History and Thought 8. Carlisle, UK; Waynesboro, GA: Paternoster, 2003.

Naylor, Peter. *Calvinism, Communion and the Baptists: A Study of English Calvinistic Baptists from the Late 1600s to the Early 1800s*. Studies in Baptist History and Thought 7. Carlisle, UK; Waynesboro, GA: Paternoster, 2003.

______. *Picking Up a Pin for the Lord: English Particular Baptists from 1688 to the Early Nineteenth Century*. London: Grace Publications Trust, 1992.

Nettles, Thomas J. "Andrew Fuller (1754–1815)." In Haykin, *The British Particular Baptists*, 2:97–141.

______. *The Baptists: Key People Involved in Forming a Baptist Identity*. Fearn, UK: Christian Focus Publications, 2005.

______. *By His Grace and For His Glory: A Historical, Theological, and Practical Study of the Doctrines of Grace in Baptist Life*. 20th anniversary ed. Cape Coral, FL: Founders Press, 2006.

______. "Christianity Pure and Simple: Andrew Fuller's Contest with Socinianism." In Haykin, *'At the Pure Fountain of Thy Word'*, 138–173.

Nichols, Stephen J. *Jonathan Edwards: A Guided Tour of his Life and Thought*. Phillipsburg, NJ: P&R, 2001.

Nicholson, J.F.V., "The Office of 'Messenger' Amongst British Baptists in the Seventeenth and Eighteenth Centuries." *Baptist Quarterly* 17, no. 5 (January 1958): 206–25.

Nuttall, G.F. "The Baptist Churches and their Ministers in the 1790s: Rippon's Baptist Annual Register." *Baptist Quarterly* 30, no. 8 (October 1984): 383–87.

_____. "John Ash and the Pershore Church." *Baptist Quarterly* 22, no. 5 (January 1968): 271–76.

_____. "Letters from Robert Hall to John Ryland 1791-1824." *Baptist Quarterly* 34, no. 3 (July 1991): 127–31.

_____. "Northamptonshire and The Modern Question: A Turning-Point in Eighteenth-Century Dissent." *Journal of Theological Studies* 16, no. 1 (April 1965): 101–23.

_____. "The State of Religion in Northamptonshire (1793) by Andrew Fuller." *Baptist Quarterly* 29, no. 4 (October 1981): 177–79.

O'Brien, Susan. "A Transatlantic Community of Saints: The Great Awakening and the First Evangelical Network, 1735–1755". *American Historical Review* 91, no. 4 (October 1986): 811–32.

O'Gorman, Frank. *The Long Eighteenth Century British Political and Social History 1688–1832.* Oxford: Oxford University Press, 1997.

Old, Hughes Oliphant. *The Reading and Preaching of the Scriptures in the Worship of the Christian Church.* Vol. 4. Grand Rapids, MI: William B. Eerdmans, 2002.

_____. *The Reading and Preaching of the Scriptures in the Worship of the Christian Church.* Vol. 5. Grand Rapids, MI: William B. Eerdmans, 2002.

Oliver, Robert W. "Andrew Fuller and Abraham Booth." In Haykin, *'At the Pure Fountain of Thy Word'*, 203–22.

_____. "The Emergence of a Strict and Particular Baptist Community Among the English Calvinistic Baptists, 1770–1850." DPhil thesis, London Bible College, 1986.

_____. *History of the English Calvinistic Baptists 1771–1892: From John Gill to C. H. Spurgeon.* Edinburgh, UK; Carlisle, PA: Banner of Truth, 2006.

Oussoren, A. H. "William Carey, Especially his Missionary Principles." PhD thesis, Leiden: A.W. Sijthoff's Uitgeversmaatschappi 1945.

Payne, Ernest A. "Abraham Booth, 1734-1806." *Baptist Quarterly* 26, no. 1 (January 1975): 28–42.

_____. "Andrew Fuller as a Letter Writer." *Baptist Quarterly* 15, no. 7 (July 1954): 290–96.

______. "Baptists and the Laying on of Hands." *Baptist Quarterly* 15, no. 5 (January 1954): 203–15.

______. "Baptists and the Ministry." *Baptist Quarterly* 25, no. 2 (April 1973): 51–58.

______. *The Baptist Union: A Short History*. London: Kingsgate, 1959.

______. *The Great Succession: Leaders of the Baptist Missionary Society During the Nineteenth Century*. London: Carey Press, 1938.

______. "The Ministry in Historical Perspective." *Baptist Quarterly* 17, no. 6 (April 1958): 256–66.

______. "Who were the Baptists?" *Baptist Quarterly* 16, no. 8 (October 1956): 339–42.

Plumb, J.H. *England in the Eighteenth Century*. Middlesex, UK: Penguin Books, 1963.

Porter, Roy. *English Society in the Eighteenth-Century*. Middlesex, UK: Penguin Books, 1982.

Postman, Neil. *Building a Bridge to the 18th Century: How the Past can Improve our Future*. New York: Vintage Books, 1999.

Price, Seymour. "Abraham Booth's Ordination, 1769." *Baptist Quarterly* 9, no. 4 (October 1938): 242–46.

Priest, Gerald L. "Andrew Fuller's Response to the 'Modern Question'—a Reappraisal of The Gospel Worthy of all Acceptation." *Detroit Baptist Seminary Journal* 6 (2001): 45–73.

______. "Andrew Fuller, Hyper-Calvinism, and the 'Modern Question.'" In Haykin, *'At the Pure Fountain of Thy Word'*, 43–73.

Rathel, David Mark. "John Gill and the charge of hyper-Calvinism: assessing contemporary arguments in defense of Gill in light of Gill's doctrine of eternal justification." *The Journal of Andrew Fuller Studies* 1 (September 2020), 11–29.

Reed, Edwin Allen. "A Historical Study of Three Baptist Doctrines of the Atonement as seen in the Writings of John Smyth and Thomas Helwys, John Gill, and Andrew Fuller" ThM thesis, Golden Gate Baptist Theological Seminary, 1965.

Renihan, James M. "Out from Hyper-Calvinism: Andrew Fuller and the Promotion of Missions" *Reformed Baptist Theological Review* 1, no. 1 (January 2004): 45–65.

Reymond, Robert. *A New Systematic Theology of The Christian Faith*. 2nd ed. Nashville: Thomas Nelson, 1998.

Roberts, Philip R. *Continuity and Change: London Calvinistic Baptists and the Evangelical Revival: 1760–1820*. Wheaton: Richard Owen Roberts, 1989.

______. "Andrew Fuller." In *Theologians of the Baptist Tradition*, rev. ed., edited by Timothy George and David S. Dockery, 34–51. Nashville: Broadman & Holman, 2001.

Robinson, H. Wheeler. *The Life and Faith of the Baptists*. London: Methuen, 1946.

Robison, O.C. "The Particular Baptists in England: 1760-1820." DPhil thesis, Regent's Park College, Oxford, 1986.

Rushton, William, Jr. *A defence of particular redemption; wherein the doctrine of the late Mr. Fuller, relative to the atonement of Christ, is tried by the word of God. In four letters to a Baptist minister.* 1834. Reprint, New York: Primitive Publications, 1973.

Sell, Alan P.F. "Andrew Fuller and the Socinians." *Enlightenment and Dissent* 19 (2000): 91-115.

______. "*The Gospel Its Own Witness*: Deism, Thomas Paine, and Andrew Fuller." In *Enlightenment, Ecumenism, Evangel: Theological Themes and Thinkers 1550-2000*, Studies in Christian History and Thought, 111-143. Carlisle, UK; Waynesboro, GA: Paternoster, 2005.

______. *The Great Debate: Calvinism, Arminianism, and Salvation.* Eugene, OR: Wipf & Stock, 1998.

South, Thomas Jacob. "The Response of Andrew Fuller to the Sandemanian View of Saving Faith." ThD diss, Mid-America Baptist Theological Seminary, 1993.

Stanley, Brian. *The History of the Baptist Missionary Society: 1792-1992*. Edinburgh, UK: T&T Clark, 1992.

Stone, Lawrence. *The Family, Sex, and Marriage in England 1500-1800*. Abridged ed. New York: Harper and Row, 1979.

Talbot, Brian R. *Searching for a Common Identity: The Origins of the Baptist Union of Scotland 1800-1870*. Studies in Baptist History and Thought 9. Carlisle, UK: Paternoster Press, 2003.

Taylor, G.H. "The Reverend John Ash, LL.D. 1724-1779." *Baptist Quarterly* 20, no. 1 (January 1963): 4-22.

Taylor, Rosemary. "English Baptist Periodicals, 1790-1865" *Baptist Quarterly* 27, no. 2 (April 1977): 50-82.

Toon, Peter. *The Emergence of Hyper Calvinism in English Nonconformity 1689-1765.* London: Olive Tree, 1967.

______. "Hyper-Calvinism." In *New Dictionary of Theology*, edited by Sinclair B. Ferguson, David F. Wright, and J.I. Packer, 324. Leicester, UK; Downers Grove, IL: Inter-Varsity Press, 1988.

Thompson, Ronald W. *Heroes of the Baptist Church.* London: Carey Kingsgate Press, 1948.

Trevelyan, G.M. *Illustrated English Social History Volume Three: The Eighteenth Century*. Harmondsworth, UK: Penguin Books, 1964.

Tull, James E. *Shapers of Baptist Thought.* Valley Forge, PA: Judson Press, 1972.

Underwood, A.C. *A History of the English Baptists*. London: Kingsgate, 1947.

Underwood, W. *The Life of the Rev. Dan Taylor*. London: Simpkin, Marshall, 1870.

Vanhoozer, Kevin J. *The Bible, The Reader, and the Morality of Literary Knowledge: Is there meaning in this text?* Grand Rapids, MI: Zondervan, 1998.

Walker, Austin. *The Excellent Benjamin Keach*. Dundas, ON: Joshua Press, 2004.

Ward, W.R. "The Baptists and the Transformation of the Church, 1780-1830." *Baptist Quarterly* 25, no. 4 (October 1973): 167-84.

Watts, M.R. *The Dissenters: From the Reformation to the French Revolution*. Oxford: Oxford University Press, 1978.

______. *The Dissenters: The Expansion of Evangelical Nonconformity 1791-1859*. Oxford: Oxford University Press, 1995.

Wells, David F. *No Place for Truth, or Whatever Happened to Evangelical Theology?* Grand Rapids: Eerdmans, 1993.

Wheeler, Nigel D. "Andrew Fuller's Ordination Sermons" *Eusebeia: The Bulletin of the Andrew Fuller Center for Baptist Studies* 9 (Spring 2008): 167-182.

White, B.R. *The English Baptists of the Seventeenth Century: A History of the English Baptists*. Vol. 1. London: Baptist Historical Society, 1983.

______. *The English Baptists of the Seventeenth Century: A History of the English* Baptists. Vol. 1. Rev. ed. Edited by Roger Hayden. Oxford: Baptist Historical Society, 1996.

______. "Samuel Eaton (d.1639) Particular Baptist Pioneer" *Baptist Quarterly* 24, no. 1 (January 1971): 10-21.

Whitley, W.T. *A History of the British Baptists*. London: Charles Griffin, 1923.

Williams, Basil. *The Whig Supremacy (1714-1760)*. London: Oxford University Press, 1949.

Winter, E.P. "Who may Administer the Lord's Supper" *Baptist Quarterly* 16, no. 3 (July 1955): 128-33.

Wolever, Terry, ed. *The Life and Works of Joseph Kinghorn*. Vol. 1. Springfield, MO: Particular Baptist Press, 1995.

Young, Doyle. "The Place of Andrew Fuller in the Developing Modern Missions Movement." PhD diss, Southwestern Baptist Theological Seminary, 1981.

Long Eighteenth-Century Ordination Sermons

1681. *A Sermon Preached at the ordination of an Elder and Deacons in a Baptised Congregation in London by Nehemiah Cox*. London, 1681.

February 19, 1705-1706. "Sermon III. Preach'd at the Ordination of the Revd. Mr. David Rees and Two Deacons; in a Church of

Christ at Limehouse, Feb. 19, 1705–6." In *The Works of the late Reverend and Learned Mr. Joseph Stennett*, vol. 2, 114–122. London, 1731.

March 28, 1734. "The Duty of a Pastor to his People. Preached at the Ordination of the Reverend George Braithwaite, M.A. March 28, 1734." In *A Collection of Sermons and Tracts: In Two Volumes. Volume II. Ordination Sermons. Several of which were never before Printed. By the late Reverend and Learned John Gill, D.D. To Which are Prefixed, Memoirs of the Life, Writings, and Character of the Author*, 1–13. London, 1773.

March 5, 1735. *A Sermon preached at an Ordination of Deacons. March 5, 1735.* London, 1735.

1758. "The Work of a Gospel-Minister recommended to Consideration. A Charge delivered at the Ordinations of the Reverend Mr. John Gill, Mr. James Larwill, Mr. Isaac Gould, Mr. Bonner Stone, and Mr. Walter Richards." In *A Collection of Sermons and Tracts: In Two Volumes. Volume II. Ordination Sermons. Several of which were never before Printed. By the late Reverend and Learned John Gill, D.D. To Which are Prefixed, Memoirs of the Life, Writings, and Character of the* Author, 14–29. London: George Keith, 1773.

July 26, 1750. Brine, John. *The Solemn Charge of a Christian Minister Considered. A Sermon Preach'd at the Ordination of the Revd Mr John Ryland, on the 26th of July, 1750.* London, 1750.

March 28, 1754. Fall, James. *The Charge of God to Feed the Flock of Slaughter. A Sermon Preach'd at the Ordination of the Reverend Mr. James Fall, of Goodman's-Fields, London, On the 28th March, 1754. In the late Rev. Mr. William Bentley's Meeting-House, in Crispin-Street, Spital Fields. To which is added, A True, and Candid Narrative of the Churches Proceedings, in the Affair of their Separation, given at the time of ordination, by Capt. Thomas Best, one of their Worthy Deacons.* London, 1754.

September 4, 1755. Wallin, Benjamin. *The Obligations of a People to their Faithful Minister. Represented in a Discourse Preached at the Ordination of the Revd. Mr. Samuel Burford, September 4, 1755.* London, 1755.

December 15, 1756. Brine, John. *Diligence in Study Recommended to Ministers. In a Sermon, Preached at the Ordination of the*

Reverend Mr. Richard Rist, in Harlow, Essex. December 15, 1756. London, 1757.

August 6, 1760. Crabtree, William. "The Regard Which The Churches Of Christ Owe To Their Ministers. A Sermon, Preached At The Ordination Of The Rev. Joshua Wood, Of Halifax, August 6, 1760." In *Memoirs of the late Rev. Wm. Crabtree, first pastor of the Baptist Church at Bradford, Yorkshire. To which is added a sermon, preached to the church at the ordination of the Rev. Joshua Wood, of Halifax, August 6, 1760*, by Isaac Mann. London, 1815.

August 15, 1764. Gill, John. "The Doctrine of the Cherubim Opened and Explained. A Sermon at the Ordination of the Reverend Mr. John Davis, at Waltham-Abbey. Preached August 15, 1764." In *A Collection of Sermons and Tracts: In Two Volumes. Volume II. Ordination Sermons. Several of which were never before Printed. By the late Reverend and Learned John Gill, D.D. To Which are Prefixed, Memoirs of the Life, Writings, and Character of the Author*, 30–48. London, 1773.

1766. "The Form of Sound Words to be Held Fast. A Charge Delivered at the Ordination of the Rev. Mr. John Reynolds." In *A Collection of Sermons and Tracts: In Two Volumes. Volume II. Ordination Sermons. Several of which were never before Printed. By the late Reverend and Learned John Gill, D.D. To Which are Prefixed, Memoirs of the Life, Writings, and Character of the Author*, 49–64. London, 1773.

August 18, 1767. Stennett, Samuel, and John Tommas. *A Charge and Sermon, Together with an Introductory Discourse, and Confession of faith, Delivered at the Ordination of the Rev. Mr. Caleb Evans, August 18, 1767, in Broad-Mead, Bristol.* Bristol, 1767.

February 16, 1769. Wallin, Benjamin. *A Charge and Sermon together with an Introductory Discourse and Confession of Faith Delivered at the Ordination of the Rev. Mr. Abraham Booth Feb. 16, 1769, in Goodman's Fields.* London, 1769.

November 20, 1771. "God's Approbation The Study of Faithful Ministers. A Sermon delivered at the Ordination of the Rev. George Moreton, Pastor of the Baptist Church at Kettering. Nov. 20th 1771." In *The Complete Works of the Late Rev. Robert Hall, Arnsby, Leicestershire. Consisting* *of Sermons, Essays, and Miscellaneous Pieces*, edited by J.W. Morris. London, 1828.

August 4, 1773. Evans, Caleb, and Hugh Evans. *A Charge and Sermon, Delivered at the Ordination of the Rev. Thomas Dunscombe, at Coate, Oxon, August 4th, 1773.* Bristol.

October 7, 1773. Turner, Daniel, and Caleb Evans. *A Charge and a Sermon, Delivered at the Ordination of the Rev. Mr. Job David, October 7, 1773, at Frome, Somersetshire.* Bristol.

August 18, 1773. Evans, Hugh. *The Able Minister. A Sermon Preached in Broad-mead, Before the Bristol Education Society, August 18, 1773.* Bristol.

May 26, 1774. Fawcett, Benjamin and Andrew Kinsman. *Preaching Christ and not Self. A Sermon preached at Tuckers-Street-meeting, Bristol, at the Ordination of the Reverend Mr. Thomas Janes. May 26th, 1774.* Bristol.

August 13, 1777. Turner, Daniel. *The Divine Appointment, and Great Importance of the Christian Ministry Considered, in a Sermon, Preached in Broad-mead, Bristol, before the Bristol Educational Society, August 13, 1777.* Bristol.

March 25, 1784. *Three Discourses Addressed to the Congregation at Maze-Pond, Southwark, on their Public Declaration of having chosen Mr. James Dore their pastor. March 25th, 1784.* Cambridge, 1784.

July 13, 1785. "Pastoral Cautions: An Address to the Late Mr. Thomas Hopkins, when Ordained Pastor of the Church of Christ, in Eagle Street, Red Lion Square, July 13, 1785." In *The Works of Abraham Booth, Late Pastor of the Baptist Church Assembling in Little Prescott Street, Goodman's Fields, London. With Some Account of His Life and Writings in Three Volumes*, vol. 3. London, 1813.

October 18, 1786. Taylor, Dan. "The Service of God, in the Gospel of his Son, explained and illustrated. A Charge Delivered at the Ordination of the Rev. Mr. George Birley, October 18, 1786, at St. Ives." In *A Charge and Sermon, Together with a Confession of Faith, Delivered at the Ordination of the Rev. Mr George Birley, on Wednesday, October 18, 1786 at St. Ives, Huntingdonshire.* London. [General Baptist]

October 1786. "A Discourse Preached at the ordination of George Birley, at St Ives, Huntingdonshire, Oct. 1786." In *Miscellaneous Works of Robert Robinson, late pastor of the*

Baptist Church and Congregation of Protestant Dissenters, at Cambridge; in Four Volumes: To Which are prefixed Brief Memoirs of his Life and Writings. Vol. 4, 39–59. Harlow, 1807.

December 7, 1796. Ryland, John, and S. Pearce. *The Duty of the Ministers to be Nursing Fathers to the Church; and the Duty of Churches to Regard Ministers as the Gift of Christ: A Charge, Delivered by the Rev. John Ryland, D. D. of Bristol; and a Sermon, Delivered by the Rev. S. Pearce, M.A., of Birmingham; in the Dissenters Meeting-House, Angel-Street, Worcester, at the Ordination of the Rev. W. Belsher, to the Pastorate of the Baptist Church, meeting in Silver-Street, in the same city: Together with an Introductory Address, by the Rev. G. Osborn, and also Mr. Belsher's Declaration of Religious Sentiments*. Bristol.

August 14, 1799. Deacon, Samuel. *A Sermon Delivered at the Ordination of Mr. George Hardstaffe, to the Pastoral care of the General Baptist Church, at Kirkby-Woodhouse, near Mansfield Nottinghamshire, August 14, 1799.* London. [General Baptist]

November 17, 1801. Ryland, John, and James Hinton. *The Difficulties and Supports of a Gospel Minister; and the Duties incumbent on a Christian Church: A Charge by John Ryland, D.D. And a Sermon, by James Hinton; Delivered Nov. 17, 1801, At the Ordination of Thomas Coles, A.M. to the Pastoral Care of the Baptist Church, at Bourton-on-the-Water, Gloucestershire*. Bristol.

June 23, 1802. Ryland, J., and Andrew Fuller. *The Difficulties of the Christian Ministry, and the Means of Surmounting them; with the Obedience of Churches to their Pastors Explained and Enforced: A Charge, by the Rev. J. Ryland, D.D. and a Sermon by the Rev. Andrew Fuller; Together with an Introductory Address, by the Rev. J. Sutcliff; Delivered June 23, 1802, At the Ordination of Thomas Morgan, To the Pastoral Office over the Baptist Church, meeting in Cannon-street, Birmingham: And, also, Mr. Morgan's Declaration of Religious Sentiments.* Birmingham, 1802.

[1812]. "On the Discouragements and Supports of the Christian Minister: A Discourse, Delivered to the Rev. James Robertson, at his Ordination over the Independent Church at Stretton, Warwickshire." In Olinthus Gregory and Joseph Belcher, eds., *The Works of the Rev. Robert Hall, A.M. with A Memoir of his Life by Dr. Gregory; Reminiscences, by John Greene, ESQ.: and his*

Character as a Preacher, by the Rev. John Foster. Vol. 1. New York, 1849.

January 19, 1814. "An Address to the Rev. Eustace Carey, On His Designation as a Christian Missionary to India." In *The Works of the Rev. Robert Hall, A.M. with A Memoir of his Life by Dr. Gregory; Reminiscences, by John Greene, ESQ.: and his Character as a Preacher, by the Rev. John Foster*, vol. 1, edited by Olinthus Gregory and Joseph Belcher. New York, 1849.

June 23 / August 3, 1814. Kinghorn, Joseph. *Advice and Encouragement to Young Ministers—Two Sermons, Addressed Principally to the Students of the Two Baptist Academies at Stepney and at Bristol. The First Preached June 23, 1814, At the Rev. Dr. Rippon's Meeting, Carterlane, Southwark; The Second, August 3, 1814, At the Rev. Dr. Ryland's, Broad Mead, Bristol.* Norwich, 1814.

November 8, 1815. "The Substance of a Charge, Delivered at the Ordination of the Rev. J. K. Hall, at Kettering, November 8, 1815." [From the notes of the Rev. S. Hillyard, of Bedford.] In *The Works of the Rev. Robert Hall, A.M. with A Memoir of his Life by Dr. Gregory; Reminiscences, by John Greene, ESQ.: and his Character as a Preacher, by the Rev. John Foster*, vol. 4, edited by Olinthus Gregory and Joseph Belcher. New York, 1854.

October 21, 1818. Steadman, William. *The Qualifications Necessary for the Discharge of the Duties of the Christian Ministry. A Pastoral Charge, Addressed to Mr. George Sample, on his Ordination over the Baptist Church, Assembling at West-Gate, Newcastle upon Tyne, October, 21, 1818.* London, 1819.

Fuller's Ordination Sermons

The following sermons are found in Fuller, Andrew. *The Complete Works of the Rev. Andrew Fuller, With a Memoir of his Life by the Rev Andrew Gunton Fuller. A New Edition in Five Volumes.* Vol. 4. London: William Ball, 1837.

The Qualifications and Encouragement of a Faithful Minister of Illustrated by the Character and success of Barnabas. 25–39.

The Obedience of Churches to their Pastors Explained and Enforced. 111–119.

Pastors Required to Feed the Flock of Christ. 446–448.

Spiritual Knowledge and Holy Love Necessary for the Gospel Ministry. 448–453.

On an Intimate and Practical Acquaintance with the Word of God. 453–458.

Date Completed	Name

www.ingramcontent.com/pod-product-compliance
Ingram Content Group UK Ltd.
Pitfield, Milton Keynes, MK11 3LW, UK
UKHW041856190726
13854UKWH00002B/938

9 781989 174968